CONTRIBUTORS

Peter J. Casarella, Ph.D., is an Associate Professor of Theology at the University of Notre Dame.

John C. Cavadini, Ph.D., is a Professor of Theology and Director of the Institute for Church Life at the University of Notre Dame.

Larry Chapp, Ph.D., is Manager of The Dorothy Day Catholic Worker Farm in Harveys Lake, PA and a retired Professor of Theology at DeSales University.

Monsignor John Cihak, S.T.D., S.T.L., is a priest of the Archdiocese of Portland in Oregon who serves as an official at the Holy See and teaches Theology at the Pontifical Gregorian University.

Father Christopher Collins, S.J., S.T.D., is Director of Catholic Studies and Assistant Professor of Theology at St. Louis University.

Father Emery de Gaál, Ph.D., priest of Eichstätt, Bavaria, Germany is Chairman and Professor of Dogmatic Theology at Mundelein Seminary in Illinois.

Father Michael Paul Gallagher, S.J., Ph.D., is Professor Emeritus of Theology at the Gregorian University, and Rector of the Collegio Bellarmino, Rome.

Sister Gill Goulding, S.T.L., Ph.D., is an Associate Professor of Theology and Spirituality with Regis College, at the University of Toronto.

Daniel A. Keating, D.Phil., is an Associate Professor of Theology at Sacred Heart Major Seminary in Detroit.

Tracey Rowland, Ph.D., is Dean at John Paul II Institute for Marriage and Family in Melbourne, Australia.

D. Vincent Twomey, S.V.D., Ph.D., is a Professor Emeritus of Moral Theology at Maynooth (Ireland).

NIHIL OBSTAT: Father Matthew J. Gutowski, JCL

IMPRIMATUR: Most Reverend George J. Lucas
                   Archbishop of Omaha, Nebraska
                   July 14, 2014

THE INSTITUTE FOR PRIESTLY FORMATION
IPF Publications
2500 California Plaza
Omaha, Nebraska 68178
www.IPFPublications.com

Printed in the United States of America
ISBN-13: 978-0-9887613-2-2

Cover design by Timothy D. Boatright
Marketing Associates, USA
Tampa, Florida

THE INSTITUTE FOR PRIESTLY FORMATION
MISSION STATEMENT

The Institute for Priestly Formation was founded to assist bishops in the spiritual formation of diocesan seminarians and priests in the Roman Catholic Church. The Institute responds to the need to foster spiritual formation as the integrating and governing principle of all aspects for priestly formation. Inspired by the biblical-evangelical spirituality of Ignatius Loyola, this spiritual formation has as its goal the cultivation of a deep interior communion with Christ; from such communion, the priest shares in Christ's own pastoral charity. In carrying out its mission, the Institute directly serves diocesan seminarians and priests as well as those who are responsible for diocesan priestly formation.

THE INSTITUTE FOR PRIESTLY FORMATION
Creighton University
2500 California Plaza
Omaha, Nebraska 68178
www.priestlyformation.org
ipf@creighton.edu

TABLE OF CONTENTS

FOREWORD

This is a book about the intersection of spirituality and theology. The essays collected here are united by a common idea, namely, that the God who speaks to our hearts in prayer and sacrament is the same God we seek in theology, and that the study of theology ought to be shaped and enriched by the love that grows in spiritual practice. The authors of these essays draw from the abundant wisdom of the Church, and bring together a range of perspectives from the ancient to the contemporary on the connection between loving God and knowing him in the work of theology. To their efforts, I add my own perspective, not as a theologian but as the president of the national university of the Catholic Church.

When Pope Benedict XVI visited Catholic University's campus in 2008, he spoke about the mission of Catholic education. He said a Catholic university was a place where people "first and foremost . . . encounter the living God who is Jesus Christ."[1] The Pope's words were a reminder of how Catholic education stands apart from its secular counterpart. The God we seek to know is also the one who created and redeemed us, and whom we encounter in the sacraments. We want to know God, not just know about Him.

All of Catholic education, for that matter all of Catholic thought, hinges on this relationship with God and is transformed by it. A really Catholic education is motivated not by curiosity or a generic desire to know, but by love. Love and knowledge—and, therefore, love and education—are fundamentally intertwined. Our search to better understand God and his creation is enriched by our love for him, and our love for Him is deepened by understanding.

In the contemporary academy, this Catholic pairing of love and education has tended to draw suspicion. It runs counter to some widely accepted assumptions about what counts as real knowledge. We inherited from the Enlightenment a hope that, if we could separate reason from faith, we could improve understanding by making education more rigorous. What we really did was to narrow the range of our understanding, and marginalize faith in academic discourse.

Today, the academy accepts this pheresis as a mark of progress. The faith we once relied on to help us understand things we could not otherwise explain has been replaced by a more rarified reason. We do not need faith anymore, we are told, because we are smarter and more rigorous than we used to be. Apart from being forgetful of the debt modern intellectual traditions owe to religion, this account of progress in human thought fails to see how much narrower we have made the horizons of intellectual discourse. One aspect is the near eradication of theology from the standard curriculum. But we have lost much more than that. Faith shapes the path of inquiry from science to the arts. Its absence has empowered a raw materialism in biology; circumscribed imagination in the arts, and left the humanities searching for a principle of unity.

Faith was once a method of understanding, complementary to reason. Now, it is supposed to cloud and hinder thought. Faith and reason were once thought of like two wings of a dove; in today's academy, faith is a threat to reason. And though it was secular education that began the assault on faith, religious schools have found themselves involved in the war. Not all take the same side. When religious colleges and universities subscribe to the view of their secular counterparts, they lose the resource that made them distinctive. Much of the Catholic intellectual discourse is now cramped under the weight of rationalist influences. Theology's stature has been reduced and its importance, deemphasized.

Perhaps, the most damaging effect of the triumph of rationalism is the separation of the search for truth from love. As Pope Benedict reminded Catholic University's students on his visit in 2008, Catholic thought is characterized not only by the added intellectual discipline that faith brings, but also by the love that shapes our faith. We seek to know the God who has touched our hearts as well as our minds. Like the ancient philosophers who sought truth because they loved it, we seek to know because of what we love.

For Christians, this is not a metaphorical way of speaking because truth is a person. God is not something *that* we love; he is someone *whom* we love. Our desire to know and understand Him stems from a desire for a deeper relationship with Him. The great achievements of religious thought were cultivated not simply by the rigors of reason, but by the tenderness of love. We are transformed by this knowing and loving, as Benedict XVI explains. For "those who meet him are drawn by the very power of the Gospel to lead a new life characterized by all that is beautiful, good, and true; a life of

Christian witness nurtured and strengthened within the community of our Lord's disciples, the Church."

It is fitting that the effort to restore the connection between knowing and loving God should begin in theology. Catholic education has traditionally honored theology as the queen of the intellectual disciplines, a role that implies a special responsibility for steering the university's course. The essays collected here draw from the Church's wealth of thought to reveal the historical and theological significance of bringing prayer, spiritual discipline, and growth in the love of God to the search to understand Him and His creation. The authors are united in a common hope that by joining our efforts to God's grace, we may reunite in the theology of the church what the intellectual trends of the modern world have put asunder.

John Garvey
President
The Catholic University of America

NOTES

1.   Pope Benedict XVI, "Meeting with Catholic Educators,"
April 17, 2008, *Libreria Editrice Vaticana*, http://www.vatican.va/
holy_father/benedict_xvi/speeches/2008/april/documents/
hf_ben-xvi_spe_20080417_cath-univ-washington_en.html.

INTRODUCTION

JOHN CAVADINI

It is a daunting task to try to add anything by way of introduction to the excellent essays in this volume, since they speak so well for themselves and have amply covered their ground, namely, the necessary, but currently attenuated, connection between theology and spirituality. If theology is "faith seeking understanding," then what is seeking, namely, "faith," must be something capable of "seeking." It must not simply be an objective body of teaching, the "*fides quae*," the faith which is believed; but it must, at the same time, be a state of mind, the "*fides qua*," the faith by which one believes the teaching. This faith is a *virtue*, as John Cihak reminds us, orienting the mind toward the truths it receives; it is a *hermeneutic*, as Tracy Rowland reminds us, a light afforded the mind by its orientation toward these truths; and a *clinging*, as Christopher Collins reminds us, a clinging to the Cross through clinging to the truths believed. In other words, faith is, itself, already an existential state of mind. As such, it is already a spiritual state.

The essays show that there is not so much a need to reconnect something called "spirituality" with something called "theology." Rather, there is a need for a deepening awareness of the specific "seeking" that is theology, where theology is a particular specification of the spiritual disposition "faith," namely, as it "seeks understanding" of what it believes. So theology, because it is faith as it seeks understanding, not only entails a spirituality, but is, in a way, already a spirituality.

The essays display the manifold dimensions of this spirituality. In doing so, they also remind us that it is preconceived notions of what "spirituality" is, just as much mistaken notions of what theology is, that can cause us to set up a dichotomy between "spirituality" and "theology," and then find ourselves in the predicament of having to re-unite the two. "Spirituality" can seem by clichéd turns something sanctimonious, emotional, superficial, sentimental, anti-intellectual, ponderous or triumphalist, reactionary or alternative, disconnected or contextually over-determined; and then, when theologians are called to embrace a "spirituality," it seems as though they are being scolded for not having enough of *that*, whatever the spirituality *du jour* may be. Whatever it is, it always seems extrinsic to theology, an add-on intended to suit some non-theological interest that finds theology either too critical or too pious.

As bothersome as such a clichéd understanding of spirituality might be, it is only a reflection of a truncated understanding of what theology is. Larry Chapp's essay, following Balthasar, provides a thumbnail sketch of the separating out of something that came to be called "spiritual theology" from "dogmatic theology." This separation did not occur, as some have alleged, with the advent of Scholasticism, but later, especially "after the Reformation, the scientific reformation, and the Enlightenment," as a "hypertrophy of the deductive moment within theology." It led to the degeneration of theology to "full defensive mode, intent on 'proving' the truth of faith to the nonbelievers through a putatively 'certain' philosophical propaedeutic, with an equally rationalistic rigor applied to the theological debates with the Protestants."

These comments by Chapp are echoed by Collins, reminding us of Ratzinger's analysis of this split. It produced a "neo-scholastic theology" which, "while not erring in any essential way, still left the reader a bit cold with its 'crystal clear logic … too closed in on itself, too impersonal and ready-made.'" Rowland, also taking up Ratzinger's legacy, shows how the subject doing theology has been whittled from its proper locus, the "heart," down to something more exclusively rationalistic, as though the *"mens"* of St. Augustine had been narrowed down to "intellect" only. Paul Claudel, Rowland notes, spoke of the Jansenist influence in this regard. Holding "'noble faculties of imagination and sensibility in contempt,'" they produced a theological subject with a "'starved imagination.'"

In other words, what is called the separation of "spirituality" and "theology" is really the result of a truncation of the subject of the "faith" that is "seeking understanding." But faith engages the whole *mens*, not just the intellect. If we follow Augustine's way of thinking, it includes the memory of the embodied human being, and his or her will. The life of faith is the renewal of this mind, the image of God, as it is engaged in remembering, understanding, and loving God; and, therefore, the mind in faith is already in a relationship with God, or to use the term that many of our essays prefer, is already in *dialogue* with God.

Theology, as faith seeking understanding, proceeds from

the dialogical nature of faith. It is, thus, a specifically *dialogical* seeking. Emery de Gaál provides an invaluable tour through Joseph Ratzinger's homilies on the occasion of a priest's first Mass. These homilies invoke the dialogical stance proper to *faith itself*. Priestly ministry arises out of the same fundamental disposition of all believers, whose life, "Christ-centered," puts him or her in solidarity with the joys and hopes of all human beings, feeling their fears and their doubts without contempt for them, acknowledging that all of these fears and doubts could cross even our own hearts as believers. The priest does not become "'servant to the servants of God'" by abstracting himself from this solidarity, but out of the midst of it, the one whose hand is "not there to curse and to hit … but to bless," and, thereby, to mediate to the people of God the "unsurpassable beauty" of "the Cross of Jesus Christ, who through the Eucharist continues to impart on us the strength to persevere amid life's vicissitudes and give everything its most sublime meaning in Christ."

In this connection, Vincent Twomey reminds us of Joseph Ratzinger/Benedict XVI's idea of "sacramental mysticism." Faith is, once again, not simply intellectual assent to certain propositions, but more: it has an ecclesiological and Eucharistic form. The believer has communion "with God through sharing in Jesus's self-gift, sharing in his body and blood." Thus, he has communion with all for whom Jesus offered Himself, "entertaining" even "the doubts of the day" to the point that one has become "*vulnerable*" to them, identifying with them so that there is the deepest possible engagement of them with the Word of God. The resulting theology "offers the possibility of appropriation of divine revelation that meets the challenges of the day and transforms them," as

Collins puts it. The "seeking to understand" that is theology arises as an appropriation into oneself of the suffering of others intrinsic to the stance of faith.

In the words of Peter Casarella, the dialogical spirituality of theology is a spirituality of *encounter*. In faith, the whole person encounters the Lord who is *light*, *life*, *truth*, and *way*; and this encounter orients the person toward a "spiritual exchange between conscience, community, and culture in myriad ways." It is social without being collapsed into the world, and spiritual without renouncing social bonds, but rather seeks transformation of them, from within them. Casarella cites Luigi Sturzo and Félix Varela as theologians who sought to understand what they believed by working out its social implications. If faith is an encounter with the one who is *true life*, then "understanding" this *life* will entail investigating its requirements in the contemporary world where slavery and other forms of fragmentation of social and familial ties are alive and well.

I was pleased to see that Daniel Keating's essay mentions the teaching role of the theologian. Most of us theologians, are, in fact, teachers; and the "doubts of the day" most likely to reach us are those of our own students. The teacher who can descend to the doubts, the troubles, the malaise, and the worries of his or her students, who can feel them as his or her own, is the one who will engage the dialogue out of which theology arises. Michael Gallagher reminds us of Newman's injunction to be "real," meaning, to be willing to work out of that faith which is not simply intellectual assent but a personal commitment and a continuing openness to conversion. Every existential question a student asks is an invitation to share his difficulties and own them, lest we "stay locked in what Newman calls 'bigotry' [and] … never reach out in dialogue to different positions because [we] cannot 'learn another disposition.'" If we accept the struggle against the "rigidity" that might give a quick formulaic answer, allowing for the "enlargement" of heart to which faith calls us, will we not discover that we are "seeking understanding" of the truths we believe precisely in seeking to engender understanding in others? We do not change the truths to which we are clinging. Instead, our very clinging to them gives rise to an articulation of them that seeks to engender understanding in those we are teaching. Would this not be the essence of a science that arises directly from the dialogic character of faith, as faith "seeks understanding?"

Perhaps, it is in the context of teaching, of "doctrina," that theology will find its renewal, not re-joined to something called "spirituality," but *as* a spirituality, *as* a specification of the dialogic character of the faith as it seeks understanding. It strikes me that this is a quintessentially Augustinian insight. However, before I wear out my welcome as Introducer by venturing too far into my own opinions, I must release the reader to enjoy the wisdom of this splendid collection, courtesy of the careful editing of James Keating, to whom, in closing, we owe a debt of thanks.

PART I

THEOLOGY AND SPIRITUALITY

HOW DOES SPIRITUALITY SUPPLY THEOLOGICAL STUDY WITH THE CORRECT METHOD?

TRACEY ROWLAND

In his 1768 work, *Dei fondamenti della religion e dei fonti dell'empietà*, the Italian Dominican Antonio Valsecchi wrote (as cited in Fabro), "The source of impiety is not in the intellect but in the heart."[1] More recently, in *Porta Fidei* (2011), the Apostolic Letter announcing the Year of Faith, Pope Benedict XVI wrote that "Knowing the content [of the faith] to be believed is not sufficient unless the heart, the authentic sacred space within the person, is opened by grace that allows the eyes to see below the surface and to understand that what has been proclaimed is the word of God."[2]

As a Catholic of the immediate post-conciliar generation, I often thought that those theologians who dissented from magisterial teaching were often "lusting after Modernity," to use a phrase coined by E. Michael Jones.[3] Jones diagnosed the Catholic intellectuals of the sixties as suffering from a massive inferiority complex, desperately wanting to be welcomed into the halls of the prestigious non-Catholic academies. Their most fundamental desire was for the Church to be accepted by the world and for them to escape the social milieu of pre-conciliar Catholicism, which they regarded as a ghetto. Their hearts craved something like acceptance by non-Catholic social elites. The key pastoral project of this generation was correlationism—the idea that the faith is best presented by attaching it, or correlating it, to fashionable elements in the contemporary culture that are deemed to be receptive to it. Accordingly, theologians focused on searching for these allegedly Christian-friendly elements within the culture and repackaging the faith with reference to them. In all of this there was a tendency for the personal relationship of the individual Catholic to the Persons of the Trinity to be occluded. Today, the correlationist project is being updated. Instead of correlating the faith to the culture of modernity, theologians of the *Katholieke Universiteit Leuven*, faithful to the theological vision of Edward Schillebeeckx, are working on a project to "re-contextualise the Catholic faith to the culture of post-modernity."[4] Both projects—correlationism and recontextualisationism—take their bearings from the fashionable intellectual currents of the world, not from Trinitarian theology.

Joseph Ratzinger, Henri de Lubac, and Hans Urs von Balthasar stood apart from the dominant orientation of the sixties generation by arguing for the foundational status of the Trinity. Their alternative to correlationism was the development of a Trinitarian, Christocentric anthropology that situated human actions within the context of a relationship between the human person and each of the Persons of the Trinity. Central to this relationship is an understanding of the missions of the Persons of the Trinity in the life of the world, including the work of the theological virtues—faith, hope, and love—on the faculties of the human soul, as well as the soul's receptivity to goodness, truth, and beauty. The Trinitarian encyclicals of the papacy of St. John Paul II (*Redemptor Hominis, Dives in Misericordia,* and *Dominum et Vivificantem*) and the theological virtues trilogy of the papacies of Pope Benedict XVI and Pope Francis (*Deus Caritas Est, Spe Salvi,* and *Lumen Fidei*) outline the major principles of this Trinitarian Christocentric anthropology. In addition, Hans Urs von Balthasar's essays "Theology and Sanctity" and "Spirituality" in his first volume of *Explorations in Theology: The Word Made Flesh* offer something of a pathology report on how spirituality and academic theology became severed from their relationship to one another in the collapse of the medieval theological syntheses. Von Balthasar's sixteen-volume *magnum opus* (divided into theological aesthetics, theo-dramatics, and theo-logic) further charts the severance of the true, the beautiful, and the good from one another, and offers a positive account of how the human person might reconnect with the life of the Trinity.[5] When taken together, these works, including their patristic and medieval antecedents, provide a blueprint for the renewal of theological anthropology and, within that, the development of a spirituality that is sufficiently rich and multidimensional to foster theological renewal in general.

The Primacy of a Clean Heart

The primary point to be made about this theological anthropology is that it does not view the intellect as operating in a Kantian vacuum, detached from faith and Tradition. In his exegesis on the Beatitude, "Blessed are the clean of heart, for they will see God" (Mt 5:8), Pope Benedict XVI notes that the organ for seeing God is the heart; the intellect alone is not enough. He suggests that "in order for man to become capable of perceiving God, the energies of his existence have to work in harmony . . . His will must be pure and so too must the underlying affective dimension of his soul, which gives intelligence and will their direction. Speaking of the heart in this way means precisely that man's perceptive powers play in concert, which also requires the proper interplay of body and soul, since this is essential for the totality of the creature we call man."[6] Von Balthasar made a similar point in his essay, "Sanctity and Theology": "If I am to hear properly . . . I must not come before the word with specially selected acts of reason and will: I must encounter the word with my whole conscience, or rather, with my whole person. For faith, the organ of hearing has to do with the whole person, not [with] the [individual] 'faculties of the soul.'"[7]

The primary importance of a pure heart was also emphasized by John Henry Newman who, according to Alfred Läpple, was Ratzinger's hero when he was a seminarian. In his famous "Sermon 12," Newman wrote:

> What, then, is the safeguard [of faith], if Reason is not? I shall give an answer, which may seem at once commonplace and paradoxical, yet I believe it is the true one. The safeguard of Faith is a right state of [the] heart. This it is that gives it birth; it also disciplines it. This is what protects it from bigotry, credulity, and fanaticism. It is holiness, or dutifulness, or the new creation, or the spiritual mind, however we word it, which is the quickening and illuminating principle of true faith, giving it eyes, hands, and feet. It is Love which forms it out of the rude chaos into an image of Christ; or, in scholastic

language, justifying Faith, whether in Pagan, Jew, or Christian, is *fides formata charitate*.[8]

In his doctoral dissertation on the "Spiritual Christology of Joseph Ratzinger," Peter McGregor argues that, for Ratzinger, the heart is the "place" of integration for the intellect, will, passions, and senses of the body and the soul.[9] After analyzing the idea of the heart in biblical, patristic, and medieval works, as well as in the writings of Blaise Pascal, John Henry Newman, Karl Rahner, Romano Guardini, Dietrich von Hildebrand, and Pius XII, McGregor concludes that Ratzinger's interpretation of the heart is closest to that of Guardini and Newman.

Indeed traces of Newman and Guardini can be found all over Ratzinger's anthropology. When Ratzinger speaks of a spirituality that is a necessary prerequisite to a correct theological method, he is speaking as a loyal student of Guardini. Guardini was a lecturer for von Balthasar at the University of Berlin and for Ratzinger at the University of Munich. He understood that scholastic maxims were an inadequate medium for addressing the existential anguish of those who lived through two world wars and a depression. In her translator's preface to Romano Guardini's work *Sacred Signs*, written in the immediate pre-conciliar era of the 1950s, Grace Branham writes:

> Our religious education addresses itself to the intellect and will,—our "spiritual faculties." It has resulted (no mean achievement) in moral firmness and mental precision. But the formulas of the Catechism do not enable us to read the two great works provided by God for our education—created nature and the written Word.

In these are addressed not only our intelligences and wills, but the entire human creature, body and soul, with his imagination, passions, appetites, secular experiences, the whole complex in which intellect and will are inextricably mingled. Cultivated apart, and as it were out of context, our noblest faculties may grow dry and superficial. Man being of a piece, if his appetite for beauty, joy, freedom, love, is left unnourished, his so called spiritual nature contracts and hardens.[10]

A number of elements are implicit here. The first is the idea that the Boethian definition of the human being as an individual substance of a rational nature is completely inadequate.[11] Not only is the human being inadequately described as a rational animal, but the human being is also insufficiently understood if pared down to the interplay of a rational intellect and a free will. When Guardini thinks of a human person, he is thinking of "the entire human creature, body and soul, with his imagination, passions, appetites, secular experiences, the whole complex in which intellect and will are inextricably mingled."[12] Secondly, Guardini's human person has an appetite for beauty, joy, freedom, and love. These appetites need to be nourished if the intellect and will are not to "contract and harden."

In emphasising the need for a more expansive anthropology than that which is typified by the scholastic manuals of the pre-conciliar era, Guardini was very much in tune with members of the lay Catholic literati such as Paul Claudel, who complained about Jansenists holding the "noble faculties of imagination and sensibility in contempt, to which, [he said], certain lunatics would have added reason itself." Claudel believed that the Jansenists had created a crisis, not so much of the intellect, but of "a starved imagination."[13]

Thirdly, it follows from this problem of a starved imagination that the development and nourishment of the human capacity for mythopoetic thinking is a necessary component of a truly human spiritual formation. In scholastic language, there is *intellectus* as well as *ratio*; in German, *Vernunft* as well as *Verstand*; or intuition as well as logical analysis. This was a key theme in the works of another of young Ratzinger's heroes, the philosopher Peter Wust. Mythopoesis nourishes the imagination and thereby nurtures the capacity for connatural judgment.[14]

Apropos Grace Branham's aversion to a rigid, contracted, or one might say "pinched," spiritual nature, for which the anthropology of Guardini was a pre-conciliar antidote, in the famous *Ratzinger Report* of 1985, Cardinal Ratzinger stated that a "theologian who does not love art, poetry, music and nature can be dangerous" because "blindness and deafness toward the beautiful are not incidental: they are necessarily reflected in his theology."[15] Moreover, in *A New Song for the Lord*, wherein he was critical of what he called "parish tea party liturgy" and "emotional primitivism," Ratzinger further acknowledged that an implication of this is that seminaries need to be a place of broad cultural formation. While he conceded that "no one can do everything," he nonetheless implored ecclesial leaders "not to surrender to philistinism."[16]

A related anthropological insight may be found in Benedict Groeschel's book *Spiritual Passages.*[17] Groeschel believes that human beings tend to have a "primary transcendental," that is, a natural attraction to that which is true, beautiful, or good. Aquinas is the obvious example of someone focused

on truth; St. Francis of Assisi was clearly deeply attracted
to goodness; and St. Augustine and St. Bonaventure are the
Doctors of the Church most associated with beauty. Groeschel believes that it is important for spiritual directors to discern what a person's primary transcendental is. This will give
the director an insight into a person's likely spiritual strengths,
and where work will probably need to be done. One can even
apply this theory to recent popes. It could be argued that St.
John Paul II's primary transcendental was truth; Pope Benedict XVI's, beauty; and Pope Francis's, goodness.

Assuming that Groeschel is on to something here, it
raises a further question of the relationship between one's
primary transcendental, one's spiritual life, and one's study of
theology. The fact that von Balthasar's *magnum opus* addressed
the issue of the nature of the Trinity from the perspective of
all three transcendentals would seem to suggest that he was,
at least, aware of the need to broaden the theological enterprise beyond the objective side of objectivity and capital "V,"
veritas, important and essential though this is.

In summary, it may be argued that the combined insights
of Newman, Guardini, Ratzinger, Wust, Groeschel, and von
Balthasar converge on the principle that sound theological
work requires a pure heart (the heart in this context being
something like the place of integration for the intellect, will,
imagination, passions, senses, body, and soul in pursuit of the
true, the beautiful, and the good); and further, that if spiritual
directors ignore the development of any of these dimensions of the human person, then the resulting spirituality can
be anemic.[18]

This more humanistic anthropology is not the only
intellectual contribution Romano Guardini made to young

Ratzinger's formation. Ratzinger has written that Guardini taught him that the essence of Christianity is not an idea, a system of thought, or a plan of action. The essence of Christianity is Jesus Christ Himself. This principle became enshrined in the conciliar document *Dei Verbum* (1965), which Ratzinger helped to draft, and it formed the central theme of his first encyclical, *Deus Caritas Est* (2007). Ratzinger also credited Guardini for giving him an approach to the spiritual interpretation of Scripture: "Guardini recognized that the liturgy is the true, living environment for the Bible and that the Bible can be properly understood only in this living context from which it first emerged. The texts of the Bible, this great book of Christ, are not to be seen as the literary products of some scribes at their desks, but rather as the words of Christ himself delivered in the celebration of the holy Mass."[19]

Pope Benedict XVI's statement that the organ for seeing God is a pure heart and that the intellect alone is not enough reiterates one of his earlier remarks in an article published in 1969 on the notion of human dignity in *Gaudium et Spes*.[20] In a broadside against eighteenth century conceptions of rationality, Ratzinger argued that "the organ by which God can be seen cannot be a non-historical 'ratio naturalis' [natural reason] which just does not exist, but only the *ratio pura*, i.e. *purificata* [purified reason] or, as Augustine expresses it echoing the gospel, the *cor purum* [pure heart]." At this time, he also observed that "the necessary purification of sight takes place through faith (Acts 15:9) and through love, at all events not as a result of reflection alone and not at all by man's own power."[21]

The Theological Virtue and Hermeneutic of Faith

Consistent with these statements, Pope Francis's first encyclical, *Lumen Fidei*, which was drafted by Pope Benedict XVI, contains the following words that highlight the link between the theological virtue of faith and the work of theology:

> Since faith is a light, it draws us into itself, inviting us to explore ever more fully the horizon which it illumines, all the better to know the object of our love. Christian theology is born of this desire. Clearly, theology is impossible without faith; it is part of the very process of faith, which seeks an ever deeper understanding of God's self-disclosure culminating in Christ. It follows that theology is more than simply an effort of human reason to analyze and understand, along the lines of the experimental sciences. God cannot be reduced to an object. He is a subject who makes himself known and perceived in an interpersonal relationship . . . The great medieval theologians and teachers rightly held that theology, as a science of faith, is a participation in God's own knowledge of himself. It is not just our discourse about God, but first and foremost the acceptance and the pursuit of a deeper understanding of the word which God speaks to us, the word which God speaks about himself, for he is an eternal dialogue of communion, and he allows us to enter into this dialogue. Theology thus demands the humility to be "touched" by God, admitting its own limitations before the mystery, while striving to investigate, with the discipline proper to reason, the inexhaustible riches of this mystery.[22]

The theological virtue of faith is, thus, a necessary prerequisite to any work of Catholic theology and this has been emphasised many times by Pope Benedict XVI in the specific context of scriptural exegesis. For example, in his Erasmus Lecture of 1989, which was titled "Biblical Interpretation in Crisis," he argued that scriptural analysis should take place within the horizons of faith itself.[23]

The Seven Theses on Christology

The moment we begin to treat faith as an indispensable element of any hermeneutical framework, we run into the territory of Trinitarian theology, the Creed as it were. In particular, we run into Christology because we know from *Gaudium et Spes* that Christ as the Second Adam "fully reveals man to man himself."[24] It is for this reason that Pope Benedict XVI noted that the Beatitude, "Blessed are the Pure of Heart," is "profoundly Christological."[25] We will see God when we enter into the "same attitude . . . in Christ Jesus" (Phil 2:5). The spiritual and academic enterprises thus become one of "entering into the mind of Christ."[26]

In this context, then-Cardinal Ratzinger offered seven theses on Christology that might orient the spiritual development of all Christians, but especially those considering using their intellects in the service of Christ.

Thesis 1: The Felial Thesis

According to the testimony of Holy Scripture, the center of the life and person of Jesus is his constant communication with the Father. Of this thesis, Ratzinger wrote: "only by entering into Jesus' solitude, only by participating in what is most personal to him, his communication with the Father, can one see what this most personal reality is; only thus can one penetrate to his identity. This is the only way to understand him and to grasp what 'following Jesus' means. The Christian confession is not a neutral proposition; it is prayer, only yielding its meaning within prayer."[27]

Thesis 2: The Soteriological Thesis

Jesus died praying. At the Last Supper, He anticipated His death by giving Himself, thus transforming His death—from within—into an act of love, into a glorification of God. Regarding this thesis, Ratzinger concludes: "Death, which, by its very nature, is the end, the destruction of every communication, is changed by him [Christ] into an act of self-communication; and this is man's redemption, for it signifies the triumph of love over death. We can put the same thing another way: death, which puts an end to words and to meaning, itself becomes a word, becomes the place where meaning communicates itself."[28] The Eucharist is, thus, the great gift of this act of love, which begins at the Last Supper but is finished on the Cross.

Here again, Ratzinger invokes Guardini in the liturgical context in order to make a point about the nexus between spirituality and theological method. In his essay "Guardini on Christ in Our Century," Ratzinger writes: "As a student, Romano Guardini had himself experienced the drama of liberalism and its collapse, and with a few friends he set out to find a new path for theology. What came to impress him in the course of this search was the experience of the liturgy as the place of encounter with Jesus. It is above all in the liturgy that Jesus is among us, here it is that he speaks to us, here he lives."[29]

Thesis 3: The Personal Thesis

Because the center of the person of Jesus is prayer, it is essential to participate in His prayer if we are to know and understand Him.

In another criticism of eighteenth-century style rationality, Ratzinger writes that prayer is not "some kind of pious supplement to reading the Gospels, adding nothing to knowledge of him or even being an obstacle to the rigorous purity of critical knowing. On the contrary it is the basic precondition of real understanding, in the sense of modern hermeneutics—i.e. the entering-in to the same time and the same meaning."[30] Even more daringly, in his analysis of this thesis, Ratzinger suggests that the New Testament provides a foundation for a theological epistemology.[31]

Thesis 4: The Ecclesial Thesis

Fellowship with the person of Jesus, which emerged from participation in His prayer, thus constitutes the all-embracing fellowship that Paul calls the "Body of Christ."[32] Therefore, the Church—the "Body of Christ"—is the true subject of our knowledge of Jesus. In the Church's memory, the past is present because Christ is present and lives in her.

The logical corollary is, therefore, that any spirituality must be nourished by the Tradition of the Church, the deposit of the faith, and not built upon a syncretic mixture of elements, or what the Germans call a *Bettelsuppe* (or Begger's broth) of ingredients. This concept rules out the recontextualists's idea of Tradition whereby each generation of Catholics is analogous to receivers of a testamentary benefit, which they then own and can modify according to their own preferences or with reference to other traditions.

In Ratzinger's words, theology has an ecclesial quality, "which is not an epistemological collectivism, not an ideology which violates reason, but a hermeneutical context which is essential to reason if it is to operate at all."[33]

Thesis 5: The Dogmatic Thesis

"The core of the dogma defined in the councils of the early Church consists in the statement that Jesus is the true Son of God, of the same essence as the Father and, through the Incarnation, equally of the same essence as us. . . . [Thus] Christology from above and from below, the theology of the Incarnation and the theology of the Cross, form an indivisible unity."[34]

Here the difficulty for the spiritual life is the tension between the theology of the Cross and the theology of the Incarnation. In an article on the interventions of Cardinal Josef Frings in the debates of the Second Vatican Council, Ratzinger observes that Frings was keen to emphasise one general principle: "For the Christian life in the world three revealed truths are always to be kept before us: creation, which teaches us to love the things of the world as God's work; the Incarnation, which spurs us on to dedicate to God all the things of the world; the cross and resurrection, which leads us in the imitation of Christ to sacrifice and continence with regard to the things of the world."[35]

In other words, spiritualities can become pathological if the tension between creation, Incarnation, and the Cross and Resurrection is loosened, and one gains dominance over the others. For example, Jansenism is fixated on the Cross, while what Ratzinger called bourgeois Pelagianism is fixated on the goodness of creation and could do with a dose of the theology of the Cross.

Thesis 6: The Volitional Thesis

The Neo-chalcedon theology, which is summed up in the Third Council of Constantinople (680–681), was an important contribution to the proper grasp of the inner unity of biblical and dogmatic theology, of theology and religious life. Here, one might say that Ratzinger's reference to the Third Council of Constantinople is code for saying that the works of Maximus the Confessor are an excellent antidote to Nestorian tendencies, which may have dire consequences for one's understanding of the relationship between nature and grace.[36]

Thesis 7: The Hermeneutical Thesis

The historical-critical method and other modern scientific methods are important for understanding Holy Scripture and Tradition. Their value, however, depends upon the hermeneutical (philosophical) context in which they are applied.[37] This was the point of Ratzinger's "Erasmus Lecture," and this principle may be found in a more expanded form in the document, "The Interpretation of the Bible in the Church," a publication of the Pontifical Biblical Commission during a period when Ratzinger was its president.[38] For Ratzinger, only the hermeneutic of faith itself is sufficient to maintain the inner unity of the corpus of the Old and New Testaments and to achieve a synthesis of the two. He also argues that only the doctrine of the two natures of Christ joined together in one person is able "to open up a vista in which apparent contradictions found in the tradition each have enough scope and can be moulded together into a totality."[39]

Devotion to the Sacred Heart

In his doctoral dissertation on Ratzinger's spiritual Christology (based on these seven theses), Peter McGregor drew attention to an observation first made by Sara Butler that the subsection on the Christological Councils in the *Catechism of the Catholic Church* concludes with a paragraph on the Sacred Heart.[40] He also noted that Ratzinger's collection of essays published as *Behold the Pierced One* included a reflection on *Haurietas Aquas*, the 1956 encyclical of Pope Pius XII, which celebrated the centenary of Pope Pius IX's declaration of a Feast of the Sacred Heart of Jesus.[41]

One might, therefore, conclude that a it would be valuable intellectual exercise to comb through the writings of saints and scholars who have had a strong devotion to the Sacred Heart to see what insights they have to enrich a specifically Trinitarian Christocentric anthropology. One thinks, for example, of St. Mechtilde, St. Claude de la Colombière, and Jules Chevalier, the founder of the Missionaries of the Sacred Heart.

One of the great missionaries of the Sacred Heart was Archbishop Alain de Boismenu, a friend of Paul Claudel, who was sent to open Catholic missions in Papua New Guinea. De Boismenu was a leonine style of bishop. He famously remarked that there were only two people in the world to whom he was ever unconditionally obedient (the Pope and his sister, Augustine, who had brought him up after their mother died). It was under de Boismenu's influence that the Australian poet James McAuley was converted to the Catholic faith and McAuley was later to write a hymn which in four verses encapsulates de Boismenu's spirituality of the sacred heart. The first verse contains the lines "Jesus in your heart we find love of the Father and mankind, these two loves to us impart, Divine love in a human heart'."[42]

The Importance of Friendship

McAuley's friendship with de Boismenu, de Boismenu's friendship with Claudel, von Balthasar's friendship with Adrienne von Speyer, and Joseph Ratzinger's friendships with von Balthasar, von Hildebrand, and Josef Pieper (to name but a few of his friends), illustrate a further principle: the epistemic importance of friendship.

In *Fides et Ratio*, St. John Paul II argues that "truth is attained not only by way of reason but also through trusting acquiescence to other persons who can guarantee the authenticity and certainty of the truth itself," adding that "the ancient philosophers proposed friendship as one of the most appropriate contexts for sound theological enquiry."[43]

In his book *On the Way to Jesus Christ*, Ratzinger further notes that "evangelisation is never merely intellectual communication [this is the error of the rationalist]; it is a process of experience, the purification and transformation of our lives, and for this to happen, company along the way is needed."[44]

In his 1995 work of homage to Romano Guardini, *Reform from the Source*, von Balthasar speaks of the "bombed out spiritual and intellectual landscape that surrounds us today."[45] Those of us who work within this bombsite need the support of friends to supplement the kind of Carmelite asceticism that is required of faithful Catholics in this dark night of our civilization. After the devastation of the sixteenth century, the rationalist attacks of the eighteenth century, the romantic nihilism of the nineteenth century, Bismark's

Kulturkampf against the Catholic faith in Germany, the French and Soviet revolutions and their militant atheism, the Nazi regime, followed by two generations of post-conciliar chaos, a new generation of theologians is helping one another piece together the debris. Symposia such as those sponsored by The Institute for Priestly Formation are, therefore, an important element in the spiritual development of Catholic scholars and the work of the new evangelization.[46]

The Role of the Holy Spirit

Finally, in *Fides et Ratio*, St. John Paul II not only speaks of the importance of friendships but also of the significance of the work of the Holy Spirit. The gifts of the Holy Spirit, especially wisdom, understanding, counsel, and knowledge, are necessary components of any spirituality deep enough to sustain the study of theology. Matthias Scheeben eloquently expresses this idea in his book, *The Mysteries of Christianity*: "The Holy Spirit anoints with his light the spiritual eye, and so imparts a moral receptivity enabling us to attain a fuller and purer comprehension of the content of faith; and so our knowledge only comes to full strength and life through the realizing of the supernatural life flowing out within us from the Spirit."[47]

Von Balthasar cites Scheeben's quotation in his essay on spirituality where he links it to Scheeben's nuptial mysticism. Theology, von Balthasar asserts, "proceeds always as a continuous dialogue between Bridegroom and bride. The Bridegroom gives and the bride receives, and only in this acceptance of faith can the miracle of the pouring forth of the Word, which is both sower and seed, be accomplished."[48] In a full frontal assault on Kantian epistemology, von Balthasar concludes that there is "no neutral standpoint outside the encounter between Bride and Bridegroom."[49] As a consequence:

> It is of the utmost importance to see that what is lacking [in the relationship between spirituality and theology] is not just a piece of material that can be easily incorporated into the existing structure, or else a sort of stylistic quality to be reproduced anew. . . . The fact is that the spiritual dimension can only be recovered through the soul of man being profoundly moved as the result of his direct encounter with revealed truth, so that it is borne in upon him, once and for all, how the theologian should think and speak, and how he should not. This holds good for both the estranged disciplines, dogmatic theology and spirituality.[50]

The Need for "Complete Personalities"

In a recently published work on the theological vision of Jean Danielou, Marc Nicholas concluded that "the answer to the gap, between the disciplines [of spirituality and theology] is not bridged through methodological or academic orientation, but rather is achieved by realizing who we are."[51] What people like Danielou, de Lubac, and von Balthasar understood was that the alternative to the atheistic humanisms of the nineteenth and twentieth centuries was a doxological humanism set within a Trinitarian, Christocentric anthropology. From this perspective—unless one gets the foundational anthropology right—the spirituality is likely to be defective. The intellect goes off the rails; the imagination becomes impoverished; the will is misguided, and the heart is impious. Nicholas suggested that "we need examples of an integrated anthropology or, 'complete personalities' to use von Balthasar's parlance, who exemplify the re-weaving of spirituality and theology."[52] Ratzinger is arguably the leading candidate to illustrate this integration. Other candidates include de Lubac and Danielou, Jesuit-scholar victims of the Nazis like Alfred Delp and Yves de Montcheuil, and heroic missionaries like Alain de Boismenu. Each of these could easily recite St. Ignatius's prayer: *Take Lord, and receive all my liberty; my memory, my understanding, my entire will, all that I have and possess, You have given all to me, To you, Lord, I return it. All is yours. Give me only your love and grace. That is sufficient for me.*

An ability to recite this prayer and mean it would seem to be evidence of a heart that is, at least, attempting to be pure.

NOTES

1.   Antonio Valsecchi, *Dei fondamenti della religion e dei fonti dell'empietà, Dei fondamenti della religion e dei fonti dell'empietài* (Charleston, South Carolina: Nabu Press, 2011). Cited in Cornelio Fabro, *God in Exile: Modern Atheism*, trans. Arthur Gibson (Toronto: Newman Press, 1964), 483.

2.   Pope Benedict XVI, *Porta Fidei* (2011), sec. 10.

3.   E. Michael Jones, Living Machines: Bauhaus Architecture as Sexual Ideology, (San Francisco: Ignatius Press, 1995). 42.

4.   G. Hoskins, "An Interview with Lieven Boeve: Recontextualising the Christian Narrative in a Postmodern Context," *Journal of Philosophy and Scripture*, Vol. 3(2), (Spring 2006): 31-37.

5.   Hans Urs von Balthasar, *The Word Made Flesh*, vol. I of *Explorations in Theology* (San Francisco: Ignatius, 1989).

6.   Pope Benedict XVI, *Jesus of Nazareth* (New York: Doubleday, 2007), 92–93.

7.   Hans Urs von Balthasar, *Prayer* (San Francisco: Ignatius, 1986), 229.

8.   John Henry Newman, Sermon 12, "Love the Safeguard of Faith against Superstition." In *Fifteen Sermons Preached before the University of Oxford* (London: Longmans, Green and Co, 1909): 222-250 at 239.

9.   Peter McGregor, "Spiritual Christology of Joseph Ratzinger," (PhD diss., Australian Catholic University, 2013).

10.   Grace Branham, preface to *Sacred Signs* by Romano Guardini, (St. Louis: Pio Decimo Press, 1955), 5.

11.   This argument was made by Joseph Ratzinger is his essay "Concerning the Notion of the Person in Theology," *Communio: International Catholic Review*, 17 (Fall, 1990): 439–454.

12.   Grace Branham, Preface to *Sacred Signs* by Romano Guardini, op. cit. 5.

13.   Paul Claudel, *Positions et Propositions* (Paris: Gallimard, 1926), 175.

14.   For a recent article on this subject, see Daniel McInerny, "Poetic Knowledge and Cultural Renewal," *Logos: A Journal of Catholic Thought and Culture*, 15:4, (Fall, 2012): 18.

15.   Joseph Ratzinger, *The Ratzinger Report* (San Francisco: Ignatius, 1985), 130.

16.   Joseph Ratzinger, *A New Song for the Lord* (New York: Crossroad, 1996), 175.

17.   Benedict Groeschel, *Spiritual Passages: The Psychology of Spiritual Development* (New York: Crossroad, 1984).

18.   For a very extensive analysis of the biblical and patristic understandings of the concept of a pure heart see the publications of Juana Raasch.

19.   Joseph Ratzinger, "Guardini on Christ in Our Century," *Crisis Magazine*, (June 1996): 14–15 at 14.

20.   Joseph Ratzinger, "On the Dignity of the Human Person," in *Commentary on the Documents of the Second Vatican Council*, ed. Herbert Vorgrimler (London: Burns and Oates, 1969), 155.

21.   Ibid.

22.   Pope Francis, *Lumen Fidei* (2013), sec. 36.

23.   Joseph Ratzinger, "Biblical Interpretation in Crisis: On the Question of the Foundations and Approaches of Exegesis Today," in *Biblical Interpretation in Crisis: The Ratzinger Conference on Bible and Church*, ed. Richard John Neuhaus (Grand Rapids: Eerdmans: 1989), 1–24.

24.   Pope Paul VI, *Gaudium et Spes* (1965), sec. 22.

25.   Joseph Ratzinger, *Jesus of Nazareth*, (New York: Doubleday, 2007): 95.

26.   Ibid, 95.

27.   Joseph Ratzinger, *Behold the Pierced One* (San Francisco: Ignatius, 1986), 19.

28.   Ibid., 25.

29.   Ratzinger, "Guardini on Christ in our Century," 14.

30.   Ratzinger, *Behold the Pierced One*, 26.

31.   Ibid.

32.   Ibid., 27.

33.   Ibid., 32.

34.   Ibid.

35.   Joseph Ratzinger, "Frings's Speeches During the Second Vatican Council: Apropos of A. Muggeridge's *The Desolate City*," *Communio: International Catholic Review*, Cardinal 15, no. 1 (1988): 131–47.

36.   An in-depth analysis of this topic may be found in recent publications by Aaron Riches of the Edith Stein Institute in Granada.

37.   Joseph Ratzinger, "Seven Theses on Christology and the Hermeneutic of Faith," *Letter and Spirit* (2007): 189–209.

38.   Pontifical Biblical Commission, "The Interpretation of the Bible in the Church," April 15, 1993. Available on Holy See website.

39.   Ratzinger, *Behold the Pierced One*, 45.

40.   Peter McGregor, "The Spiritual Christology of Joseph Ratzinger," 26.

41.   Joseph Ratzinger, *Behold the Pierced One*, 47-71.

42.   James McAuley, "Jesus in Your Heart we Find," *The Living Parish Hymn Book*, Anthony Newman (ed), (Sydney: Living Parish Series, 1965):133.

43.   St. John Paul II, *Fides et Ratio* (1998), sec. 31.

44.   Joseph Ratzinger, *On the Way to Jesus Christ*, trans. Michael J Miller (San Francisco: Ignatius Press, 2005), 50.

45.   Hans Urs von Balthasar, *Romano Guardini: Reform from the Source* (San Francisco: Ignatius, 2010), 9.

46.   This book is one in a series of books from The Institute for Priestly Formation as the fruit of its Annual Seminar for Theologians held at Creighton University. The theologians whose essays are contained in this book were invited to ponder how spirituality might impress upon theology a correct method for its fruitful execution.

47.   This translation is von Balthasar's. In the English version of *The Mysteries of Christianity* translated by Cyril Vollert (New York: Herder, 1954), the treatment of the Holy Spirit is found in pages 149–189.

48.   Balthasar, *The Word Made Flesh*, 201.

49.   Ibid, 36.

50.   Ibid., 201.

51.   Marc Nicholas, *Jean Daniélou's Doxological Humanism: Trinitarian Contemplation and Humanity's True Vocation* (Eugene, OR: Pickwick Publications, 2012), 8.

52.   Ibid.

Ratzinger on Theology as a Spiritual Science

D. Vincent Twomey

Pope Benedict XVI, writing to the participants of a meeting held on October 6, 2005 to celebrate the centenary of the birth of Hans Urs von Balthasar, stressed that: "Spirituality does not attenuate the scientific charge, but impresses upon theological study the right method for achieving a coherent interpretation." Behind this assertion is a lifelong battle by theologians such as von Balthasar and Ratzinger to define theology in the traditional sense amid the transformation of theology that occurred in the past half-century into just one more academic subject among many. This transformation was characterized by its aim to be purely scientific or academic (*wissenschaftlich*) and so, as a corollary, to be free from what was considered to be the "heterogeneous" authority of the Church. In other words, the vision of theology shared by von Balthasar, Ratzinger, and others (such as de Lubac and Bouyer) was and is, to put it mildly, contested in the world of contemporary theology. Two radically different views of what constitutes theology are at stake.

Before looking more closely at Ratzinger's own

understanding of theology, I would like to introduce the topic by recalling an incident that (I was told) took place at the University of Regensburg during my time there in the early 1970s. A first-year student of theology came reeling out of one of her first lectures in a daze. She was deeply upset by what she had heard in the lecture and said to a friend who had been studying theology some years, "Did you hear what he said?" The friend replied, "Oh, don't take it too seriously. After a few more lectures you will have lost your faith." Theology had become so radically critical of what young people at the time still took as Gospel—the faith they had received from their Catholic parents and schools—that it undermined it. Of course, theology can be upsetting insofar as it challenges misinterpretations of the Christian faith, but such a widespread undermining of the faith would mean that all but professional theologians had gotten it wrong.

According to Ratzinger, what actually went wrong was the exclusive use of the so-called scientific approach to theology, an approach that was predicated on questionable philosophical assumptions. This method was, by its nature, inimical to the faith because it was basically positivistic and eliminated consideration of the metaphysical dimension. In the attempt to establish its claim to be considered scientific, theology embraced the methods of critical exegesis. While good and useful in themselves, these methods effectually reduced the study of Scripture and the documents of Tradition to a kind of antiquarianism, namely a search to describe as exactly as possible the origins of texts in their historical development.[1] Because of the hermeneutical and philosophical presuppositions of the historical-critical method, the truth claims of the text were left aside.[2] Taking their place was a more or less radical questioning of the Church's doctrines that tended to unsettle the faith of the so-called "simple faithful," to use a phrase that is easily misunderstood.

Simplicity (*haplotes*) has a wide range of meanings in the New Testament: "simplicity, sincerity, purity or probity of mind and liberality (arising from simplicity and frankness of character)."[3] It expresses the effect of a mature faith, a faith that knows no barriers—social, cultural, or racial (Gal 3:28). Christianity rejects any suggestion that there are (as the Gnostics held) two classes in the Church, the enlightened (or learned) elite and the masses. We are all one in Christ. It is characteristic of the Christian faith that, echoing Augustine, "faith in Him who had become man opened to all men the royal way of the philosopher [the allusion is to Plato's exclusivist notion of truth] and made it a real way [for everyone]."[4] Ratzinger recalls Bonaventure's astonishment at meeting an elderly woman of deep faith who possessed more wisdom than the greatest scholars. Augustine, in the tumultuous months leading up to his conversion, "discovered to his deep amazement that his mother, that simple and unlearned women, had reached the pinnacle of philosophy by virtue of her discernment and the simplicity of a life rooted within."[5]

In an essay entitled "Faith and Learning,"[6] Ratzinger clarifies what is meant by the simplicity of mature faith, which not infrequently carried with it an implicit criticism of learning or scholarship. Skepticism with regard to learning, as found in Thomas A. Kempis's *The Imitation of Christ*[7] and in the works of St. Francis of Assisi, is also echoed in the New Testament. In 1 Corinthians 1:18–25, St. Paul contrasts the wisdom of the Greeks with the simplicity of the Christian message. The tradition finds its origin in the words of the

Lord: "I give praise to you, Father, Lord of heaven and earth, for although you have hidden these things from the wise and the learned you have revealed them to the childlike" (Mt 11:25). "In these words, we find the root of that reserve with regard to culture and learning that appears again and again throughout the history of the Church; they also explain the profound seriousness of the question we are discussing."[8]

This raises the question: "How does Paul reconcile his scorn for the wisdom of the Greeks with his own spiritual struggle to comprehend the content of the faith—a struggle that would have been unthinkable without the legacy of Hebrew and Greek learning?"[9] Ratzinger's answer is found in what he calls the missionary element of the faith (see 1 Tim 2:4). "The love that is required by faith and that belongs to its innermost nature does not exclude the other's need for truth. . . . The faith that reaches out to the other reaches out of necessity to his questioning as well, to his need for truth."[10] By entering into the other's questioning, one is forced to pose the same questions to oneself and, in the process, comes to know other aspects of the faith that had previously remained unnoticed. For this reason, "faith needs philosophy because it needs man who questions and seeks."[11] By this process of trying to give a reason for the hope that is in us (1 Pet 3:15), theology is born.

Commenting on 1 Peter 3:15, the *locus classsicus* of theology in the Middle Ages, Ratzinger points out that the Greek text is more revealing than the translation: "Believers are enjoined to give an *apo-logia* regarding the logos of our hope to whoever asks for it. The *logos* must be so intimately their own that it can become *apo-logia*; through the mediation of Christians, the Word [*Wort*] becomes response [*Antwort*] to man's questions."[12] What is at stake here is not simply the legitimate need to explain one's beliefs to others, but the missionary nature of Christian faith.

Faith has a right to be missionary only if it transcends all traditions and constitutes an appeal to reason and an orientation towards the truth itself. However, if man is made to know reality and has to conduct his life, not merely as [one's own cultural or religious] tradition dictates, but in conformity to the truth, faith also has the positive duty to be missionary. With its missionary claim, the Christian faith sets itself apart from the other religions which have appeared in history; this claim is implicit in its philosophical critique of the religions and can be justified only on that basis.[13]

From the outset, Christian thinkers found their allies in the philosophers' critiques of the dominant myths and rituals of the time. Here philosophy must be understood in the original sense—what Ratzinger often calls the first Enlightenment—that spirit of radical criticism and self-criticism by the Greeks that led to the breakthrough from the world of traditional myths and rituals toward ultimate reality and, thus, to God. This is a restless criticism of common assumptions being treated as empty rituals, while traditional doctrines are being fossilized into ideologies.

Due to its reduction of reason to what can be scientifically verified, today's world is marked by an increasingly closed Western mind[14]; this excludes *a priori* the metaphysical questions that touch on the nature of our humanity, its origin and goal, and God, as well as the source of moral criteria. Ratzinger maintains that this closing of the Western mind has also affected theology, as seen, for example, in the stress on *orthopraxis*, on the one hand, and the more bourgeois version of ecclesial activity on the other, both of which treat the question of truth with indifference. This is often justified by an appeal to a salvation–history approach to theology rather than to theology proper. Ratzinger comments: "I am convinced, in fact, that the crisis we are experiencing in the Church and in humanity is closely allied to the exclusion of God as a topic with which reason can properly be concerned—an exclusion that has led to the degeneration of theology first into historicism, then into sociologism, and, at the same time, to the impoverishment of philosophy."[15]

To return to the notion of simplicity, we must ask the question: What is the relationship between simplicity and learning (or academic theology)? The answer gives us our first indication of what Ratzinger meant by spirituality in the topic under discussion.

> For the Christian, the learned person is not the one who knows and can do the most but the one who has become most and more purely [human]. But one can neither become nor be that without letting oneself be touched by him who is the ground and measure of man and all his being. That is why a very simple person who bears within himself a sense of values and, thus, a sensitivity toward others, towards what is right and beautiful and true, is immeasurably more learned than the most experienced technocrat with his computer brain. Augustine experienced this in the case of his mother.[16]

Spirituality, as understood by Ratzinger, seems to be summed up in this phrase: allowing "oneself [to] be touched by him who is the ground and measure of man and all his being." How does this relate to theology? In two ways, it would seem. First of all, the great saints—men and women who had been "touched by God" in a remarkable fashion—influenced theologians. Athanasius would be unthinkable without St. Anthony the Great, Augustine without Monica, St. John Paul II without that remarkable tailor-cum-mystic, Jan Tyranowski. Secondly, it seems that the theologian must, likewise, be touched by God and be on the way, as it were, to acquiring that simplicity which is the goal of all our lives. This will profoundly affect his or her way of studying theology.

Theology has its own implicit spirituality. Ratzinger often quotes 1 Peter 3:15: "Always be ready to give an explanation to anyone who asks you for a reason for your hope." Ratzinger claims that was the express aim of the medieval theologians, and it was his own aim from the start, namely to discover and present the reasonableness of faith to today's world. The topic he chose for his Inaugural Lecture as Chair of Fundamental Theology on the Catholic Theology Faculty of the University of Bonn is significant: "The God of Faith and the God of the Philosophers: A contribution to the problem of *theologia naturalis*."[17] He shows that the breakthrough in Greek thought, when reason discovered God as he who transcends man's religious world, was paralleled around the same time by the breakthrough made by the Prophets under Divine Inspiration. Both kinds of "enlightenment," as Ratzinger shows, intermingled in the late wisdom literature, preparing the way for divine reason to become flesh. When early Christian thinkers such as the second century's St. Justin Martyr were called upon by their contemporaries to give a reason for their hope, they found welcome allies in the Greek thinkers.[18] However, these theologians did not simply take over Greek thought; they purified and transformed it and, in the process, deepened the Church's own grasp of the divine mysteries.[19] The Church's doctrine of the Trinity is the most significant instance of that centuries-long struggle to articulate the central mystery of our faith in human language;[20] the notion of "person" is perhaps the most significant cultural product of the same process.[21]

Theology is the exercise of reason in the realm of faith:[22] faith seeking (ever deeper) understanding, always aware that, in the final analysis, "if the painful history of the human and Christian striving for God proves *anything*, it surely proves that any attempt to reduce God to the scope of our comprehension leads to the absurd."[23] Referring to Bonaventure's other justification for theology, Ratzinger writes that it amounts to "Love seeks understanding. It wishes to know even better the one whom it loves. It 'seeks his face,' as Augustine never tires of repeating."[24] Love, Ratzinger says, "is at the same time eros for truth and only so does it remain sound as agape for God and man."[25]

For Ratzinger, Revelation is primarily an event; more precisely, it is the person of Jesus Christ, true God, and true man. Scripture and Tradition allow us to encounter Christ's person, but He transcends both. History is marked by the transforming effect of Divine intervention on humanity to which it is addressed. Revelation is not just about God but involves man, the recipient of Divine Revelation, who cooperates in shaping Revelation.[26] Man's capacity to be addressed by God, and so be transformed by God's self-revelation, is based on the fact that man is made in the image and likeness of God. God addresses man's reason and will (embedded in a body and, therefore, in a particular culture and language) when He reveals Himself for the salvation of humanity, so that man's reason is caught up in the act of faith.[27] Theology is the result of man's inadequate but real grasp of what is revealed; it is therefore intrinsic to faith. Theology is not an added extra, but is part of the foundation of revealed faith.[28] Faith expresses itself in theological terms that are forged out of a language and culture common to the theologian and his contemporaries.[29] Faith is, thus, communicated through one person's theological perspective—meaning through the mind of one theologian who has grasped something of faith's unfathomable meaning and can communicate it in his or her own language.

In the opening essay of Part Three of *Principles of Catholic Theology*, which deals with "The formal principles of Christianity and the method of theology," Ratzinger asks, "What is theology?" The context is a *laudatio* for bishop and theologian Cardinal Herman Volk on the occasion of his seventy-fifth birthday. Taking his cue from Bishop Volk's own motto, "God is all in all," and his renown as one who tended to ask questions that got to the heart of the matter, Ratzinger's main thesis asserted that "Theology has to do with God, and, in that way, it also fulfils the ultimate task of philosophical speculation." He clarifies this by stressing, "If theology has to do primarily with God, if its ultimate and proper theme is not salvation history or Church or community but simply God, then it must think in philosophical terms,"[30] (by which he means in metaphysical terms). Ratzinger stresses that philosophy is not absorbed into theology but retains its own integrity; however, that is not the main point here. The main point is, to quote St. Thomas Aquinas: "the object of this science is God."[31] Ratzinger held this against the more common view at the time that theology was about the economy of salvation that "finds in what is positive, [for example] in the Church, the reflection of God's nature and being."[32] This way of thinking, Ratzinger adds, characterized the assumptions of the Second Vatican Council. The medieval controversies about the nature of theology—whether a *scientia speculativa* (the Thomist view) or a *scientia practica* (the Franciscan view)—reflect the more radical, contemporary use of the terms "orthodoxy" and "orthopraxis" in the attempts to give theology a new orientation after the Council. When orthopraxis, the preferred option today, is pushed to its radical extremes, theology "becomes then no more than a guide to action, which, by reflecting on praxis, continually develops new modes of praxis."[33] As a result, not only redemption but truth itself becomes the product of man. Even when not pushed to this extreme, "less militant—what we might call Western-bourgeois—forms of the undivided sovereignty of *scientia practica* are ultimately marked by the same loss of truth."[34] Today, truth is *a priori* considered inconceivable and any claim to truth is seen as an attack on tolerance and pluralism, while "the decision about what to communicate is decreed in terms of how it is to be communicated."[35] Anyone who has anything to do with teacher training, for example, knows the confusion caused by the primacy of pedagogical skills over objective content. Behind this confusion is a lack of trust in the truth of the faith.

Defending the Thomistic position, Romano Guardini spoke in the early 1920s about the primacy of *logos* over *ethos*, namely the primacy of God's truth over his actions throughout history. More precisely, it means "a view of theology in which the meaning of Christocentrism consists in transcending oneself and, through the history of God's dealings with mankind, making possible an encounter with the being of God."[36] The whole point of the Incarnation, as St. Irenaeus pointed out, was to enable man to encounter the Holy One (who up to then was beyond man's reach), and to destroy "the insurmountable wall that had separated mankind from the being and the truth of God."[37] Christology becomes a real theology only to the extent that the metaphysical reality of God is discussed which, in turn, opens up the need for metaphysics. Theology must transcend history and ultimately speak of God.[38]

Influenced by Pseudo-Dionysius, Bonaventure came to understand theology in terms of the Greek distinction between *qeologia* (theology) and *qeologikh* (the study of theology), where those who were called theologians could be regarded as the voice of the deity. For this reason, "Scripture alone is theology in the fullest sense of the word because it truly has God as its subject; it does not just speak of him but is his own speech."[39] Theology, Ratzinger concludes, is a spiritual science. "The normative theologians are the authors of Holy Scripture. This statement is valid not only with reference to the objective written documents they left behind but also with reference to their manner of speaking, in which it is God himself who speaks."[40]

Commenting on Jerome's saying, "Ignorance of the Scriptures is ignorance of Christ," Pope Benedict XVI stresses the importance of every Christian living in contact and in personal dialogue with the Word of God given to us in Sacred Scripture. "This dialogue . . . must be a truly personal dialogue because God speaks with each one of us through Sacred Scripture and it has a message for each one. We must not read Sacred Scripture as a word of the past [as in the historical-critical method] but as the Word of God that is also addressed to us, and we must try to understand what it is that the Lord wants to tell us."[41] In the same catechesis, he warns against any individualist approach: the personal word is also intended to build community, the Church.

Ratzinger concludes his article, "What is Theology?" with the comment: "It seems to me that it was only after World War II and completely after Vatican Council II that we came to think that theology, like any exotic subject, can be studied from a purely academic perspective from which one acquires knowledge that can be useful in life and earn a living from it. But just as we cannot learn to swim without water, so we cannot learn theology without the spiritual praxis in which it lives."[42] It is worth recalling that the *locus classicus* for theology, 1 Peter 3:15, begins with the injunction, "Sanctify Christ as Lord in your hearts."

Here, I will make two brief points about the nature of spiritual praxis. The first point applies to the asceticism inherent in the search for truth. "To the extent that men allow themselves to be guided and cleansed by the truth, they find their way not only to their true selves but also to the human 'thou.' Truth, in fact is the medium by which men make contact . . . Accordingly the movement towards the truth implies temperance."[43] It purifies man from egotism and from the illusion of absolute autonomy, giving him the courage to be humble. Further—and this indicates philosophy's central role in spiritual praxis—Ratzinger argues that, "to think through the essence of truth is to arrive at the notion of God. . . . Ultimately, therefore, reverence for the truth is inseparable from that disposition of veneration that we call adoration."[44]

The second point is that the spiritual praxis that is

the humus of theology is both personal and ecclesial by nature because it is rooted in the act of faith. In his paper, "The Spiritual Basis and Ecclesial Identity of Theology,"[45] Ratzinger sets out to demonstrate the intrinsic relationship between theology as an academic subject and the teaching authority of the Church. That relationship is rooted in the radical nature of Christian faith and the related nature of conversion. His starting point is the statement in the Letter to the Galatians where Paul describes that distinctive element of Christianity as a personal experience, which revolutionizes everything and is, at the same time, an objective reality: "Yet I live, no longer I, but Christ lives in me," (Gal 2:20).[46] This expresses both an intense individual experience that simultaneously "declares what Christianity is for everyone,"[47] namely a death-event, when one subject (the autonomous "I") is fitted into a new subject (the greater "I" of Christ, the Church, the risen body of Christ). "The 'Yet I live, no longer I' does not describe a private mystical experience but rather defines the essence of baptism."[48] In Romans, Paul "describes baptism as an experience of being committed to the standard of doctrine," to which the subjective response is "an obedience coming from the heart (Rom 6:17)."[49] That spiritual praxis peculiar to theology is, of its very essence, ecclesial, and so involves sincere submission to the Church's doctrine as that which is ultimately assured by the Spirit of God present and working in the Church through the apostolic succession. The ultimate criterion is not the theologian's insight, but the Church's teaching.

Stephan Otto Horn claims that Galations 2:20 is the key to Pope Benedict XVI's spirituality.[50] There are many instances of great saints—such as St. Anthony the Great, St.

Augustine, or Romano Guardini—being moved by hearing
a word of Scripture at a decisive moment in their lives, and
so, in the life of the Church. Horn argues that Galations 2:20
had a similar significance for Ratzinger, even as a young theologian, when he was studying Augustine. Ratzinger regularly
cites Galations 2:20 and interprets it in an original way, often
reflecting on his own personal experiences. Horn argues that
this text had a decisive influence on Ratzinger's theology.
Horn describes three dimensions of the phrase, "Yet I live,
no longer I, but Christ lives in me" (Gal 2:20).

The first dimension concerns the surrender of one's
autonomy.[51] "No longer I" means cancelling the ego and
living within a new subject, the Church, a process, as we
have seen, that only happens through the encounter with
Jesus Christ made possible by the Church as the Body of
Christ. The third dimension, only implicit in Galations 2:20,
is an inner transformation, which union with Christ in the
Eucharist effects is the believer, who thereby finds oneself
anew through participation in Christ's love for the world, the
missionary dimension as it were."[52]

The second dimension, the significance of union with
Christ, requires greater explanation: "Christ lives in me."
Here, according to Horn, Ratzinger enters into the mysticism
of the Apostles and makes it the center of his own spirituality. "Ratzinger's theological and spiritual insights demonstrate
that Christian mysticism is not a private interior experience
but rather an experience of faith, which occurs in baptism
and Eucharist and in the life shaped by them, and thus are
most closely tied to our being Christian. In baptism and
Eucharist we are touched directly by God, indeed we become
one with him."[53] In his catechesis on St. Paul, Pope Benedict

XVI speaks of the mutual compenetration between Christ and the Christian, which is characteristic of Paul's teaching and even speaks of an element that we might describe as "mystical" because it entails identifying ourselves with Christ, as well as Christ with us.[54]

This identification is realized through prayer. Let us look more closely at what this simple statement means for Ratzinger. In the introduction to the first volume of *Jesus of Nazareth*, he concludes as follows:

> Again and again the Gospels note that Jesus withdrew "to the mountain" to spend nights in prayer "alone" with his Father. These short passages are fundamental for our understanding of Jesus; they lift the veil of mystery just a little; they give us a glimpse into Jesus' filial existence, into the source from which his action and teaching and suffering sprang. The "praying" of Jesus is the Son conversing with the Father: Jesus' human consciousness and will, his human soul, is taken up into that exchange, and in this way human "praying" is able to become a participation in this filial communion with the Father.[55]

Further along Ratzinger adds, "'He who sees Jesus sees the Father' (Jn 14:9). The disciple who walks with Jesus is thus caught up with him into communion with God. And this is what redemption means: this stepping beyond the limits of human nature, which had been a possibility and an expectation in man, God's image and likeness, since the moment of creation."[56]

Prayer has its source and summit in the Eucharist. In *Deus Caritas Est*, Pope Benedict XVI writes, "The Eucharist draws us into Jesus' act of self-oblation. More than just statically receiving the incarnate Logos, we enter into the very dynamic of his self-giving. The imagery of marriage between God and Israel is now realized in a way previously inconceivable: it had meant standing in God's presence, but now it becomes union with God through sharing in Jesus' self-gift, sharing in his body and blood. The sacramental 'mysticism,' grounded in God's condescension towards us, operates at a radically different level and lifts us to far greater heights than anything that any human mystical elevation could ever accomplish."[57]

Pope Benedict XVI describes the distinctive character of this mysticism in his treatment of the Beatitude, "Blessed are the pure in heart, then they will see God." How is the heart—"the organ of seeing God," man's inner eye—purified? The mystical tradition speaks of a "way of purification," ascending to final "union." We meet the motif of purity in Psalm 24, reflecting the Liturgy at the entrance to the Temple. "Who may go up the mountain of the Lord?" The answer is the man of clean hands and pure heart; that is, moral rectitude. One fundamental condition of purity is that "those who would enter into God's presence must inquire after him, must seek his face (Ps 24:6)."[58] Pope Benedict XVI comments:

> On Jesus' lips, though, these words acquire a new depth. For it belongs to his nature that he sees God, that he stands face-to-face with him, in permanent interior discourse—in a relationship of sonship. In other words, this Beatitude is profoundly Christological. We will see God, when we enter into the "mind of Christ" (Phil 2:5). Purification of heart occurs as a consequence of following Christ, of becoming one with him: "It is no longer I who live, but Christ who lives in me" (Gal 2:20). At this point something new comes to light: the assent to

God occurs precisely in the descent of humble service, in the descent of love, for love is God's essence, and is thus the power that truly purifies man and enables us to perceive God and to see Him. In Jesus Christ, God has revealed himself in his descending: [quote from Phil 2:6–9].[59]

Benedict then adds, "These words mark a decisive turning point in the history of mysticism. They indicate what is new in the Revelation of Jesus Christ. God descends to the point of death on the Cross. And precisely by doing so, he reveals himself in his true divinity. We ascend to God by accompanying him on this descending path."[60]

In his message on the centenary of the birth of Hans Urs von Baltahasar, Pope Benedict XVI affirmed that theology, as Balthasar conceived it, had to be married to spirituality; only in this way, in fact, could it be profound and effective.

Reflecting on this precise aspect, [Balthasar] wrote: "Does scientific theology only begin with Peter Lombard? And yet: who spoke more satisfactorily of Christianity than Cyril of Jerusalem, Origen in his homilies, Gregory of Nazianzus or the Areopagite, that master of theological reverence? Who would dare take exception to any one of the Fathers? People knew then what theological style was, the natural, obvious unity both between the attitude of faith and the scientific attitude and between objectivity and reverence. As long as theology was the work of saints, it remained prayerful theology. This is why its rendering in prayer, its fruitfulness for prayer and its power to generate prayer were so immeasurably immense." [61]

Pope Benedict XVI concludes: "These words lead us to reconsider the proper place of research in theology. Its need for a scientific approach is not sacrificed when it listens religiously to the Word of God and lives the life of the Church, strong in her Magisterium. Spirituality does not attenuate the scientific charge, but impresses upon theological study the right method for achieving a coherent interpretation." [62] The history of dogma illustrates this point in abundance; I want to draw attention to just one example.

When discussing the history, structure, and content of the Creeds of Nicaea and Constantinople, Ratzinger highlights the role played by the Cappadocian Fathers in making the theological breakthrough that led to the resolution of the post-Nicene crisis at the Council of Constantinople (381). That crisis in the Church was caused by the, at times, violent resistance of the majority of Eastern bishop/theologians (supported by the Emperor) to accept the formula of Nicaea. Ratzinger underscores that, even though they were a tiny minority before Constantinople, "The new theology of the Cappadocians, which made possible the triumph of Constantinople, rested in fact on the new [spiritual] experience that owed its existence to the Nicene faith. It is unthinkable without the suffering of the martyrs who defended their faith against the state church and, in a time of crisis, had recourse to a deep-rooted reliance on prayer and on the liturgy of the Church." [63] In other words, the suffering of the minority bishops for the faith of Nicaea provided the existential ground for the acceptance of the Cappadocian theology by the Bishops assembled at Constantinople. But that theology was, in turn, inspired by the experience of Christian prayer. Ratzinger points out that the source of the theology of St. Basil of Caesarea, the true "Father" of Constantinople, was the Liturgy: "Basil developed his concept of the Holy Spirit, his concept of Christian monotheism, entirely from the liturgy of the Church; his book about the Holy Spirit is, at bottom, nothing other than a theology of the liturgy. . . . In the biblical context of baptism, Basil found the fundamental law of Christian life and prayer. The reality of Christian prayer was the guideline for philosophy."[64]

As Prefect of the Congregation for the Doctrine of the Faith, Cardinal Ratzinger issued the *Instruction on the Ecclesial Vocation of the Theologian*.[65] In a later theological commentary on this text, he wrote:

[The *Instruction*] is ultimately concerned with an anthropological problem: if religion and reason cannot be brought into the proper correspondence, man's spiritual life disintegrates into a flat rationalism dominated by technique, on the one hand, and into a dark irrationalism on the other. . . . Positivism contests man's capacity for truth, for it holds that his knowledge is restricted to the producible and verifiable; meanwhile, irrational forces triumph outside the domain of production. For this reason, the Instruction places the subject of theology within the broad horizon of the question of man's capacity for the truth and of his true freedom. . . . [F]aith responds to the primordial question of man regarding his origin and goal. . . . But what distinguishes theology from the philosophy of religion and from secular religious science? The answer is that man's reason knows that it has not been left to its own devices. It is preceded by a Word which, though logical and rational, does not originate from reason itself but has been granted it as a gift and, as such always transcends it. It remains a task that we never completely fulfill in history. Theology is pondering what God has said and thought before us. If it abandons this secure ground, it annuls its own constitution.[66]

NOTES

1. See Scott Hahn, *Covenant and Communion: The Biblical Theology of Pope Benedict XVI* (Grand Rapids, MI: Brazos Press, 2009), in particular Chapter 2, "The Critique of Criticism," 25-40.

2. See Joseph Ratzinger, *Behold the Pierced One: An Approach to a Spiritual Christology*, trans. Graham Harrison (San Francisco: Ignatius Press, 1986), 42f. See also Joseph Ratzinger, "Theology and Church Politics," in *Church, Ecumenism, and Politics*, trans. Michael J. Miller, et al. (San Francisco: Ignatius Press, 2008), 150: "The Christian theologian does not merely interpret texts but enquires about the truth itself and he regards man as capable of apprehending the truth."

3. *The Analytical Greek Lexicon*, New and Revised Edition (London: Samuel Bagster and Sons, N.D.).

4. Joseph Ratzinger, *The Principles of Catholic Theology: Building Stones for a Fundamental Theology*, trans. Mary Francis McCarthy (San Francisco: Ignatius Press, 1987), 362.

5. Ibid.

6. "Glaube und Bildung," translated as "Faith and Education" in Ibid., 333–342.

7. Thomas A. Kempis, *The Imitation of Christ* (Minneapolis: Filiquarian, 2005).

8. Ratzinger, *The Principles of Catholic Theology*, 336.

9. Ibid., 337.

10. Ibid.

11. Joseph Ratzinger, *The Nature and Mission of Theology: Approaches to Understanding Its Role in the Light of Present Controversy*, trans. Adrian Walker (San Francisco: Ignatius Press, 1995), 29.

12. Ibid., 26.

13. Ibid., 26–27.

14. This is the end product of the process of "de-Hellinization" that Pope Benedict XVI succinctly outlined in his Regensburg Address (September 12, 2005). See also Tracey Rowland, *Ratzinger's Faith: The Theology of Pope Benedict XVI* (Oxford: University Press, 2008), 108–12.

15. Ratzinger, *The Principles of Catholic Theology*, 316. See, in particular, his introduction to *Fides et Ratio* in the chapter, "Truth and Tolerance."

16. Ibid., 341. "Christian naiveté consists in holding fast to the question of truth and referring learning to truth. If it fails to do so, it becomes indeed soulless and dangerous—we all know this and have experienced it," (Ibid., 338).

17. Pope Benedict XVI, *Der Gott des Glaubens und der Gott der Philosophen. Ein Beitrag zum Problem der theologia naturalis*, ed. Heino Sonnemans (Trier: Paulinus, 2006); see Emery de Gaàl, *The Theology of Pope Benedict XVI:*

The Christocentric Shift (New York: Palgrave Macmillan, 2010), 73–77 for a summary and evaluation. See also Joseph Ratzinger, "The God of Faith and the God of the Philosophers," in *Introduction to Christianity*, trans. J. R. Foster (San Francisco: Ignatius Press, 2004), 137–150.

18.   See Thomas Finan, "The Desired of All Nations," in Thomas Finan and Vincent Twomey, *Studies in Patristic Christology* (Dublin: Four Courts Press, 1998), 1–22.

19.   See also Ratzinger, *The Nature and Mission of Theology*, 27. Ratzinger also acknowledges that "sometimes the Church fathers were not sufficiently critical in appropriating philosophical concepts," (de Gaàl, *The Theology of Pope Benedict XVI*, 76).

20.   See Ratzinger, *The Principles of Catholic Theology*, 112–121 and Joseph Ratzinger, "Belief in the Triune God," in *Introduction to Christianity*, trans. J. R. Foster (San Francisco: Ignatius Press, 2004), 162–190.

21.   See also Ratzinger, *Introduction to Christianity*, 166–167; 181–184.

22.   "Consequently, seeking its own reason—and therein reason itself [the Logos], the reasonableness of reality—must be an essential part of the Christian faith," (Ratzinger, *Church, Ecumenism, and Politics*, 149).

23.   Ratzinger, *Introduction to Christianity*, 171.

24.   Ratzinger, *The Nature and Mission of Theology*, 27.

25.   Ibid.

26.   See Joseph Ratzinger, "The Biblical Belief in God," in *Introduction to Christianity*, trans. J. R. Foster (San Francisco: Ignatius Press, 2004).

27.   Ratzinger succinctly expresses this point in his commentary on St. John Paul II's Encyclical, *Fides et Ratio*, in Joseph Ratzinger, *Truth and Tolerance: Christian Belief and World Religions*, trans. Henry Taylor (San Francisco: Ignatius Press, 2004), 198–202.

28.   I think that Ratzinger would give his assent to Edward Farley, *Theologia: The Fragmentation and Unity of Theological Education* (Eugene, OR: Wipf and Stock Publishers, 2001), 153: "Theology in its primary meaning . . . is a personal and existential wisdom or understanding." Farley demonstrates, among other things, how the growing "scientific" approach to theology tended to detach itself from that "existential wisdom," becoming fragmented post-Schleiermacher, and only held together by making theology subservient to the training of clergy in all denominations. Any reform of the theological curriculum needs to pay attention to his analysis and suggestions.

29.   "Even dogmatic formulas such as 'one being in three Persons' include this refraction of the human element; they reflect in this case the man of late antiquity; whose questions and experiments are governed by the categories of late antique philosophy," (Ratzinger, *Introduction to Christianity*, 177).

30.   Ratzinger, *The Principles of Catholic Theology*, 316.

31.   Saint Thomas Aquinas, *STh* I q 1 a 7.

32.   Ratzinger, *The Principles of Catholic Theology*, 317.

33.   Ibid., 318.

34.   Ibid.

35.   Ibid., 319.

36.   Ibid.

37.   Ibid.

38.   See also Ibid., 320.

39.   Ibid., 321.

40.   Ibid. See also Scott Hahn, "The Spiritual Science of Theology," in *Covenant and Communion: The Biblical Theology of Pope Benedict XVI* (Grand Rapids, MI: Brazos Press, 2009), 63–90.

41.   Pope Benedict XVI, "General Audience," *Libreria Editrice Vaticana*, November, 7, 2007, http://www.vatican.va/holy_father/benedict_xvi/audiences/2007/documents/hf_ben-xvi_aud_20071107_en.html.

42.   Ratzinger, *The Principles of Catholic Theology*, 322.

43.   Ratzinger, *The Nature and Mission of Theology*, 39.

44.   Ibid., 40.

45.   Ibid., 45–72.

46.   Ibid., 50.

47.   Ibid., 51.

48.   Ibid., 52.

49.   Ibid., 53.

50.   Stephan Otto Horn ,"Zur Spiritualität von Joseph Ratzinger/Papst Benedikt XVI," in *Ein hörendes Herz: Hinführung zur Theologie und Spiritualität von Joseph Ratzinger/Papst Benedikt XVI*, Michaela Christine Hastetter and Helmut Hoping eds. (Regensburg: Friederich Pustet, 2012), 90–104.

51.   By way of contrast, in his book *The Principles of Catholic Theology*, Ratzinger critiques Karl Rahner's theology (anonymous Christianity), culminating in the claim that "The real problem seems to me to be in the spiritual formulation, for it is only in the spiritual formulation which has its source in the abstract concept, that we find the real test of theological speculation," (166). For Rahner, that spiritual formulation amounts to one's self-affirmation: "To be a Christian is to accept yourself," (166). The logic of such a spiritual formulation, Ratzinger shows, leads to nihilism. "Just to accept one's humanity as it is (or even 'in its unconditionality')—that is not redemption; it is damnation. For what does it mean to be human? Not [in the sense] that merely accepting humanity is the last word. Against such a conclusion, the question arises: Why are we as we are? And from that there flows the longing to become other than we are," (167).

52.   Stephan Otto Horn, "Zur Spiritualität von Joseph Ratzinger/Papst Benedikt XVI," 97.

53.   Ibid., 95.

54.   Pope Benedict XVI, "General Audience," *Libreria Editrice Vaticana*,

November 8, 2006, http://www.vatican.va/holy_father/benedict_xvi/
audiences/2006/documents/hf_ben-xvi_aud_20061108_en.html.

55. Pope Benedict XVI, *Jesus of Nazareth: From the Baptism in the Jordan to the Transfiguration*, trans. Adrian J. Walker (New York: Doubleday, 2007), 7. See also Ratzinger, *Behold the Pierced One*, especially 13–46.

56. Pope Benedict XVI, *Jesus of Nazareth*, 8.

57. Pope Benedict XVI, *Deus Caritas Est* (2005), sec. 13.

58. Pope Benedict XVI, *Jesus of Nazareth*, 94.

59. Ibid, 95

60. Ibid.

61. Hans Urs von Balthasar, *Verbum Caro: Saggi Teologici I* (Brescia, 1970), 228.

62. Message of His Holiness Benedict XVI for the Centenary of the birth of Fr. Hans urs von Balthasar, Oct 6, 2005.

63. Ratzinger, *The Principles of Catholic Theology*, 119–120. The German term *"geistlich"* is incorrectly translated as "intellectual;" it should instead be "spiritual."

64. Ibid., 120.

65. Joseph Ratzinger, *Donum Veritatis* (1990).

66. Ratzinger, *The Nature and Mission of Theology*, 102–103.

THE ESSENTIAL INTERRELATION BETWEEN THEOLOGY AND SPIRITUALITY

DANIEL A. KEATING

"Although our outer self is wasting away, our inner self is being renewed day by day." (2 Cor 4:16)

The Weariness of the Theological Task

The trigger for these reflections on the essential inter-relationship between theology and spirituality is a selection from Pope Benedict XVI, writing at Pentecost in 1998 about the advent of new movements in the Church. Recounting his initial experiences with several of these new movements, he speaks of:

> the early 1970's, a time when Karl Rahner and others were speaking of a winter in the Church. And it did seem that, after the great blossoming of the Council, frost was creeping instead of springtime, and that exhaustion was replacing dynamism. The dynamism now seemed to be somewhere else entirely—where people, relying on their own strength and without resorting to God, were setting about creating a better world of the future. That a world without God could not be good, let alone a better world,

71

was obvious to anyone who had eyes to see. But where was God in all this? Had not the Church in fact become worn-out and dispirited after so many debates and so much searching for new structures? What Rahner was saying was perfectly understandable. It put into words an experience that we were all having. But suddenly here was something that no one had planned. Here the Holy Spirit himself had, so to speak, taken the floor.[1]

This is a striking assessment of what was happening, not only in the Church at large but in theology as well. A "frost was creeping in" instead of the anticipated springtime that was promised. "An exhaustion" was replacing the initial dynamism. Moreover, the Church appeared to be "worn-out and dispirited." Why? Because, according to Pope Benedict XVI, we were seeking to create new things from our own ideas and by our own strength. We were being powered by the enthusiasm of our own visions and had simply run out of energy. All of this calls to mind the searching text of Isaiah 40:30–31: "Though young men faint and grow weary, and youths stagger and fall, They that hope in the LORD will renew their strength, they will soar on eagles' wings; They will run and not grow weary, walk and not grow faint." In the narrative recounted here by Pope Benedict XVI, the Holy Spirit "took the floor" by stirring up many young people in numerous movements to display the life and power of God. This story is still very much in process.

It is not difficult to see that this "creeping frost" and "exhaustion" can occur in the sphere of theology. When theology is fueled and energized, mostly by a human vision, it may start with great speed and make its way down the track with alacrity. However, this is just a momentum created by human enthusiasm and it quickly fades. It has no animating center or staying power and soon becomes exhausted. With no spiritual core, it looks to other motivations and sources of energy and "recenters" itself—taking on a new DNA, so to speak, and becomes something entirely different in nature. We do not have to strain to recognize this pattern in the past generation or two in some American Catholic theologies.

I would like to extend this observation and take it in a new direction. Theology, of course, can and does run dry for the reasons given by Pope Benedict XVI—those doing theology cease looking to the Lord and attempt to construct their own theological structures with materials of their own making. The road can become long and weary even for those who maintain their sure faith in God and seek to serve him in the theological task. The task of theology can become somewhat cold and hard. Theology's servants can suffer exhaustion and become worn-out and dispirited. Theologians need ongoing refreshment, so that they are renewed *in the midst of* the theological effort and find springs of life as a wayfarer along the way. Again, Paul's description of our life aptly applies to the task of theology in this age: "[The] outer self is wasting away, [but the] inner self is being renewed day by day" (2 Cor 4:16). Left to itself, I submit, the theological task tends toward "wasting away" and is in need of "being renewed day by day."

What are some of the root causes of this tendency toward exhaustion in the theological task? First, there is the inherent challenge of trying to grapple with the immensity of the subject matter itself—God and his dealings with the world. To borrow a phrase from Paul, "Who is qualified for this?" (2 Cor 2:16). The greatness of God, the breadth and complexity of His working in the world, the inherent limitations of our minds and language to express these things—all of this can lead to a weariness over time. This might be called the intrinsically steep "slope" of the theological task: no one can ascend this slope for long without falling prey to weariness. The temptation is to exit this steep slope and find another path that is less demanding, thus diverting oneself from the proper theological task to other ancillary disciplines that are easier to manage on natural human energy (for example, political issues, human development, historical research, and psychology, and so on).

A second cause of weariness is the headwind that comes from constant theological controversy. Almost no theological work is done in a vacuum but finds itself in the midst of swirling debate. This controversy may at times exist only at the academic level—which can be demanding enough—but the theological task normally includes controversy more broadly within the Church and in the world around the Church. There is a very real sense in which the theologian is called to engage in a fight, to battle for the truth of the Gospel and its proper explication. This can be a wearisome task and even the most vigorous combatants grow tired of the fight over time. Moreover, these battles can also provoke one to anger and frustration, and can narrow one's expression of charity. In short, the battle can harden us; and we need something to "soften" us in the midst of battle lest we become casualties of the struggle.[2]

A third source of weariness comes from the countless challenges presented by the modern world and the discouragement that can set in when one's best efforts seem like so much water poured out on sand. The power of a media that seems to have an inexorable force in the culture, especially among the young, can lead to profound disheartening that one's efforts will not amount to much in the end. We are tempted to conclude that our theological labors are in vain, like a whisper carried away by a great wind. We need to hear and take heart from the words of the Apostle, "Therefore . . . be firm, steadfast, always fully devoted to the work of the Lord, knowing that in the Lord your labor is not in vain" (1 Cor 15:58).

A fourth reason has to do with how theology functions in the life of the university. To a great extent, theology functions like any other discipline within the academy—the goal is to have a proper distance and perspective on the object of study. However, God can never be approached simply as an "object" like other created realities. He is also always the "subject" who is speaking and acting, even in the life of the one doing research concerning the things of God. The recent encyclical from Pope Francis, *Lumen Fidei*, makes this point with great force:

> Clearly, theology is impossible without faith; it is part of the very process of faith, which seeks an ever deeper understanding of God's self-disclosure culminating in Christ. It follows that theology is more than simply an effort of human reason to analyze and understand, along the lines of the experimental sciences. God cannot be reduced to an object. He is a subject who makes himself known and perceived in an interpersonal relationship. Right faith orients reason to open itself to the light which comes from God, so that reason, guided by love of the truth, can come to a deeper knowledge of God.[3]

While the faith-filled theologian should labor to make use of all the tools of study available to him, he or she can never simply take up the objectified and distanced approach to the "subject" that others in the academy naturally do. The pressure to "study theology" and present one's findings in the same way that one studies history, for example, is intense. The objectification inherent in the academic method (and in the entire academic atmosphere) makes it difficult to maintain a living link between theological study and spiritual life, even for the well-intentioned. Falling prey to this objectification of the theological subject is another reason why the study of theology in our day is especially prone to become dreary and tiresome.

The danger for the theologian, however, is more than just weariness; the greater snare for the theologian is a *creeping skepticism* that slowly wraps itself around the mind and soul over time. This can happen to some of the finest minds and most able intellects. They have seen too much; they have heard too many arguments on all sides; they have been scandalized once too often by those who do not show forth the fruits of the life of Christ (including themselves), and after many years in the task can end up as bitter skeptics—or at least marked by the scent of skepticism. Apart from a living and renewing source of spiritual life, they are like a great tree that has been hollowed out on the inside with precious little life left to impart to new shoots.

The point I wish to make is that, for an array of reasons and due to the circumstances surrounding the theological task, the practitioner of theology will often experience that "the outer self is wasting away," and will need to find a source of renewal "day by day."

The Mutual Refreshment Between Spirituality and Theology

With these observations in place, I would now like to draw on the writings of the great French theologian Louis Bouyer who, throughout his long and fruitful career, constantly returned to the essential interrelation of theology and spirituality. Bouyer was born in 1913 into a French Lutheran family and became an ordained Lutheran pastor in 1936. Persuaded by his extensive reading and study, he became a Catholic in 1939 and was ordained a priest of the Oratory in 1944. He lived a long and fruitful life (dying in 2004) and is best known for his writings on spirituality and Liturgy, though his dogmatic works are also worthy of attention.

Bouyer is insistent about the essential interconnection and interrelation between theology and spirituality. It is one of the marks of his thought: "There is, in fact, a very close link between theology and spirituality. . . . This is why theology and spirituality are in continuity. You cannot, then, have an authentic theology which does not lead to spirituality and which is not animated by a spiritual dynamism. Reciprocally, there is no true spirituality that does not proceed from the vision of faith that explains itself, that reflects itself, and that analyzes itself and becomes conscious in the work of theology."[4]

It is crucial to understand that Bouyer is saying *more* than that a theologian generally ought to pray and have a spiritual life. While this is certainly true, it is not sufficient for a theologian simply to have his theological work and his spiritual life exist side-by-side while relatively disconnected. This can lead to a bifurcation where the two do not mutually feed and encourage one another.

Bouyer contends that there is not only a link between the two, but also a continuity. This continuity goes in both directions—and this is essential. On the one hand, theology proceeds from a spiritual dynamism that, in turn, enriches the spiritual life of the theologian. On the other hand, true spirituality proceeds from a vision of faith and needs to be in constant dialogue with that vision—corrected, balanced, and enriched. Extending his commentary, Bouyer speaks of theology "tending toward spirituality," and "magnetizing" toward the spiritual experience of the theologian and his readers, as shown in the following selection:

> If theology is authentic, it tends of itself toward spirituality. Reciprocally, you can only have an authentic theology that, thus, magnetizes toward the spiritual experience of the one who makes this theology and of those to whom it is addressed. A theology that would not strive to lead those who study it to salvation would reveal itself by the fact that the theologian who has conceived it is not truly a theologian. The one who would not situate himself in this perspective would only end up in a pseudo-theology because there can only be theology in the faith, in the perspective of faith.[5]

Theology and spirituality must attain a certain *integration* in the life of the theologian if the two are going to mutually invigorate each other. One's spiritual life must energize and animate one's theology, and one's theology must find an outlet and application in further development of one's spiritual life.

Every doctoral student who spends hours each day (often for several years on end) immersed in theological reading and thinking knows the truth of what Bouyer is saying. The same could be said for a seminarian's long philosophical and theological training. If theological and historical research does not proceed from a spiritual source and lead back into spiritual fruitfulness, the daily process becomes semiarid. Many graduate students speak of the narrowing, even waning, of their own faith in the course of doctoral research. Is this because they cease to pray? Perhaps in some cases, but more often I believe it is because the theological research itself has no fruitful connection to spiritual life—and both suffer accordingly in the life of the person undertaking the theological task. Does this not also occur for the experienced theologian or exegete whose work is not grounded in, and in turn grounding, a lively spiritual life? When the results of scholarship have little or nothing to do with the life of faith, how can the theological work stay on task and achieve its end? Bouyer trenchantly makes this point when he writes of the theologian who fails to accomplish this link and continuity: "The theologian who claims to exercise his intellectual faculties outside of the whole current of the life of the Church, without also personally inserting himself as deeply as possible, by uniting himself in her prayer, by docilely submitting to the directives of her authority, and by opening himself to the entire spirit of the Church as it is expressed in all her Tradition, especially the liturgical and patristic Tradition and that of the great doctors—well then, this theologian would not be a theologian."[6]

Here Bouyer refers to *the proper context* for a true spiritual life. Among the many elements that comprise this context, Bouyer consistently identifies two that stand out as paramount for him: Sacred Scripture and the Liturgy. Bouyer's theology has rightly been called a theology of the Word,[7] and for Bouyer, this word is preeminently found in the Scriptures: "It is in the Bible, then, that we should look for the primary nourishment of our spiritual life."[8] Scripture fulfills this function because of its unique ability to link and integrate theological truth with real life: "This supreme and unique value of Holy Scripture becomes especially clear when we turn to spiritual theology. For in Sacred Scripture the truths of faith are immediately directed toward actual life. . . . For Christian truth, revealed truth, is not just any truth. It is truth revealed precisely to make us live, to make us live the life which God desires for us."[9] In other words, the Scripture has a unique ability to bridge theology and spirituality in the life of the theologian. By virtue of its inspired charism, the Bible mediates our faith and our spiritual life in an altogether unique way. "Holy Scripture is always the great Christian source of dogma and spirituality. The Theologians of the patristic period and those of the Middle Ages did not hesitate to say that it was the source."[10]

Bouyer is insistent that reading of the sacred text should regularly accompany prayer and vivify it: "Actually, if Christian prayer is to be nourished as it should be by the Word of God, it should always proceed from reading. This is true even when we immerse ourselves in prayer at the outset. For such prayer will be truly Christian only to the extent to which it is fed from the living store left in our memory by the divine Word, previously read or heard."[11] He modifies this requirement to allow for the reading of other liturgical and theological texts, but only with the proviso that these two lead the reader back to the Scripture and its resonances: "Such reading must always have the divine Word as its object. Yet the material does not necessarily have to be provided by the very letter of Scripture; it can equally well be a liturgical text or any other great spiritual text of Catholic tradition. It is essential, however, that the text proceed from Scripture and lead back to it; that it resemble the faithful echo which sometimes enables us to hear a far-off voice more distinctly, and which transmits only that voice, not changing it in any way with its own resonances."[12]

Is Bouyer correct here, or is he exaggerating the unique role that Scripture plays in mediating theology and spirituality, faith and life? I believe he is accurately identifying an essential feature of the Christian spiritual life, one that is easily (and ominously) overlooked by theologians. We are prone to assume that if we are studying and researching spiritual things and theological truths, then we are somehow automatically going to be spiritually influenced and impregnated by those truths. While this is sometimes—and even often—the case, it is certainly not necessarily so. It is all too easy to engage in theological polemics and argue the fine points of conceptual theology at the level of the academy while having little to no real spiritual contact with the realities we are investigating and debating.

One might respond that this is also true of the Scripture itself. Is it not plain that learned theologians and exegetes could write long tomes on the Bible and engage in voluminous study of the Bible with no real connection to its vibrant life? Quite clearly so, and Bouyer would concede the point. He is not saying that *any* kind of study of the Bible accomplishes this unique role in spiritual life, but that the prayerful and faith-filled reading of Scripture opens one to the power of the Word that can uniquely bridge faith and life.[13]

I wish to apply Bouyer's insight specifically to the work of the theologian: Scripture does and should occupy a unique place in the life of the theologian. It can be a great advantage if the theological work being undertaken directly links to the Scripture. In my doctoral work, I investigated and translated the biblical commentaries of Cyril of Alexandria. It was a great help to me that my research dealt directly with the interpretation and application of the Bible. However, even when this is not the case (such as, if one were doing a comparative theology of religions), the effort should be made to relate the topic to the Scripture, and then relate the Scripture back to one's own life and growth in faith. If the study of the sacred page is the soul of theology,[14] then Scripture ought to have a role *in the theological task itself.* If Bouyer is correct that Scripture has a unique role in mediating theology and spirituality—and I believe he is—then this has consequences for how one conceives of and carries out theological work.[15]

The role that Scripture should play in theology also has implications for how seminarians and theologians are taught the Scripture in their basic formation. We all know the barren results of a Scripture curriculum that is dominated by the historical-critical method and the various theories that predominate in this approach. Such training in Scripture can have a powerfully inoculating effect on the future theologian. If Scripture is to have its proper place in theology, then it must be modeled in the classroom and in preaching at the Liturgy.

This leads directly to the second essential element for Bouyer in linking theology and spirituality namely, liturgical and sacramental life: "I have, therefore, been encouraged to follow a line which had been spontaneously my own, to know a study of theology that is inseparable from the study of spirituality, but a spirituality completely inserted in the Church as the mystical body of Christ through the liturgical and sacramental life."[16] While participation in the liturgical life will not be a direct part of the theological task itself (as the study of Scripture can be), it is for Bouyer an essential context and accompaniment for the theologian: "There is, therefore, interaction, interconnection between the development of the understanding of the faith, which theologians work at, and the realization of the supernatural life of charity with God in the Church of which the hearth is the liturgical celebration. This celebration is itself a source of life and the means for achieving union with God who wants us to be assimilated to him in order to become his sons in the only Son."[17]

I would add here a third source of spiritual fruitfulness in the life of the theologian, namely, the blessing and refreshment that comes through teaching and expounding the truth. When the theologian discharges his or her labors through the instruction of others, a reciprocal blessing comes upon the teacher. In other words, there is a *mission* proper to theologians, and when that mission is faithfully discharged a "refreshment of the roots" often occurs.

In sum, for Bouyer, an essential requirement for the study of theology is a real and life-giving relationship with God. "The starting point of the vision that I have tried to encourage, as many before and after me have done, is the conviction that the truth of the Christian faith is a truth of life, and that this truth can only be preserved in its authenticity where this life of union with God, this life in the love of God is developed."[18] If Christ Jesus is "the way and the *truth* and the life" (Jn 14:6), then the theologian in search of the truth must have a relationship with the Holy One who is truth Himself. Thus, for Bouyer, an essential mark of the theologian is a spiritual life firmly grounded in prayer, the Sacraments, and the liturgical life of the Church.

The Relationship between Theological and Mystical Wisdom

I would now like to touch on a further development of this theme by looking at a recent publication of the International Theological Commission, *Theology Today: Perspectives, Principles and Criteria*. In Part III, the document makes a striking distinction between two forms of Christian wisdom: "theological wisdom" and "mystical wisdom." "This supernatural Christian wisdom, which transcends the purely human wisdom of philosophy, takes two forms which sustain one another but should not be confused: theological wisdom and mystical wisdom. Theological wisdom is the work of reason enlightened by faith. . . . Mystical wisdom or 'the knowledge of the saints' is a gift of the Holy Spirit which comes from union with God in love."[19]

What is the distinction between these two kinds of "wisdom" that come directly from God? Theological wisdom is the product of "faith seeking understanding," what the Commission calls "the rational labor of the theologian."[20] It is the activity of the intellect under the influence of grace working with and expounding what God has revealed. "Mystical wisdom" is a gift of the Holy Spirit that is granted to the believer through union with God in love. Through an "affective connaturality," the spiritual person is enabled "to know and even suffer things divine."[21] Importantly, the Commission emphasizes that this mystical wisdom "is a non-conceptual knowledge, often expressed in poetry," and it leads to contemplation and personal union with God.[22]

We may discuss and debate the notion of a knowledge that is nonconceptual; this would require further explanation to be persuasive to all Catholic theologians. Further, the strict division between "rational labor" and "union in love" does not adequately express how the love of God itself plays an important role in "theological wisdom." Love cannot be isolated in the province of "mystical wisdom" alone.[23] The basic distinction between two kinds of wisdom—and the two *means* by which they manifest themselves—appears sound, reflecting the experience of both the Church and the individual theologian. The Commission goes on to stress the need to distinguish, and yet interrelate, these two kinds of wisdom: "Theological wisdom and mystical wisdom are formally distinct and it is important not to confuse them. Mystical wisdom is never a substitute for theological wisdom. It is clear, nonetheless, that there are strong links between these two forms of Christian wisdom, both in the person of the theologian and in the community of the Church."[24] Insofar as mystical wisdom leads the believer (and theologian) to contemplative prayer and union with God, it need not be clothed in verbal expression in order to be genuine and bear the fruit of deification in the believer. The experience of the Hesychasts in the East would seem to be an example of this: the vision of the divine light of the Transfiguration that leads to union with God. Perhaps it was just this kind of mystical wisdom granted to Aquinas at the end of his life that led him to recognize the limitations of his vast theological effort.

Nonetheless, it would seem appropriate that the theologian would normally seek to express whatever "mystical wisdom" he or she gained in the form of theological wisdom, thinking through and expounding in words what had been experienced in prayer. One example of this is the theological study of Christ's humanity by Thomas Weinandy in his book, *In the Likeness of Sinful Flesh*.[25] In the preface, Weinandy describes how the experience of the Spirit, both personally and communally, was one of the main inspirations for translating his experience into a theology on the humanity of Christ. Another example might be Hans Urs von Balthasar's enormous effort to take the visions of Adrienne von Speyr and give them theological explication.[26]

At the same time, we would expect the theologian to take the theological wisdom given to him or her and "offer" this in prayer. Only God can directly grant mystical wisdom, but the believer can take theological knowledge and apply it to prayer (praise, thanksgiving, meditation, and supplication); and this may lead to deeper insight through mystical understanding. There ought to be *commerce* between these two kinds of wisdom in the life of the theologian, and the interrelation between these two kinds of divine wisdom is one example of the interrelation between theology and, more broadly, spirituality. Prayer and experience of God ought to fuel and enrich the theological enterprise; the genuine wisdom gained through "faith seeking understanding" ought, in turn, to nourish and impregnate one's spiritual and liturgical life. *Theology Today* expresses this interrelation eloquently: "The object of theology is the living God, and the life of the theologian cannot fail to be affected by the sustained effort to know the living God. . . . It follows that the pursuit of theology should purify the mind and heart of the theologian. . . . Thus, theology is characterized by a distinctive spirituality."[27]

Conclusion

The practice of theology, without fresh water drawn from an active spiritual life, will eventually dry up. Like our mortal nature, it will grow old and "waste away." However, renewed by the springs and fonts of a spirituality that seeks integration with the theological task, it can be "renewed day by day." Those who practice theology in this way, like the cedars of Lebanon, "shall bear fruit even in old age, they will stay fresh and green" (Ps 92:15). To penetrate to the core of this truth, we need real spiritual life, and this can only come from the Spirit of God himself. "Man's ultimate thirst cries out for the Holy Spirit. He and he alone is the fresh water without which there is no life."[28] Properly speaking, our "spirituality" does not give life; it only acts as the *vessel* and *instrument* for spiritual life. We are put into true and life-giving relationship with the Father through Jesus in the Spirit. Joseph Ratzinger points out that "to speak of 'Christian spirituality' means to speak about the Holy Spirit. He makes himself recognizable by gaining a new center for human life. Speaking about the Holy Spirit includes looking at him in man, to whom he has given himself."[29] Paul eloquently identifies the Spirit as the presence in our inner being who brings us all the riches of the divine life from the Father through the Son:

> For this reason I kneel before the Father, from whom every family in heaven and on earth is named, that he may grant you in accord with the riches of his glory to be strengthened with power through his Spirit in the inner self, and that Christ may dwell in your hearts through faith; that you, rooted and grounded in love, may have strength to comprehend with all the holy ones what is the

breadth and length and height and depth, and to know the love of Christ that surpasses knowledge, so that you may be filled with all the fullness of God (Eph 3:14–19).

It is appropriate, therefore, to end by pointing to (and invoking) the Holy One who makes both theology and spirituality possible, namely, the Spirit of God, coming from and acting in union with the Father and the Son, poured out on the Church and her members. It is only because the Spirit of God has condescended to find a dwelling place in the Church and in the life of the believer that we have true spiritual life and genuine knowledge of God:

> *Come Holy Spirit, fill the hearts of your faithful and kindle in them the fire of your love. Send forth your Spirit and they shall be created. And You shall renew the face of the earth.*

> *O, God, who by the light of the Holy Spirit, did instruct the hearts of the faithful, grant that by the same Holy Spirit we may be truly wise and ever enjoy His consolations, through Christ our Lord, Amen.*

NOTES

1.   Joseph Ratzinger, "The Theological Locus of Ecclesial Movements," *Communio* 25 (Fall 1998), 480-81.

2.   I believe that one can see *some* signs of this battle hardening in the later writings of St. Augustine against his various Pelagian interlocutors.

3.   Pope Francis, *Lumen Fidei* (2013), sec. 36.

4.   Louis Bouyer, *Le Métier de Théologien: Entretiens avec Georges Daix* (Geneva: Ad Solem, 2005), 121–22. Translations mine.

5.   Bouyer, *Le Métier de Théologien*, 147.

6.   Ibid., 61.

7.   "Throughout his writings, Bouyer will return almost untiringly to this refrain: that God gives his Word in order that he might be 'known,' not conceptually or merely intellectually, but in the biblical sense of the most intimate of relationships." Jake C. Yap, "Louis Bouyer and Unity of Theology," in *Ressourcement: A Movement for Renewal in Twentieth-Century Catholic Theology* (Oxford: Oxford University Press, 2012), 293. For a full study of Bouyer's theology of the Word, see Jake C. Yap, "'Word' and 'Wisdom' in the Ecclesiology of Louis Bouyer," (D.Phil. thesis, Oxford University, 2003).

8.   Louis Bouyer, *Introduction to Spirituality* (Collegeville, MN: Liturgical Press, 1961), 28.

9.   Louis Bouyer, *The Meaning of Sacred Scripture*, trans. Mary P. Ryan (Notre Dame, IN: University of Notre Dame Press, 1958), 2.

10.   Ibid., 1.

11.   Bouyer, *Introduction to Spirituality*, 46.

12.   Ibid., 52.

13.   Bouyer's views on the role of Scripture are confirmed by the recent publication of the International Theological Commission, *Theology Today: Perspectives, Principles and Criteria* (Washington, DC: Catholic University of America Press, 2012), which upholds the central place of the Scripture in the life and work of the theologian: "Listening to God's word is the definitive principle of Catholic theology," (sec. 4, p. 5); "Theology in its entirety should conform to the Scriptures, and the Scriptures should sustain and accompany all theological work, because theology is concerned with 'the truth of the gospel' (Gal 2:5)," (sec. 21, p. 18).

14.   Pope Paul VI, *Dei Verbum* (1965), sec. 24.

15.   Here the Fathers of the Church provide a wonderful example: in many of their works, they cite or allude to Scripture numerous times on every page. They commonly "do" theology using the idiom of the Scripture itself.

16.   Bouyer, *Le métier de théologien*, 36.

17.   Ibid., 150.

18.   Ibid., 149.

19.   International Theological Commission, *Theology Today*, sec. 91, pp. 74–75.

20.   Ibid., sec. 91, p. 75.

21.   Ibid.

22.   Ibid.

23.   For a discussion on the crucial role of love in the properly theological labor of the Christian theologian, see the chapter in this book by John Cihak, "How Faith Forges a Reason Suitable for Theology According to Saint Bonaventure."

24.   International Theological Commission: *Theology Today*, sec. 92, 75.

25.   Thomas G. Weinandy, *In the Likeness of Sinful Flesh: An Essay on the Humanity of Christ* (Edinburgh: T & T Clark, 1993), xiv.

26.   To name these two examples is not to say that they are successful in what they attempt; that is to say, the proposals of both authors are controversial at points and questions remain in debate within Catholic theology.

27.   International Theological Commission: *Theology Today*, sec. 93, pp. 76–77.

28.   Joseph Ratzinger, "The Holy Spirit as Communio: Concerning the Relationship of Pneumatology and Spirituality in Augustine," *Communio* 25 (1988), 330.

29.   Ibid., 324.

HOLINESS OF MIND AND HEART: THE DYNAMIC IMPERATIVE OF CONVERSION AND CONTEMPLATION FOR THE STUDY OF THEOLOGY

GILL GOULDING, CJ

"Theology was, when pursued by men of sanctity, a theology at prayer; which is why its fruitfulness for prayer, its power to foster prayer, is so undeniable."[1] This comment from Hans Urs von Balthasar's essay "Theology and Sanctity" gives a succinct account of the interrelationship between theology, prayer, and the struggle for holiness that he saw as a vital dynamic at the heart of all theology. Indeed, he believed that only with this conjoining could theology be both profound and effective in the lives of theologians. Maintaining this dynamic tension was imperative for him in his own study of theology and in the witness of his life and work. The facilitative tools Balthasar used for this were the call to ongoing conversion and the practice of contemplation, most notably aided by the Ignatian *Spiritual Exercises.*

Prayer is rarely seen as part of the methodology for the rigorous intellectual discipline of theology. Yet individuals such as Balthasar might cause us to see prayer as a necessary epistemological presupposition. If this is, indeed, the case then theologians need to learn to pray as part of their vocation as theologians. As the *Instruction on the Ecclesial Vocation of the Theologian* (IEVT) states, "Since the object of theology is the Truth which is the living God and His plan for salvation revealed in Jesus Christ, the theologian is called to deepen his own life of faith and continuously unite his scientific research with prayer. In this way, he will become more open to the 'supernatural sense of faith' upon which he depends, and it will appear to him as a sure rule for guiding his reflections and helping him assess the correctness of his conclusions."[2] As Gavin D'Costa makes clear in his essay "Why Theologians Must Pray," "It is not just a pious sense in which theologians must pray, but an epistemological requirement for proper engagement with the subject of study."[3]

This essay aims to underline the vital necessity of prayer as an epistemological presupposition of theology, precisely because the focus of theology is a personal and communal engagement of love with the living triune God. Trinitarian love dictates the method of the co-inherence of theology and spirituality. The essay will focus on five areas: a brief reference to key characteristics of the contemporary cultural context within which theologians and seminarians live and serve; the dynamic divine initiative of Trinitarian love as the foundation for the truth of relationship with God and others; the encounter with Christ; the gift of ongoing conversion (particularly drawing from the Ignatian *Spiritual Exercises*); and finally, contemplation as the operative dynamic of theology that informs the theologian and seminarian's mission. As Pope Francis stated, "There is no prayer in which Jesus does not inspire us to do something."[4]

The Contemporary Cultural Context

Students of theology have generally been subject to the following cultural characteristics: a confusion around reason and faith; a detachment of Christ from the Church; and a loss of the sense of sin and the graced means of addressing this both at sacramental and doctrinal levels. In addition, it is an overworked truism to say that contemporary society is dominated by technological advances, principally in the area of communications media; however, this raises certain fundamental questions with regard to the teaching of theology. Balthasar was very concerned about the way in which the mass media of his time—mainly focused through television—exerted a seductive influence[5] on young people who, "assaulted by a multitude of chaotic images flitting across the screen, are no longer capable of asking questions about the meaning of life."[6] The rapid increase of such "chaotic images" combined with the increased hours spent in artificial, computerized environments continue to raise serious questions about the possibility of any receptivity to—and, indeed, recognition of—the profound subject matter of theology. In response to such questions, it is interesting that amid current research an awareness is emerging that a balanced relationship with technology can be attained, in part, by recovering the priority of silence, understood as both an experience and an inner attitude characterized by active receptivity.[7]

Alongside these developments in technology, which have brought about a radical immanentism, the popularity of the so-called New Atheists[8] and the concurrent atheistic movements manifest a deep cultural sense that "truth" and "freedom" are threatened by the existence of God (or—perhaps more accurately—the Abrahamic religions' teachings about God). Modern philosophy's characteristic "turn to the subject" valorized human reason and conceived of truth as the correspondence between "the world" and the human person's determined, innate structures for knowing the world. To know the truth of a thing in this "modern" paradigm is, therefore, to have a clear and distinct concept of the thing and subsequently, to overcome (as far as possible) any lack of clarity, difference, or "otherness" in knowing.[9] When this notion of truth informs discussions about human freedom, whether as an inherent property of a person or within the political realm, the notion of an absolute truth (held by God or an earthly authority) must somehow be opposed or resisted because such a totalizing truth would necessarily homogenize the difference and otherness necessary for freedom.[10]

While knowledge and mystery are opposed in this "modern" notion of truth, it is possible to conceive of truth in such a way that mystery and "difference" are an intrinsic part of it. Grounded in Jesus' revelation of a triune God, Balthasar formulated a nonreductive, "dramatic" structure of truth capable of uniting independent terms into an intelligible whole, while simultaneously maintaining an abiding difference (mystery) between them. This is of considerable importance when trying to plumb the mystery of identity, person, and mission that lies at the heart of vocations and is also the subject matter of theology.[11]

The Divine Initiative[12]

"[God's] love transforms all of life. It is a love that is limitless and that precedes us, sustains us and calls us along the path of life, a love rooted in an absolutely free gift of God."[13]

Pope Benedict XVI's assertion that God's love is both the origin and the transformative principle of all life finds an echo in Balthasar's work. Both men understand that the profound truth of our existence is that all creation—and, in particular, every human person—is a result of the fecundity of God's loving activity; a love that we know from Scripture, tradition, and our own personal experience as being without limit, faithful, and everlasting. It is this love, Balthasar maintains, that is the transformative dynamic at the heart of all theology and every vocation.[14] God is not only Love—the eternal act of perichoretic indwelling between the Father and the Son hypostasized as the Spirit who is himself Love—but God also loves the human person on whom he freely chooses to disclose Divine Love in the fullness of the act of creating. The Trinity is love *ad-intra* and *ad-extra*. Accordingly, God's Love is a mutual revelation of the Divine Persons (Lover, Beloved, and Love), as well as an external revelation of love as God's nature to each human person. Such a revelation is grounded in mystery.

For Balthasar, "mystery" is intrinsic to truth; it is not an optional extra.[15] At the heart of this mystery is the truth of the Trinity. For Balthasar, the reality of the Trinity is the source from which a fullness of interpretation of human existence is derived. From our understanding of the distinctions within the Trinity (Father, Son, and Spirit) and the fullness of a relationship inherent in one God, we may postulate that distinction and otherness, as well as communion, may all be integral parts of such mystery, bursting the bounds of any subjective identification. Such an assertion is important for our contemporary understanding. Attention has been focused on the question of whether the transcendence that takes place in the process of knowing and the search for truth is achieved only through the act of the subject, or is it something that the object, being known, co-enables.[16]

The process of knowing for Balthasar, then, is primarily God's act of disclosing or unveiling objective content to the thought of the receptive human person, who then awakens to knowing in wonder and amazement. Here we see clearly the importance of prayer as the epistemological presupposition, and the work of the Holy Spirit. It is the divine initiative that inspires the process of unveiling. The true reception of such disclosure involves a spirit of wonder and gratitude that is, as it were, the "natural" Christian response to God's gift of self. Such a prayer of gratitude is to be encouraged in theologians as they wrestle with theological truths. Through this process, the receptive human subject transcends personal limitations through grace by being opened to an "other" who is beyond the subject's knowing. The focus is on engaged contemplation, as the human subject ponders the divine disclosure with wonder.

Balthasar's premise for this whole process of knowing is that all meaning and all unity lie in God. We can only know God by being "in" God. This is the goal of theology. God alone brings about being, which unveils itself within the world. The process of knowing is primarily God's action of disclosing or unveiling objective content to the receptive human person. Within this revelation is ultimately what

Balthasar calls, a "poverty of Being and of its sensibility [which] reveals that the sole treasure Being contains, is nothing other than—love."[17] Calling for relationship, this love is the divine dynamic operating deep within human reality. For the believing Christian, this relationship is an interaction with the divine life of the Trinity.[18] To say that love is the communion of Christians is not simply to enunciate an abstract principle; rather, in the Christian communion of love, we share in a personal act of God himself, the tip of which may be seen shining in the person of Christ. In its depths, this act contains the interpersonal life of the Blessed Trinity; and in its breadth, it embraces the love of God for the whole world.[19]

Love is the final truth of being[20]—in the divine essence, in the reciprocal self-gift of the Persons, and—because God the Trinity is the Creator—in the created world itself, which bears God's mark. Supremely in human persons made in the image of God, love is the final truth of human existence, for it is the creativity of Divine Love that pours itself out, as Aidan Nichols indicates, in a "glorious self-sharing love of its own divine Source."[21] In this graced sharing of Divine Love, the human person is brought to a deeper expression what it means, in reality, to be both a creature and a beloved child of God. This lies at the center of the covenant relationship to which human persons are invited; this key recognition is vital for the process of ongoing conversion and growth in holiness. Balthasar's extraordinary theological vision attempts to speak words of beauty and honor to reflect the grandeur of the mystery of God's love for human beings made known in Christ.

The Encounter with Christ

Pope Francis spoke about the importance of the definitive encounter with Christ on September 7, 2013, the day that he called for prayer and fasting for peace, particularly in Syria. "'Jesus,' he said, 'is the center. Jesus is the Lord.' And yet, he maintained, this . . . 'is not easily understood.' Jesus is not a lord of this or that, but is 'the Lord, the only Lord.' He is the center that 'regenerates us, grounds us': this is the Lord, 'the center.'"[22] The present dynamic presence of Christ as Lord—that irreducible particularity across all generations—is a key focus of Balthasar's theology. Balthasar maintains that being a Christian means to be "in Christ"; it is a participation in Christ's very being. "The 'where' of the Christian is in Christ himself, just as Christ's 'where' is in the Father,"[23] which means to be in the Father's will as was Jesus himself. Such a grounding may lead to a cruciform way of knowing, as being drawn into Christ inevitably involves some experience of the redemptive pattern of Cross and Resurrection. The question arises: What needs to die within oneself so that the life of renewed knowing might be made more manifest?

"Having given freedom to the creature," Balthasar wrote early in the *Theo-Drama*, "God, as Creator, is always 'involved' in the world, and this means that there is always a divine–human dramatic tension."[24] Indeed, Balthasar's starting point is the dramatic tension that occurs when humanity recognizes that, although the God of infinite freedom exists, we are still free to act, albeit in a limited way. Balthasar's understanding of the relationship between human and divine freedom is grounded in a Trinitarian theology of persons in unity. In the triune mystery, the three persons of God are each themselves and wholly distinct, yet fully interconnected and one.[25] Furthermore, for Balthasar, the dramatic union of the persons of the Trinity is characterized by *kenosis*: the mutual self-giving, self-emptying to and for each other. This giving of each person is undertaken in absolute freedom as gift, and the giving of each is "understood differently and according to their proper roles within the divine life."[26] It is through this infinite, kenotic, self-giving of the persons of the Trinity between and within each other, giving and sharing one another in infinite freedom and love, that they share themselves again and further in creation.[27] Just as the persons of the Trinity remain mysteriously one and distinct, so, too, are we free because we are made free by God, who guarantees our freedom. Our freedom is certain because we are created to be free by an infinite freedom. Our createdness itself, therefore, does not endanger our freedom; something else did and does.[28] This is the reality of sin in our lives.

Humanity is caught within a web of paradoxes.[29] In humanity's effort to be free without limitation, it has become bound to sin and death on the one hand, and according to Balthasar, left with the feeling of "emptiness and indifferent freedom" on the other, especially when we recognize our freedom is in fact the "space that God had originally created for himself."[30] For Balthasar, recognizing that human freedom is not absolute, but rather related to another freedom, is necessary for moving humanity beyond its inertness. He asserts that both finite and infinite freedom find their full integration in Jesus Christ, and nowhere is this more evident than in Christ's "yes" to both the Incarnation and His Passion and Death on the Cross: "as God's 'yes' to the world and the world's 'yes' to God, Jesus Christ seals and implements the truth of the relationship between God and the world in terms of a Covenant between infinite and finite freedom."[31] We need to be converted to perceive this.

Conversion

"Conversion is not something that we can promise to do; it must actually be accomplished."[32] This succinct observation from the last pages of *Epilogue* is uncompromising in the challenge it presents. For Balthasar, conversion has nothing to do with vain promises, procrastination, or even prodigious activity. It is something that actually has to be accomplished, and the successful completion always involves the Divine initiative of love calling forth a human response. Echoing throughout Balthasar's theology is the preeminent divine call to conversion, which is both a mysterious gift of grace, as well as an ongoing condition (or dynamic disposition) of dialogue with God. This work of prevenient grace is also intrinsically personal because the core action of all conversion is the dawning awareness of one's own reality through an encounter with Christ. It involves divesting the disguises and subterfuges that have become accretions to the ego, as well as renouncing self-seeking, which ultimately brings peace to the soul.

Conversion is precipitated by a call from God; it is not a monologue, but a dialogue between an individual and Christ. As Balthasar himself stated: "*Lumen Gentium cum sit Christus.* The great light of the world, for which people are searching today, is Christ."[33] Following from this, in *Lumen Gentium* we encounter the *telos* of such conversion with the assertion that all Christians are called to the perfection of love and holiness. Conversion is, out of necessity, an individual process, and yet it is also situated within the larger drama of redemption.

Conversion is focused in a dialogue between God and human persons where the entire Trinity is involved, where infinite and finite freedom engage, and where the role of the Church is made manifest.

The Graced Human Person

By Divine Grace, the human person is a being who is at once mysterious and held in tension. Clearly rooted in temporality through a corporeal reality, human beings are yet animated by an immortal spirit; therefore, they are always beings "in tension." I affirm such tension, as does Balthasar, as a positive attribute and, therefore, not requiring some quasi-efficient "resolution." Human persons are created for a distinct purpose. According to St. Ignatius of Loyola in the Principle and Foundation of the *Spiritual Exercises*, this purpose is for the "praise, reverence and service" of God. People have an interior, inbuilt disposition of longing for God, though it may be occluded by a shift of focus to material goods or transitory activities. From this foundation of longing there can grow, by the grace gift of conversion, an openness to Trinitarian Love made known in the divine acts of creation and redemption, such that human persons may be caught up in the Trinitarian exchange of love. Throughout *Love Alone is Credible*, Balthasar makes it clear that only Divine Love (the theological trilogy in microcosm), is the true principle and foundation for all that occurs in the interaction between God and the whole of creation, and thus also for the process of conversion. Divine Love is always Trinitarian and "the plausibility of God's love does not become apparent through any comparative reduction to what man has always already understood as love; rather, it is illuminated only by the self-interpreting revelation-form of love itself. And this form is so majestic that we are led to adore it from a reverent distance whenever we perceive it."[34] The primary mode of this love is Trinitarian: the Son loves the Father so much that, in loving obedience, He is willing to pass through death; the unbounded love of the Father raises Christ from the dead; and the love of the Holy Spirit maintains the relationship between Father and Son even in the face of dissolution. As Balthasar asserts, the truth is that "the Father loves the world so much that he bestows on it his only Son. That is the most profound cause of all truth, and every other truth must be referable to it."[35] Conversion is thus a Trinitarian gift of grace bestowed by the Holy Spirit, including within it the freedom to make a choice (in Ignatian terms, "the election"), which shapes the person's life. The gift of conversion is continually being given in a gradual process (though there may be decisive moments) and, therefore, calls forth an ongoing acceptance from the individual. There are ever more profound dimensions as the person is drawn into a deeper and, therefore, more fruitful relationship with God. Balthasar emphasizes that conversion is, as it were, receiving the impression of the form of Christ. It is an awakening to the wonder of relationship with God and responding with a "yes" of faith, which is continuously repeated. "Both the believer's offering of himself to God and the impressing of the Christ-form by God upon the believer connote totality."[36] Ongoing contemplation of Christ, through the work of the Holy Spirit, gradually transforms the believer into the image of Christ. We are more and more attuned to God as we "relearn what love after all really is."[37] This process both informs and illuminates our theological perspective.

In addition, clarity emerges about the nature of what it is to be a creature and a sinner, along with the challenge to embrace the poverty of this concept. "When a sinner sees and accepts that he is helpless in his poverty, this joins him to the *anawim*; as far as Jesus is concerned."[38] Such a recognition lies at the heart of the first week of the *Spiritual Exercises* and the meditations on the reality of sin within the context of God's Love made manifest in Christ. The encounter with Christ inexorably reveals the difference between what one is called to be and how one actually lives. The graced encounter with Christ reveals the radical challenge of discipleship during the second week of the *Spiritual Exercises*. As the retreatant contemplates the way in which Jesus is led by the Spirit, so she comes to recognize that her own life and mission are to be led by that same spirit. "The conferring of the mission which occurs at a particular historical moment in the life of the one called, is but the starting point of what will be thereafter a constant *being-led by the Holy Spirit*."[39] The glory of God is seen to be revealed in gentleness, humility, and loving obedience—all crucial characteristics of the person and mission of Christ to do the will of the Father. The Father is revealed in the encounter with Christ. Balthasar emphasizes that the Father's role in conversion is to bestow the individual mission, which is always a lifelong participation in the drama of human existence.[40]

The willing acceptance of a mission from God is what constitutes becoming a theological person. We grow into personhood in and through participation in the mission of Christ. Here awareness of how we are viewed by the Father is critical to how we understand ourselves and those that we teach. According to Balthasar, one of the distinctive marks of conversion is coming to see oneself as one is seen by the Father. "No one can resolve this mystery into dry concepts: show how it is that God no longer sees my guilt in me but in his beloved Son who bears it for me; or how it is that God sees that guilt transformed by the sufferings of love and loves me because I am the one the Son loves in his suffering."[41] This is the subject matter of the third week of the *Spiritual Exercises*, where it becomes clear that divine freedom guarantees human freedom and draws forth a receptive obedience, a necessary precondition for experiencing the deeper dimensions of conversion, which inexorably involves renunciation and suffering. In contemplating the passion of Christ, the individual may find the strength to face the inevitable suffering that is a component of any human life.

The Individual within the Drama of Redemption

For a theologian, the process—and, indeed, progress—of conversion involves a dramatic living into and out of the mission given by God. Balthasar uses the apocalyptic imagery of Scripture to indicate the drama of salvation and the importance of conversion in the interplay between divine and human freedom. His rendition of the battle within the individual draws on the Ignatian vision of spiritual warfare. Christ's struggle is the struggle of the Church. The key meditations of the second week of the *Spiritual Exercises* bring into sharp focus the nature of this struggle in which Christ and the Church are engaged. Ignatius saw this struggle at the heart of human history. In the meditation on the Two Standards, he gives a graphic description of the standard of Satan.[42] The satanic—the diabolical—is the antihuman, the humanly destructive; this sense of relentless, cosmic struggle

re-appropriates within the *Spiritual Exercises* the Pauline understanding of the conflict that lies at the heart of human history (Eph 6:11–18). It is Christ, however, who stands against
the "enemy of our human nature."[43] The *Spiritual Exercises*
understand the Church to be the community gathered around
Christ, engaged in this mysterious and fundamental struggle
that lies at the heart of human history. This is the intractable
conflict between the call of Christ and the influences of the
antihuman. The Church, in the *Spiritual Exercises,* is a community in struggle. Indeed it is the principal agent in the struggle
with the antihuman.

This enormous and ongoing struggle is not *between* human
beings but is *about* human beings and the very destiny of
human life. Fundamentally, it is a struggle of the human
versus the antihuman with the human heart as its battlefield.
The definitive victory of redemption has been won by Christ.
At the same time, Christ's redemptive work continues today
in and through the Church. The Church makes known the
saving grace of Christ and calls her members to share in the
struggle against all that seeks to undermine the human relationship with God.

Ignatius's insistence that the diabolical is the antihuman[44] leads to a radical critique of culture. If the Church is
to be true to itself in any culture, it will be on the alert, not
beguiled into an inauthentic peace. In any sound election, the
individual comes to participate in the Church's struggle. Such
participation unites the individual to the Church and, because
the Church is configured to Christ, so the individual is united
to Christ in His redemptive work. In this way, the struggles
of men and women carry the Church's mission forward
against all that dehumanizes. This is the challenge present in

Balthasar's *Theo-Dramatic*, as Ben Quash makes clear: "The theo-dramatics makes a claim about the overwhelmingly dramatic character of the Christian revelation, and the overwhelmingly dramatic response that it demands. It summons academic theology back from desiccated rationalism to a form and a register that is vibrant and forceful."[45]

Conversion is, thus, a dramatic challenge involving risk, a leap of faith requiring great courage. Here, Mary's fiat is exemplary of what is necessary in the spiritual combat. The defining act of the Theo-drama is the Incarnation, Christ's entrance into human existence, which profoundly affects the course of human history. "No ('epic') horizon can embrace the totality of free actors in all their mutual confrontations; yet their encounters do not create a multiplicity of independent dramas but are yoked together in a single, total drama that encompasses all the individual interactions. This is because all encounters between man and God are included in the drama of Christ."[46]

To give without reserve from a disposition of active receptivity is at the heart of conversion. This leads to a willingness to embrace the Cross and "Christ himself becomes the norm that dwells in a new way within his followers without their ever being able to control it."[47] Christ came to suffer with us, not to abolish suffering. It becomes clear, therefore, that an inevitable part of discipleship is a share of suffering, part of sharing in the redemptive work of Christ, and that true freedom for human persons is defined by being "always indebted" to God.[48] This involves a journey of discovery, "we discover God by obeying him, our fellow [human beings] by serving them, and ourselves whom we only encounter in such service and obedience."[49]

The interior action of the Holy Spirit promotes the dialogue of conversion and assists the growth in congruence of
the finite freedom of the individual to the infinite freedom
of God through an ongoing assent to grace. Indeed, the true
measure of human freedom is this docility to the Holy Spirit.
The place of encounter and dialogue occurs within the wider
community of the Church and most especially, within the
realm of individual and communal prayer where the Spirit
transforms the longings of hearts into prayer that is pleasing to the Father. Within this process, contemplative prayer
has a primary place for Balthasar. In such prayer the interior
spiritual faculties allow the possibility of seeing, tasting and
touching contemplatively, as indicated in the "Application of
the Senses" within the *Spiritual Exercises*. It is also within the
domain of contemplative prayer that the election is made, the
reality of indifference is illumined, and obedience becomes a
loving response to the ongoing call to conversion. Within the
understanding of colloquy, where heart speaks to heart, the
deepest dimensions of dialogue may be made manifest. Here,
the call to a disposition of self-emptying love in imitation of
the divine example may be more clearly heard and followed.
Indeed, for Balthasar, "the essence of being a Christian is to
be open daily and hourly to the call of God and to let oneself
be touched and guided by it."[50] Here, the sacraments are life-
giving aids.

In the Sacrament of Reconciliation, right relationships
are restored after confession, not just between the penitent
and God, but with the whole Christian community, which is
enhanced by the grace that pours forth from the encounter
with Christ. "This act of the Church which singles out the
individual so that he may be restored to the community in the

right way, was introduced by Christ himself, who called each and every person to come to him and be converted and thus healed and forgiven."[51] The Eucharist continues to nourish the life of the believer and the community, constantly calling the Church to live the reality of this timeless encounter with Christ by reaching out to the whole world. So Balthasar stated: "The Christian thing to do is to go in search of his brother, and speak to him in a way that is intelligible for today."[52] As each of the sacraments promotes the assent—the "yes"—to ongoing conversion, so the pattern of Mary's fiat is an unambiguous example of the acceptance necessary for those called to discipleship. Balthasar notes that, "each successive revelation of the divine mystery is occasioned by a fresh demand on Mary and her assent to it."[53] Indeed, Balthasar so highly prizes the obedient acceptance of God's will that Mary reveals "the Church founded on Peter is more deeply founded on Mary."[54]

Contemplative Prayer[55]

Prayer and, particularly, contemplation continue the work of the Eucharist and the other sacraments in incorporating human persons into the incarnate Word such that the sphere of our existence is in Christ.[56] There is, thus, a twofold sense of blessing (in prayer and in the gift of grace), both of which are key constituents of the relationship between God and human persons. It is, Balthasar affirms, through grace and in prayer that human persons are given a greater openness to the truth and, concomitantly, greater self-giving. "We can now see the twofold presupposition—objective and subjective—of hearing the word of Christian contemplation: the divine truth must be open to [human persons] and the hearts and minds of [human persons] open to God."[57]

Fundamentally, it is the grace of God, primarily the Father, that enables us to engage in prayer and contemplation. From this grace we derive the power and the freedom to contemplate the truth. In the twofold movement of Christ coming from the Father and returning to the Father (in the power of the Spirit), Christ makes contemplative prayer possible. When the Word became flesh there was a "concretizing" of God in the created world and, in the Ascension, there was a carrying of the whole world back to God. Both of these actions were brought about through the person of the Son who is from all eternity the Word of the Father.[58]

Contemplation is also made possible for us through the work of the Holy Spirit. Divine life and truth are brought to human persons through two parts of a single happening: the sending of the Word of God (the Son) and the imparting of the Holy Spirit. It is through the gift of faith that we are taught the truth by the Holy Spirit concerning the Son and that we can speak of that truth. The Spirit also progressively leads us into the depths, already opened up, of the truth of God present within us. This is, however, not a merely individual enterprise. "Contemplation must always be a renewed 'hearing' of what the Spirit speaks to the Church,[59] a new hearing of what the Spirit unfolds inwardly to the contemplative mind in its own spirit of faith as members of the Church."[60] Through the Spirit, the Son's return to the Father results in His becoming the head and life-giving source of the Church, in the outpouring of the Spirit's life in the sacraments, Scripture, the Liturgy, and preaching, and in the whole of Christian living.[61]

Balthasar states that "Contemplative prayer is the reception of revealed truth by one who believes and loves and therefore desires to apply to it all his powers of reason, will and sense. Consequently, the form of the truth itself must always determine and prescribe the mode of reception."[62] The preeminent form of truth is found in Christ. The life of the Trinity and the life of Christ are not mere paradigms. It is crucial, from Balthasar's appreciation, that Christian action participates in the absolute freedom of God's interpersonal love. Christ—through the Incarnation and the bestowal of His Spirit—imparts upon us participation in the infinite freedom of His Divine Sonship by which we are made capable of taking part in His Trinitarian mission. This is an invitation into the realm of divine freedom, and it is here that we overcome the false dichotomy between contemplation and action.[63] Christian action is derived from and sustained by contemplation. The source for such contemplation is the divine action: "What we are looking at when we contemplate the love of God is Christ giving himself in love."[64] By contemplating this action, we are inspired to play our part in the divine drama. Indeed, the credibility of Christian action as an encounter with God, and a consequent inspired action for the life of the world, resides in it being a grace-filled likeness to the "folly" of Divine Love. Pre-empting the inevitable criticism of such an understanding, Balthasar states: "It will be objected that such a program of action demands the character of a saint. This may well be; but from the very beginning, Christian living has always been most credible, where at the very least, it has shown a few faint signs of holiness."[65]

Conclusion

Spirituality, and particularly the practice of prayer, is of vital importance for academic ecclesial theology. Theology is not just informed by the dynamic of Divine Love, rather "God's own Trinitarian love dictates the method by which God is known and loved."[66] This methodology, cognizant of the pressures of contemporary culture, is the sustaining source of encounter with Christ and a profound encouragement for ongoing conversion. The dynamic of the *Spiritual Exercises* resonates within this process, upholding the dignity of the graced human person, drawing to a depth of conversion, and strengthening an understanding of mission. This dynamic illuminates the individual's place within the Church in the drama of redemption. Undertaken from such a foundation, theology nourishes holiness of mind and heart toward a unified witness to the operative effect of Divine Love on the graced human person. It is the privilege and responsibility of the theologian to share both their intellectual wealth and the passion of their own interiority in teaching theology. As Balthasar stated, "We need individuals who devote their lives to the glory of theology, that fierce fire burning in the dark night of adoration and obedience whose abysses it illuminates."[67]

NOTES

1.   Hans Urs von Balthasar, "Theology and Sanctity," in *Explorations in Theology I: The Word Made Flesh*, (San Francisco: Ignatius Press, 1989), 208.

2.   Congregation for the Doctrine of the Faith, *Instruction on the Ecclesial Vocation of the Theologian*, (Rome, Vatican, 1990), 2, paragraph 8. It is interesting to note that Balthasar is the only modern theologian mentioned in this document.

3.   Gavin D'Costa, "Why Theologians Must Pray," in *Theology in The Public Square: Church, Academy and Religion* (Oxford: Blackwell, 2005), 112–144 at 121.

4.   Pope Francis homily morning mass at Casa Santa Marta September 5th 2013. 'Jesus has a promise and a mission for every Christian', http://www.news.va/en/news/pope-francis-jesus-has-a-promise-and-a-mission-for.

5.   Among the seductive images of contemporary culture are those of a pornographic nature. In January 2013, it was estimated that 12 percent of websites on the Internet were pornographic, which equates to approximately 25 million sites. Three thousand dollars are spent every second on pornography. In a typical month, 70 percent of men aged 18 to 24 visit porn sites. Thirty-five percent of all downloads are pornographic. The average age when a child first sees pornographic material is 11 years old; nine out of ten boys were exposed to pornographic material before the age of 18. "Pornography Statistics: Annual report 2013," *Covenant Eyes Internet Accountability and Filtering*, accessed 11/29/2013, http://www.covenanteyes.com/pornstats/.

It is clear that, in the area of pornography, we are dealing with powers and principalities that disseminate disvalues in the culture. The added dimension of child abuse images and incitements to terrorism appears to involve a diabolical element. The very statistics, combined with experience working with those in formation, indicate likelihood that seminarians and their teachers will have been exposed to these pressures at some point in their early lives.

6.   He continues, "I remember one of the last lectures of Gabriel Marcel, at which, leaving his notes aside and glancing up at the ceiling, he said that watching television reminded him of seeing a tiny patch of the ocean floor through the hatch of a submarine, imagining it to be the whole world." Hans Urs von Balthasar, *Test Everything: Hold Fast to What is Good* (San Francisco: Ignatius Press, 1989), 26.

7.   "This attitude is not focused towards the digital field but to the Trinitarian God and to incarnate reality, and results from a recovery of the priority of 'being' over 'doing' or 'making,' an existential stance that acknowledges one's ontological contingency and creature-hood."

John D. O'Brien, "The Priority of Silence: Recovering an Anterior Sense of 'Active Receptivity' to Acquire Right Relationship with the New Digital Media Environments of Our Technological Society," (unpublished M.A. Thesis, Regis College, Toronto, 2012). See also Pope Benedict XVI, "Message for the 46th World Communications Day," *Libreria Editrice Vaticana*, (May 20, 2012), http://www.vatican.va/holy_father/benedict_xvi/messages/communications/documents/hf_ben-xvi_mes_20120124_46th-world-communications-day_en.html.

8.   Prominent among whom are: Richard Dawkins, Daniel Dennett, Sam Harris, and the late Christopher Hitchens.

9.   The reductive notion of truth also leads to significant anxiety. Amid the media pressure to focus attention on material wealth, success, and sexual pleasure as the means of self-realization, economic well-being, and immediate emotional satisfaction, there is still a pervading anxiety that these foci do not provide the lasting happiness that is sought. In his 1952 essay entitled in English, *The Christian and Anxiety*, Balthasar attempted to "re-value" Kierkegaardian anxiety so that it could be of use to the Christian, illustrating how anxiety, rightly understood, is a part of the Christian experience and making it "possible for anxiety to participate in the fruitful anguish of the Cross," (Hans Urs von Balthasar, *The Christian and Anxiety*, trans. Dennis D. Martin and Michael J. Miller (San Francisco: Ignatius Press, 2000), 79).

Balthasar opens the horizon of anxiety beyond the merely human to show its theological dimension and, in so doing, integrates anxiety into the human-divine relationship. By integrating human anxiety into the Paschal Mystery and the Son's anxiety, experienced in Gethsemane and at Calvary, Balthasar reclaimed anxiety from the monopolistic hold that existential philosophy had attempted to place on it and returned it to the loving view of the Creator.

10.   By contradistinction, Martha Nussbaum writes about certain types of truth that can only be described by love. See Martha Nussbaum, *Love's Knowledge* (Oxford: Oxford University Press, 1992).

11.   One particular effect of the growth of digital media and the popularization of the new atheism is to undermine the understanding of permanent commitment. Indeed, a life lived in this way is seen as unrealistic. By contrast, David L. Schindler indicates that the only credible response to charges of a lack of realism is the witness of "each one's entire way of life, as carried in the whole of one's countless concrete acts, thoughts and gestures." David L. Schindler, *Ordering Love: Liberal Societies and the Memory of God* (Grand Rapids, MI: Eerdmans, 2011).

12.   For a more detailed exposition of the impact of the divine initiative on vocation, see Gill Goulding, "'The Irreducible Particularity of Christ'—Hans Urs von Balthasar's Theology of Vocation," in *The Disciples'*

Call: Theologies of Vocation from Scripture to the Present Day, ed. Christopher Jamison (London: Bloomsbury, 2013), 115–138.

13.   Pope Benedict XVI, "Message for the 49th World Day of Prayer for Vocations," *Libreria Editrice Vaticana*, (April, 29 2012), http://www.vatican.va/holy_father/benedict_xvi/messages/vocations/documents/hf_ben_xvi_mes_20111018_xlix-vocations_en.html. See also St. John Paul II, *Pastores Dabo Vobis* (1992), sec. 25: "Every ministerial action—while it leads to loving and serving the Church—provides an incentive to grow in ever greater love and service of Jesus Christ the head, shepherd and spouse of the Church, a love which is always a response to the free and unsolicited love of God in Christ."

14.   See Pope Benedict XVI, *Deus Caritas Est* (2005), sec. 17: "God is indeed visible in a number of ways. In the love-story recounted by the Bible, he comes towards us, he seeks to sin our hearts, all the way to the Last Supper, to the piercing of his heart on the Cross, to his appearances after the Resurrection and to the great deeds by which, through the activity of the Apostles, he guided the nascent Church along its path. Nor has the Lord been absent from subsequent Church history: he encounters us ever anew, in the men and women who reflect his presence, in his word, in the sacraments and especially in the Eucharist." Pope Benedict XVI's comments resonate with Balthasar's work, the fruit of the longevity of their esteemed relationship as both theologians and friends.

15.   For Balthasar, everything that may be known must have some characteristic of mystery, as all objects of knowledge have a creaturely character. This leads to the conclusion that the final truth of all things is "hidden in the mind of the Creator who alone may utter [their] eternal names." Hans Urs von Balthasar, *Theo-Logic: Theological Logical Theory*, vol. 1: *Truth of the World*, trans. Adrian J. Walker (San Francisco: Ignatius Press, 2000), 17. For further detailed exploration of truth as Balthasar deals with it, see Gill Goulding, "Truth Unveiled: Balthasar and the Contemplation of Truth," in *Truth Matters: Knowledge, Politics, Ethics, Religion*, eds. Lambert Zuidervaart, Allyson Carr, Matthew J. Klassen, and Ronnie Shuke (Quebec: McGill-Queens University Press, 2013).

16.   See David C. Schindler, *Hans Urs von Balthasar and the Dramatic Structure of Truth: A Philosophical Investigation* (New York: Fordham University Press, 2004), 4.

17.   Hans Urs von Balthasar, *The Glory of the Lord: A Theological Aesthetics*, vol. 1: *Seeing the Form*, ed. Joseph Fessio and John Riches; trans. Erasmo Leiva-Merikakis (San Francisco: Ignatius Press, 1982), 407. See also Hans Urs von Balthasar, *Love Alone is Credible*, trans. David C. Schindler (San Francisco: Ignatius Press, 2004). This short book clearly explores how love is the *leitmotif* of Balthasar's work.

18.   However, such an interaction is not just focused upon relationship with the Trinity but, in and through that relationship, a renewed

engagement with other people. "The significant factor in being a Christian is that [one] does all with reference to and in dependence on the ultimate source of [one's] action, through loving first and above all things, the God who loves us in Christ in order that [one] may then, by means of and together with love, turn [one's] attention to the needs of those who are the object of the love of God." Hans Urs von Balthasar, *Engagement with God*, trans. R. John Halliburton (San Francisco: Ignatius Press, 2008), 40.

19. Ibid., 41.

20. Truth is first and foremost a transcendental property of being—rooted in love.

21. Aiden Nichols, *Say It is Pentecost: A Guide Through Balthasar's Logic*, (Washington D.C.: Catholic University of America Press, 2001), 93.

22. Vatican Radio, "Pope Francis: Overcome Temptation to be 'Christians without Jesus,'" *RadioVaticana.va*, September 7, 2013, http://en.radiovaticana.va/news/2013/09/07/pope_francis:_overcome_temptation_to_be_christians_without_jesus/en1-726498. Each individual needs to consider what it means to claim that Jesus is Lord of one's life, one's prayer, one's will. The call is to pragmatic action and experience.

23. Hans Urs von Balthasar, *The Christian State of Life*, trans. Mary Frances McCarthy (San Francisco: Ignatius Press, 1983), 212.

24. Hans Urs von Balthasar, *Theo-Drama: Theological Dramatic Theory*, vol. I: *Prologomena*, trans. Graham Harrison (San Francisco: Ignatius Press, 1988), 128–29.

25. As John O'Donnell states, "the Trinity brings us face to face with the mystery that there is real otherness in God which is not incompatible with [God's] unity. . . . Oneness is not incompatible with otherness." John O'Donnell, *Hans Urs von Balthasar*, (New York: Continuum, 2000), 66.

26. Thomas G. Dalzell, *The Dramatic Encounter Of Divine and Human Freedom in the Theology of Hans Urs von Balthasar*, (Bern:Peter Lang, 2000), 47.

27. Therefore, as O'Donnell states, "this conception of divine life as the infinite self-giving of the persons thus makes possible the reality of a free creation as well as the interchange of freedom in the divine drama between God and the world. The goal of God's free dramatic action is, in Balthasar's judgement, the setting free of the creature. In the action of creation God first of all enables an autonomous creature to be. [God] lets it be and hence be free in its very being." O'Donnell, *Hans Urs von Balthasar*, 66–67. Likewise, according to Dalzell, "the ultimate end of human freedom is understood as a taking part in God's Trinitarian life process." Dalzell, *Dramatic Encounter*, 213.

28. "Although set by God in a state of rectitude, man enticed by the evil one, abused his freedom at the very start of history. He lifted himself up against God, and sought to attain his goal apart from him. Although they had known God, they did not glorify him as God, but their senseless

hearts were darkened, and they served the creature rather than the creator. What Revelation makes known to us is confirmed by our own experience. For when man looks into his own heart he finds that he is drawn towards what is wrong and sunk in many evils which cannot come from his good creator. Often refusing to acknowledge God as his source, man has also upset the relationship which should link him to his last end; and at the same time he has broken the right order that should reign within himself as well as between himself and other men and all creatures. Man therefore is divided against himself. As a result, the whole life of men, both individual and social, shows itself to be a struggle, and a dramatic one, between good and evil, between light and darkness. Man finds that he is unable of himself to overcome the assaults of evil successfully, so that everyone feels as though bound by chains." Pope Paul VI, *Gaudium et Spes* (1965), sec. 13.

29. Michael Buckley puts paradox at the center of our questions about freedom and then writes, "the human person is fundamentally conditioned by a paradox: freedom is a question about yourself. It is not a question which the person has; it is a question which I am and with which I constitute what I am to become." Michael Buckley, "Freedom, Election and Self-Transcendence: Some reflections upon the Ignatian Development of a Life Ministry," in *Ignatian Spirituality in a Secular Age*, ed. George P. Schner (Canada: Canadian Corporation for Studies in Religion, 1984), 71.

30. Hans Urs von Balthasar, *The Christian State of Life*, trans. Sister Mary Frances McCarthy, (San Francisco: Ignatius Press, 1983), 135.

31. Aidan Nicholls, *No Bloodless Myth: A Guide Through Balthasar's Dramatics*, (Washington D.C.: Catholic University of America Press, 2000) 72.

32. Hans Urs von Balthasar, *Epilogue*, trans. Edward T. Oakes (San Francisco: Ignatius Press, 2004), 118.

33. Balthasar, *Test Everything*, 17.

34. Balthasar, *Love Alone is Credible*, 56.

35. Balthasar, *Test Everything*, 88. We also see something of this truth unpacked throughout Balthasar's *Theo-Logic*.

36. Ibid., 242.

37. Ibid., 61.

38. Hans Urs von Balthasar, *The Glory of the Lord VII: The New Covenant*, trans. Brian McNeil C.R.V., (San Francisco: Ignatius Press, 1989), 132.

39. Balthasar, *The Christian State of Life*, 406.

40. Here we might ponder how it is possible to improve the cultural capital of theologians and indeed seminarians? Reinhard Hütter gives some indications from his own experience:

Where do "young" Catholic theologians—whether still in graduate programs, or in their first teaching positions, or "late born" like myself—find the kind of intellectual and spiritual guidance and formation that allows them to pursue a vision other than that of simply being functionaries of their academic guild? . . . So where can Catholic theologians in the making be theologically and spiritually formed so that they may aspire to the most intellectually rigorous understanding of the revealed truth? Where will they be instructed with the greatest fidelity to the Church? What will help them resist the one-sided and exaggerated contemporary academic emphasis on originality and productivity? The unity and coherence of theology can be maintained only if we explicitly conceive of it as an ecclesial intellectual practice of the Church, arising from the Church's nature and mission. . . . theology is essentially ecclesial, and theologians have an essentially ecclesial vocation. . . . Ultimately, what is at stake—as Augustine realized during his own lengthy struggle with the trendy theologies of his day—is our heart's desire. We will not find what we seek in Jesus Christ unless we put ourselves under the tutelage of the "church of the living God, the pillar and bulwark of the truth," for "great indeed, we confess, is the mystery of our religion" (1 Timothy 3:15–16). As Newman reminds us again and again, "private judgment" cannot reliably interpret the Holy Spirit's work in Christ's Body. And so Catholic theology cannot establish itself as a de facto counter-magisterium, remaining in splendid isolation from the Church. Nor should it seek to win a lasting standing in the secular academy that offers it a career path like that of any other academic profession. Nor, finally, will Catholic theology flourish if it is transmuted into "religious studies" to market its remnants in a post-Christian society. Whatever one thinks about the best way to give coherent and even sophisticated shape to Catholic theology, we must acknowledge that the Church herself gives us our theological task: to assist the bishops in communicating, explaining, defending, and understanding the faith that comes from the apostles. As Henri de Lubac emphasized already in 1971, we embrace the gospel not as isolated individuals ensconced in the competitions of the academy but under the tutelage of what de Lubac called "la maternité de l'église," the motherhood of the Church." Reinhard Hütter, "The Ruins of Discontinuity: Looking for Answers to the Fragmentation of Catholic Theology in America," *First Things*, January 2011, http://www.firstthings.com/article/2011/01/the-ruins-of-discontinuity.

41. Balthasar, *Love Alone is Credible*, 84.

42. *The Spiritual Exercises of St Ignatius Loyola*, trans. George E. Ganss S.J. (Chicago: Loyola University Press, 1992) 64-5, Ex. 140-142. "Consider how he summons uncountable devils, disperses some to one city and others to another, and thus throughout the whole world, without missing any provinces, places, states or individual persons. Consider the address he makes to them: How he admonishes them to set up snares and chains; how first they should tempt people to covet riches [as he usually does in most cases], so that they may more easily come to vain honor from the world, and finally to surging pride. In this way, the first step is riches,

the second is honor and the third is pride and from these three steps the enemy entices them to all the other vices."

43.   Ibid., Ex. 146. The characteristics of Christ are to invite to poverty, as opposed to riches [and especially spiritual poverty]; reproaches and contempt as opposed to honor from the world; and humility as opposed to pride; "then from these three steps they should induce people to all the other virtues," Ibid. The contrast of virtues and vices are clearly outlined in this depiction of the different strategies of the rival groups. Ignatius again underlines the serious nature of this battle between human and antihuman within the heart of all human persons.

44.   The very title of this meditation is entitled, "Lucifer, the deadly enemy of our human nature," (*Spiritual Exercises*, 136).

45.   Ben Quash, "The Theodrama," in *The Cambridge Companion to Hans Urs von Balthasar*, eds. Edward T. Oakes and David Moss (Cambridge: Cambridge University Press, 2004), 144.

46.   Hans Urs von Balthasar, *Theo-Drama: Theological Dramatic Theory*, vol. IV: *The Action*, trans. Graham Harrison (San Francisco: Ignatius Press, 1994), 62.

47.   Balthasar, *Epilogue*, 76.

48.   Hans Urs von Balthasar, *Theo-Drama: Theological Dramatic Theory*, vol. III: *Dramatis Personae: Persons in Christ*, trans. Graham Harrison (San Francisco: Ignatius Press, 1992), 36.

49.   Ibid., 271.

50.   Balthasar, *The Christian State of Life*, 435.

51.   Hans Urs von Balthasar, "Conversion in the New Testament," *Communio* I, no 1, (1974) 47-59, [55].

52.   Hans Urs von Balthasar, *The Moment of Christian Witness*, trans. Richard Beckley (San Francisco: Ignatius Press, 1994), 74.

53.   Balthasar, "Theology and Sanctity," 197.

54.   Balthasar, *The Christian State of Life*, 492.

55.   I would just note here the criticisms that Karen Kilby makes about the way Balthasar integrates theology and spirituality, particularly with regard to the question of prayer. She states: "In my judgment, though there is indeed something distinctive about the atmosphere of Balthasar's theology, it is not in fact so much reminiscent of one who prays as it is of one who directs the prayer of another. . . . One can quite easily hear in his works the overtones of the retreat director, speaking intimately, directly, confidently to his audience, working to bring them to the point of breaking down their barriers, of becoming open afresh to the gospel. . . . This gives the director of the retreat a very peculiar kind of authority." Karen Kilby, *Balthasar: A (Very) Critical Introduction* (Grand Rapids, MI: WB Eerdmans, 2012), 161. This comment is in tune with the general thrust of her argument that "there is something quite peculiarly over-reaching about Balthasar; that his work is routinely prone to silently assuming an

extraordinary, and unwarranted, authority; that his is an authorial voice that regularly seems to speak to us from an impossible position," (Ibid., 162). Interestingly, Kilby uses few sources to justify her statements. For example, regarding her criticism of Balthasar's so-called "kneeling theology," she uses only one essay, "Theology and Sanctity." Her argument makes interesting reading, but this author finds it sweeping in its scope and ironically adopting the same over-reaching stance regarding knowledge of Balthasar and the corpus of his work that she seeks to criticise in her subject.

56. Prayer enables access to both Christological mediation and the Trinitarian archetype.

57. Hans Urs von Balthasar, *Prayer*, trans. A.V. Littledale, (London : SPCK, 1975), 39.

58. "The act of faith is man's acknowledgement and agreement that he has been from time immemorial, encased in the love of the God revealed to him, and this faith comprises everything in the historical sphere that the believer encounters *a posteriori* as 'facts [or truths] of revelation.'" Ibid., 51.

59. See Revelation 2:7.

60. Balthasar, *Prayer*, trans. trans. A.V. Littledale, (London : SPCK, 1975), 59.

61. "To pray in the truth does not mean to begin by viewing it in a kind of detached way, as if we were first, by reflection, to convince ourselves that the Word of God we are actually contemplating is the truth, and then to assent to it on that ground. It means, rather, to set out from the affirmation of it as something already given long ago, and to give up and reject whatever in us militates against it. It is to live in the knowledge that the truth, which is the Spirit dwelling in us is more interior to us than we are to ourselves since, in God and in his truth, we were predestined and chosen, before the foundation of the world, before our own creation, to be his children, pure and unstained." Ibid., 63–64.

62. Ibid.

63. In Balthasar's understanding, "the life of the Trinity is . . . a union of contemplation and action. The three persons exist in an unbroken gaze of love and yet they are supremely active in their mutual self-giving." John O'Donnell, *Hans Urs von Balthasar* (New York: Continuum 2000), 158.

64. Hans Urs von Balthasar, *Engagement with God: The Drama of Christian Discipleship*, trans. R. John Halliburton, (San Francisco: Ignatius Press, 2008), 47.

65. Ibid., 61.

66. Gavin D'Costa, "Why Theologians Must Pray," 132. See also James Keating, "Theology as Thinking in Prayer," *Chicago Studies* 53 no. 1 (2014), 70-83.

67. Hans Urs von Balthasar, *Explorations in Theology: The Word Made Flesh* (San Francisco: Ignatius Press, 1989), 160.

Realization of Wisdom: Fruits of Formation in the Light of Newman

Michael Paul Gallagher, SJ

The keyword of my title is adapted from Newman, in the sense of "making real." "Real" for Newman is akin to what we might call "existential" today. It is the opposite of what he calls the "notional" or the "unreal" in the sense of ideas that remain merely abstract, distant, or theoretical. For him, theology that is isolated from spirituality would be a situation of the cart before the horse. If Newman were asked to comment on spirituality as the correct method for the study of theology, he might translate it in these terms: How can we foster a real connection (one of his other favorite words) between religion as lived and theology as reflection on religion?

With this framing of the question, I will first draw on Newman as a principal witness, and then more briefly on Aquinas and Lonergan. To ground the emerging convergence, I will finally revisit a central practice of Ignatian spirituality. Throughout, I will stress that spirituality cannot be limited to personal prayer, but invites us to a gradual contemplative integration of our Christian adventure as lived day by day.

Almost a century ago, Friedrich von Hügel in his famous book *The Mystical Element of Religion* spoke of three dimensions of religion as connected with childhood, youth, and adulthood. Children, he proposed, could grow up naturally and happily within an "institutional" kind of faith, where belonging to a church tradition shapes their images of life. A young person, however, later runs into new questions and needs a more "critical" approach to religion through reasons that make sense. For von Hügel, a third (or adult) stage of faith goes beyond the institutional and the rational dimensions to a more "mystical" phase. By this, he meant that religion needs to be experienced in depth, to be felt rather "than seen or reasoned about," and to be "loved and lived rather than analyzed"; and Von Hügel summed up his vision in one beautifully concise sentence: "I believe because I am told, because it is true, because it answers to my deepest interior experiences and needs."[1]

Translating those three dimensions into other words, our first roots are in a community of belonging, a tradition in history that carries, embodies, and celebrates a love story. But we also need to give reasons for our hope, to reflect and mediate the meaning of faith for a changing self and a changing culture. Finally, and more deeply, we try to live a spiritual adventure of encounter and surrender, a space of relationship with the Lord, a growing intimacy beyond words. In brief, von Hügel pointed to a lived convergence between ecclesial vocation, theology (as a reflection on faith), and spirituality (as the zone of action of the Spirit within us).

These three dimensions are crowned by the integrating gift we can call "wisdom."

Newman's University Sermon on Wisdom

On this theme of wisdom, I turn to a more famous figure who was, in fact, personally acquainted with von Hügel, drawing upon one of John Henry Newman's Oxford University sermons entitled, "Wisdom, as Contrasted with Faith and with Bigotry." The last in his series of five sermons on faith and reason, dating from 1841, it shows him at the peak of his powers. Echoing a long tradition, Newman sees the gift of wisdom as ordering or unifying the various dimensions of life. For our purposes, what Newman terms "wisdom" is an important quality of maturity that is not easy to foster.

In previous university sermons, Newman had argued against reducing reason to its logical or argumentative forms, instead insisting that faith involves a different version of reason that is "implicit," "spontaneous," "instinctive," and "prior" to "proof." (2, 5).[2] Here, he asks how this reflection on faith develops into a mature "habit" of "wisdom." How does the intellectual dimension of faith grow without avoiding two opposite dangers: theology becoming merely intellectual theory or faith becoming rigid in various forms of closure or fear (6)? By way of an answer, Newman introduces his key word for this sermon: "enlargement" (a term that he uses no less than nineteen times). We need "enlargement" toward a unifying and transforming "meaning," which goes beyond any mere accumulation of separate experiences (16). Wisdom, if it is to be what he calls "philosophical," creates an ever-expanding spiritual horizon, a capacity for "living knowledge" that discovers connections and moves toward integration of what one is learning (21, 28). Wisdom goes beyond fragments of information—like a tourist with no sense of history or a student full of ideas but without appropriation (24–26). If knowledge is to be a real philosophy of life, it will need to converge on a "true centre," offering the ability to patiently "discern" the "whole work of God" (29). Along this road of enlargement, faith receives and develops the larger gift called "wisdom."

Indeed, if religious people do not embrace this call to wisdom, they can be easily tempted by a "narrowness of mind" (32), which today includes fundamentalism and various forms of inflexibility. Newman views this distortion of religion as wanting easy and secure clarities instead of the necessary journey to truth through "darkness" (36). This distorted religion offers analysis, but avoids discovery (28). It sees everything "only in one way" and prefers its fixed positions to the adventure of true faith (38). A narrow take on religion has "nothing to learn" and "sees no difficulties," whereas a genuinely enlarging wisdom deepens with the challenge of a changing culture or from new scientific questions (39, 41, 46). Those who stay locked in what Newman calls "bigotry" can never reach out in dialogue to different positions because they cannot "learn another disposition" (42). They live with resentment of new realities or get angry when they cannot win an argument on their terms (46). At the end, Newman invites us to admit that this struggle between rigidity and enlargement exists in all of us: it is a prison of egoism that faith invites us to gradually "unlearn" (47).

In fact, the biblical text from which Newman begins this sermon comes from St. Paul: "The spiritual person, however, can judge everything" (1 Cor 2:15). The absence of wisdom is associated with a fragmented worldview, whereas spiritual wisdom is a gradually appropriated capacity to cope with complexity within a faith perspective. In this sense, Newman's theme in 1841 is close to our concerns today. Let me end this introduction not simply with half-quotation and paraphrase but with Newman's own account of the dangers and potentials in this area. Here, he talks about existence as tourism (as we might say in our postmodern way), comparing the inability of sailors to integrate their experiences of the world to students who fail to develop any lasting or unifying foundations in their studies:

Seafaring men . . . range from one end of the earth to the other; but the multiplicity of phenomena which they have encountered, forms no harmonious and consistent picture upon their imagination: they see, as it were, the tapestry of human life on the wrong side of it. They sleep, and they rise up, and they find themselves now in Europe, now in Asia; they see visions of great cities and wild regions; . . . and nothing which meets them carries them on to any idea beyond itself. Nothing has a meaning, nothing has a history, nothing has relations. Every thing stands by itself, and comes and goes in its turn, like the shifting sights of a show, leaving the beholder where he was (25).

[Similarly], undigested reading shows us that knowledge without system is not Philosophy. Students who store themselves so amply with literature or science, that no room is left for determining the respective relations which exist between their acquisitions . . . are rather said to load their minds than to enlarge them (26).

[By contrast,] a comprehensive mind, or wisdom . . . implies a connected view of the old with the new . . . without which there is no whole, and could be no centre. It is the knowledge, not only of things, but of their mutual relations. It is organized, and therefore living knowledge (21).

Newman's mention of science is worth noting: it is surely the fundamental error of today's arrogant atheistic scientism that it remains with the bigotry of empiricism. If this is accepted as the criterion of certainty, then we must abandon any quest for a specifically religious wisdom.

Imagination, Disposition, and Vulnerability

Before moving on from Newman, I want to touch briefly on his originality concerning three qualities that are relevant for students of theology: *imagination, disposition,* and *vulnerability.* It is widely known that Newman insisted on the importance of a real assent to religious truth, where "real" implies a personal commitment and conversion. It is less known that, in early versions of the manuscript for *An Essay in Aid of a Grammar of Assent,* he used the expression "imaginative assent" in place of "real assent," only changing it at a late stage and probably out of fear of being misunderstood by people who would confuse "imaginative" with "imaginary." In the final text of *An Essay in Aid of A Grammar of Assent,* there are occasions when the older phrase survives: "I have wished to trace the process by which the mind arrives, not only at a notional, but at an imaginative or real assent."[3]

Recalling the central role that Newman gave to imagination is also relevant for our interest in building bridges between theology and spirituality. Newman always proposed an integration of rationality, heart, and imagination, seeing the whole self as an instrument of truth. Akin to the role of imagination in Ignatian exercises, Newman speaks of "the theology of a religious imagination" as capable of having a "living hold on truths" because people find that truths about God "live in their imagination" (117).[4] When the imagination is not "kindled," belief remains notional (126). Imagination serves two other functions in the development of faith: it nourishes "our emotional and moral nature" and, in turn, becomes "a principle of action" (214). Human beings are made for action and moved by feeling. In this context, Newman quotes one of his Anglican period texts: "the heart is commonly reached, not through the reason, but through the imagination" (292). In short, Newman's epistemology of imagination sees it as a vital means of experiencing the real and hence, of "realizing" religious reality in the ordinary life of faith. Obviously, this emphasis invites us to reflect on the potential role of imagination as a key mediator between theology and spirituality, as a self-involving vehicle of affectivity, ensuring that study is in less danger of remaining merely notional. Concluding this topic (which could, of course, be explored much further with reference to modern thinkers such as Paul Ricoeur or William Lynch), I simply offer my favorite quotation on the faculty of transformation from Emily Dickinson: "The possible's slow fuse is lit by imagination."

"Dispositions for Faith" was the title of one of Newman's Dublin sermons in 1856. The question of our receptivity represents another key element in Newman's psychology of faith, one that can have a vital role in developing a more spiritual method for studying theology. Newman insists that we are responsible for the quality of our fundamental attitudes of open-mindedness or closed-mindedness. When we recall two of his metaphors, we may ask, "Should a person be 'on the lookout' for God or sitting complacently at home waiting for a divine visitor to turn up?"[5] Newman holds that the real reasons for religious belief are largely a question of "antecedent considerations."[6] Hence, his pedagogy of faith does not begin with arguments but with paying attention to preconceived spiritual attitudes. At the age of twenty-four, the young John Henry told his difficult atheist brother Charles, "You are not in a state of mind to listen," because Charles was suffering from "a fault of the heart, not of the intellect."[7] In the same spirit, at least five of Newman's sermons speak of an essential "preparation of heart." For instance, in a university sermon from 1839, we are told that the fatal error of the world is to approach "religious truth without preparation of heart."[8] The application to our theme seems evident once again: if any fruitful healing of the divorce between academic theology and personal spirituality is to happen, it will involve this pre-religious zone of disposition.

Finally, I would like to mention an extraordinary passage of Newman's from an 1839 sermon entitled "Christian Sympathy." Here, he challenges us to risk an honest vulnerability as essential to making our religious faith "real." It is close to a more modern and well-known article by Father Michael Buckley entitled "Are You Weak Enough To Be a Priest?"[9] Let me quote Newman directly with some abbreviations:

> Perhaps the reason why the standard of holiness among us is so low, why . . . our view of the truth so dim, our belief so unreal, our general notions so artificial and

external is this, that we dare not trust each other with the secret of our hearts. We have each the same secret, and we keep it to ourselves, and we fear that, as a cause of estrangement, which really would be a bond of union.

We do not probe the wounds of our nature thoroughly; we do not lay the foundation of our religious profession in the ground of our inner man. . . . We are amiable and friendly to each other in words and deeds, but our love is not enlarged, our bowels of affection are straitened, and we fear to let the intercourse begin at the root; and, in consequence, our religion viewed as a social system, is hollow. The presence of Christ is not in it.[10]

This passage translates to a strong warning against skimming the surface of theology or spirituality and of avoiding any confession of fragility or struggle. Newman seems to be reminding us of the personal courage needed to do justice to the full range of faith, involving darkness and light, presence and absence, grace and sin, commitment and doubt. All of this is rooted in a certain nonsubjectivist spiritual autobiography.

Lights from Thomas Aquinas and Pope Benedict XVI

In order to offer a different perspective on the interaction between theology and spirituality, I would like to bring together two unusual texts of St. Thomas Aquinas, both inviting us to expand the tent of our theology beyond narrow rationality. On at least one occasion, he offers a surprisingly strong defense of the need for an imaginative strand within theology. In the prologue to his commentary on the *Sentences of Peter Lombard*, he poses the question whether theology should be *artificialis*. Putting it in modern language, Aquinas asks whether theology needs an artistic dimension; and he answers in the affirmative. As always, it is intriguing to read his objections in order to appreciate the contrary view that he is about to undermine. For instance, Aquinas argues (against his final position) that, because poetry works by means of metaphoric expression, theology as a science must necessarily avoid such wavelengths. When it is a question of overcoming error, he answers affirmatively and states that clear arguments are needed; however, Aquinas broadens the agenda and suggests that confronting intellectual difficulties is not the principal purpose of theology. Insofar as theology invites us toward the "contemplation of truth," we need to develop not just a rational, but also a symbolic theology (*symbolica teologia*).[11] Going further, Aquinas argues that because the Christian faith is grounded in a "narrative of signs," reflection on faith will require "metaphorical, symbolical and parabolical" approaches.[12] He then answers the objection that poetry suffers from a defect of rational truth and, therefore, is not a proper model for theology. On the contrary, he concludes that because theology also seeks to explore beyond reason, a "symbolic method is common to both" (*modus symbolicus utrique communis est*).[13] This insight reminds us not to forget or neglect the challenge of artistic embodiments of the human drama of faith. To quote the well-known contemporary poet Christian Wiman, "art is so often better at theology than theology is."[14]

Another Aquinas text similarly warns us not to reduce theology to a provider of clarity or excessive certitude. It also speaks about the damage to the student if this model of theology monopolizes the field. In *Quaestiones quodlibetales*, Thomas Aquinas offers a pedagogical critique of what he sees as a limited, and ultimately unhealthy, approach to theology.[15] Echoing his commentary on the *Sentences of Peter Lombard* on the distinction between combating errors more clearly and nourishing faith more deeply, Aquinas accepts that—where the challenge is to clarify the content of faith—an appeal to biblical or ecclesial authority is correct and appropriate. However, Aquinas indicates a deeper task for the student of theology than finding certitude about doctrines. To undertake a genuine road to understanding requires "going to the root of the truth."[16] Without this more ambitious wavelength, says Aquinas, students may arrive at some "certitude" about truths, but if they "acquire no knowledge or understanding, they will go away empty" (*nihil intellectus acquiret et vacuus abscedet*).[17]

Let me expand on this point from a different and perhaps surprising perspective. When Pope Benedict XVI visited the Gregorian University in November 2006, he gave an unpublished speech to the Jesuits where he criticized what he called the "intellectual sterility" of "ecclesial positivism."[18] Faced with the cultural crisis and "the great existential questions of today," he called for a "restructuring of theology."[19] Pope Benedict XVI advocated for a "creative and spiritual theology" rooted in witness, lifestyle, and liturgy because "true theology matures here" and, in this way, becomes more than a "merely intellectual exercise."[20] His critique of "ecclesial positivism" seems parallel to Aquinas's concern that students could remain empty if they found security about their doctrinal bearings only in a propositional form (as if that were the only goal of theology). Once again, we find a strong invitation to create deeper connections between theology, spirituality, and indeed, the challenges of the culture.

Allowing for the different and relational quality of all religious truth, what kind of rationality does faith need in today's culture? It will need, in an expression of Saint John Paul II, "to move from phenomenon to foundation,"[21] through what Pope Benedict XVI so often called an enlarged rationality, capable of doing justice to personalist and epistemological dimensions. Faith today will also be marked by a certain humility, resulting from the long tradition of negative theology, because, as Aquinas so often insisted, faith knowledge is different and radically imperfect in this life. Here is a striking comment from Aquinas's book on the *Sentences*: "the certitude proper to faith is beyond the category of knowledge, belonging rather to the field of affectivity."[22] Thus, a worthy rationale for theology will admit the disturbing strangeness of mystery, the fragility of all our expressions, and the unique interaction of intellect, will, and feeling involved in the adventure of faith. And yet, it will have to be a rationality that is capable of defending the possibility of truth.

Perspectives from Lonergan

At this point, it seems suitable to briefly and selectively draw on the work of Bernard Lonergan. To state my proposal with utter brevity, Lonergan offers a map of the operations of theology, one that grounds them in both a coherent cognitional structure and the graced life of faith. Lonergan insists that theology reflects on religion, a claim that can seem obvious but one that reveals itself as both surprising and fruitful. Religion involves the whole adventure of our exodus from ego and our encounter with God. In this place, the love story that is Revelation is lived out. Here, Transcendent Love "dismantles" self-transcendence.[23] Theology as human inquiry can explore the data of Scripture and the history of Church, but theology as a mediating ministry and mission starts from this transforming gift of God's love. From this peak, it descends into history with a message of healing or redemption. Thus, theology first situates itself on the level of our spiritual and affective freedom before moving down to the levels of truth or reflection. Rooted in gift, it involves different phases or specializations. What Lonergan calls the fourth, or existential, level is crucial for understanding the relationship of theology and spirituality. Here, theology is foundational in the sense that theologians need to take a stance in a cultural battle zone of ideas and images. They seek clarity about the roots of conflicts and even about how these roots exist in the theologian himself or herself. This pursuit requires personal and spiritual honesty about one's own horizon, as well as about one's constant struggle for authenticity and against inauthenticity. Here, the theologian has to face the costly road of three conversions. Without a real religious conversion—without being loved into love by God's love—the heart is not transformed and theology lacks its essential spiritual foundation. Blessed with religious conversion, "Christian experience" enjoys "the fruits of being in love with a mysterious, uncomprehended God."[24] Moreover, as lived, this conversion will pervade imagination, enrich understanding, guide judgment, and reinforce decisions. Without moral conversion, we drift in an immaturity of self-satisfactions; but if we can grasp that we are responsible for what we make of ourselves, we at least begin to shift from living for self to living for values.

The third conversion is intellectual, but it is also essential for the spiritual life of a theologian and, indeed, for the very credibility of faith. Intellectual conversion involves a breakthrough concerning the real. From modernity, from our surrounding culture, and often from our lifestyle, we are infected with a childish myth that identifies the real with the visible and that imagines objectivity as somehow "out there now" to be encountered.[25] If so, God remains un-real, and theology is in deep trouble. To counter this widespread and dangerous fallacy, Lonergan's study of cognitional structure updates Aquinas's position that truth is born from judgment. Lonergan also insists that we move from the empirical world of immediacy to recognize a much "larger world" where we live out our lives and which is "mediated by meaning."[26] Without this shift, a student of theology can remain shaky and confused about truth, objectivity, subjectivity, and certainty. With this deepening of horizon, he or she will enjoy intellectual security and, indeed, spiritual consolation.

There are other floors in the Lonergan building that we do not have time to visit. He speaks of three more operations in theology that are born, and descend, from the gift of the Spirit: dogmatic truth, systematic understanding, and pastoral communication on the level of experience. I have concentrated on the existential level because it is here that Lonergan, in his own way, responds to the damaging separation of theology from spirituality.

We have seen something of the great ideal that Newman called "wisdom" as a unifying and expanding gift for reflection on faith. With Aquinas (and indeed Pope Benedict XVI), we heard a warning not to identify theology with its easier aspects of magisterial affirmations. The invitation was to be simultaneously more creative and more contemplative. With Lonergan, we discovered a way to locate the spiritual in the work of theology. But how is this method to be encouraged in the context of studying theology? The theory can be beautiful, but the practice needs to be embodied.

Saint Ignatius of Loyola: A Pause for the Paraclete

To draw toward a conclusion, I want to adapt a spiritual figure that is not usually accused of being too theoretical, indeed someone who is sometimes accused of being too methodical—St. Ignatius of Loyola. Many aspects of his spirituality could be relevant, including, of course, his sense of the battleground of imagination as famously depicted in his meditation on the Two Standards. However, I am thinking mainly of the exercise called an "Examination of Conscience (or Consciousness)," and which I want to rename and update as "A Pause for the Paraclete." I propose this as a highly practical exercise for daily spiritual integration.

Obviously, the promises of the Paraclete (or defense advocate in John's Gospel) are relevant here, in particular the promise of the Spirit as a recognizable presence with us, and within us, guiding us (Jn 14:17; 16:13). Slightly changing the order of what is offered in the *Spiritual Exercises*, this "Pause for the Paraclete" can be seen as having five moments: asking for light, giving thanks, reviewing the movements of the day, seeking healing where needed, and looking forward with the Lord to situations to come.[27] As the overall approach is well known, I will comment only briefly on some of the key points.

First, there is an underlying theology or spirituality that God is active in the flow of my day, indeed that ordinary living is my main place for encountering God—through the daily drama of God's call and my response. In other words, some of the great Christian mysteries continue today and are at work in each life: revelation and creation, redemption and resurrection. Their fruits can be recognized within my mixture of moods, experiences, and dispositions. This exercise invites one to focus on attitudes rather than actions, learning to see through the daily drama of God's call and one's response. In the spirit of the famous discovery of Jacob: "Truly, the Lord is in this place and I did not know it!" (Gen 28:16).

In practice, the five steps can be summarized as follows:

1. "In your light we see light" (Ps 36:10). Ask for Spirit-guided insight into the hours I have just lived. See these hours with God's eyes.

2. "If you knew the gift of God" (Jn 4:10). All of life is blessed with God's presence, so I seek to discover where God is leading me.

3. Review the day with the Lord, attending to the ebb and flow of moods as consolation or desolation. What way is the wind blowing?

4. Seek pardon for "missing the mark." For instance, in light of the healing of the vision of the man at Bethsaida who learns to see more clearly (Mk 8:22).

5. Literally looking forward with the Lord, ask to adjust the compass of your desires "that our God may make you worthy of his calling" (2 Thess 1:11) for these coming hours.

In my view, this fifth point has often been minimized to making a quick resolution to "pull up one's socks." Instead, it is vital as a lesson of transformation under the Spirit. It is possible to imagine what will turn up in the coming hours, to become alert to dangers, to seek new eyes with which to see all with the Lord. Where will I most need God's guidance?

In short, this exercise can serve as a crucial bridge between prayer and life, between theology as study and theology as wisdom. It involves a prayerful reflection that remembers the larger Christian drama, that sees daily life as part of God's action, and that, when practiced regularly, helps one to make choices guided by the companion Paraclete. This is a daily version of what Newman meant by wisdom, what Lonergan meant by conversion, and what Pope Benedict XVI meant by a place where theology matures.

NOTES

1.   Friedrich von Hügel, *The Mystical Element of Religion As Studied in Saint Catherine of Genoa and Her Friends*, vol. 1 (London: JM Dent and Sons, 1927) 53–54.

2.   References to the paragraphs of this Newman sermon will be given in parentheses in the text. The original is found in John Henry Newman, *Fifteen Sermons Preached before the University of Oxford between 1826 and 1843* (London: Longmans, Green and Co., 1890), 278–311.

3.   John Henry Newman, *An Essay in Aid of a Grammar of Assent* (London: Longmans, Green and Co., 1909), 119.

4.   Page references to *An Essay in Aid of a Grammar of Assent* in this section will be given in parentheses in the text.

5.   John Henry Newman, *Sermons Preached on Various Occasions* (London: Longmans, Green, and Co. 1908), 66.

6.   Newman, *Fifteen Sermons*, 187.

7.   Ian Ker and Thomas Gornell, eds., *The Letters and Diaries of John Henry Newman*, vol. I (Oxford: Clarendon, 1978), 212–216.

8.   Newman, *Fifteen Sermons*, 198.

9.   Michael J. Buckley, "Are You Weak Enough to Be a Priest?" *New York Province of the Society of Jesuits,* accessed on 01/06/2014, http://nysj.org/s/316/images/editor_documents/content/AscensionJesus%20is%20no%20longer%20limited%20by%20time%20and%20space.%20The%20A./Weak%20Enough.pdf.

10.   John Henry Newman, *Parochial and Plain Sermons*, vol. 5 (London: Longmans, Green, and Co., 1908), 126–127.

11.   San Tommaso d'Aquino, "Prologus, q. 1, a. 5" in *Commento alle Sentenze di Pietro Lombardo*, vol. I (Bologna: Edizioni Studio Domenicano, 2001), 150–155. Author translation.

12.   Ibid.

13.   Ibid.

14.   Christian Wiman, "Varieties of Quiet," *Image*, no. 73 (2012): 90.

15.   Saint Thomas Aquinas, *Quaestiones quodlibetales*, IV, q. 9, a. 3.

16.   Ibid.

17.   Ibid.

18.   Pope Benedict XVI, (informal lecture to Jesuit community, without prepared text, Gregorian University, November 3, 2006). Author notes.

19.   Ibid.

20.   Ibid.

21.   Blessed John Paul II, *Fides et Ratio* (1998), sec. 83.

22.   III *Sent.*, d. 23, q. 2, a. 3, *questiuncula* 3.

23.   Bernard Lonergan, *Method in Theology* (London: Darton Longman & Todd, 1972), 105.

24. Ibid., 242.
25. Ibid., 238.
26. Ibid., 77.
27. Saint Ignatius of Loyola, *Spiritual Exercises*, sec. 43.

PART II

THEOLOGY, SPIRITUALITY, AND PRIESTLY FORMATION

How Faith Forges a Reason Suitable for Theology According to Saint Bonaventure

Monsignor John R. Cihak

In praising the theological achievement of Hans Urs von Balthasar, Pope Benedict XVI asserted that spirituality impresses the right method upon theology.[1] I imagine that the Holy Father was well aware that the polyvalent nature of "spirituality" would invite discussion. However, with the phrase "right method," he clearly emphasized theology's formal aspect—that is, how theology should proceed. I think most would agree that, although rationality is essential to theology in order to demonstrate the intelligibility of faith, theology cannot merely be a rational exercise, given its subject matter: the Living God of Revelation. What does such an idea look like in terms of an articulated theological method?

In this essay, I would like to retrieve and reflect upon an insight from Saint Bonaventure, as the teaching of this giant of scholastic theology runs through the bedrock of both Hans Urs von Balthasar and Pope Benedict XVI and their way of thinking. A rich and compelling determination of "spirituality" impressing the "right method" upon theology can be found in Bonaventure's doctrine of the transformation of human reason by grace to arrive at what would be considered a properly theological cognition. It seems that examining any adequate theological method would naturally highlight the role of faith, the *sine qua non* of theology. Therefore, I will present the role that faith plays in forging a reason suitable for theology, focusing on Bonaventure's explicit treatment of faith in the third book of his *Commentaria in Quatuor Libros Sententiarum*.[2] I will situate that reflection within the wider context of the Seraphic Doctor's teaching on knowing God, which extends beyond what would be considered academic theology. Within this wider context, I will rely on the work of Gregory LaNave who has already written extensively and well on the subject, even if some of his Thomistic sensibilities might not be universally shared by Bonaventurians.[3] Having presented Bonaventure's teaching, I will conclude by offering five implications of this teaching, especially as they pertain to the intellectual formation of priests. From these reflections, it will hopefully be evident how the Seraphic Doctor specifically conceives spirituality as essential to theological method, and that his teachings offer a key for rediscovering the intrinsic role that spirituality plays in theology.

Theology and the Role of Sanctifying Grace

For Bonaventure, theology is the science of knowing the God of Revelation, specifically Jesus Christ ("the whole Christ").[4] It is the human understanding of revealed realities. What is striking about the Seraphic Doctor's conception of theology—taken by LaNave as a major interpretive key—is the emphasis that Bonaventure gives to the formative and directive force that the unique "object" of theology exerts upon the way theology proceeds. In other words, theology is guided not only by its *principles*, as other sciences are, but most especially by its *relation* to its object. This emphasis on the object comes as no surprise, considering the central event that serves as the irradiating nucleus driving and informing Bonaventure's theology: St. Francis's stigmatization on Mount La Verna. In this powerful mystical event, St. Francis, who for Bonaventure supplants the great Peter Lombard as "The Theologian," is not simply *thinking about* the things of faith; rather, something is happening to him. In soul and in body, he is being *conformed* into the likeness of the Crucified through love. In this event, Bonaventure sees an image and pattern of how the human soul comes to know the God of Revelation in Jesus Christ. This knowing involves the very transformation of the knower, leading him into loving union with the Blessed Trinity.

Theology, therefore, is neither purely speculative nor purely practical; it is, rather, an "affective science," a science of love. This kind of science is located between speculative science, which perfects the intellect in itself (*in se*), and practical science, which perfects the intellect by extending it toward doing something (*ad opus*). In affective science, the intellect is perfected by being extended toward the *affectus* (*ad affectum*). Theology proceeds rationally in faith according to its specific object, whereby the things of faith are brought into understanding. It considers what is believed in light of the principles of understanding. Given the unique object of theology and the relationship created by that very object, the culmination of this affective science must be more than knowledge (*scientia*). Its end is the attainment of wisdom (*sapientia*), a knowledge that passes into love where the demands of truth and love are harmoniously fulfilled. Theology, then, is a sapiential science, a science *secundum pietatem*, whose nature is determined by its love for its object. Therefore, while insisting on the rational nature of theology, Bonaventure, nevertheless, argues that, given the unique object of theology and the relationship established by that object through faith, human reason itself must be transformed by grace into a reason suitable for theology. Only then is one capable of apprehending some of the realities treated by theology. Only through the transformation of reason can (mere) knowledge become wisdom, the knowing that best corresponds to the object.

The passage from knowledge to wisdom happens through holiness (*sanctitas*),[5] which can be found in the Seraphic Doctor's general doctrine of sanctifying grace. Its aim is the perfection of the human person through union with God. In other words, holiness begins with a yearning for wisdom, becoming a personal disposition toward moral discipline. Yearning followed by discipline produces love. A pure love is holiness whose effect is the deiformity of the creature. This deiformity enables one to achieve wisdom.[6] Fundamentally, Bonaventure's teaching on holiness pertains to the virtue of justice, a right ordering of love, which necessarily involves rectifying, reforming, cleansing, illuminating, perfecting, vivifying, making steadfast, elevating, likening, and joining man to God.[7]

Sanctifying grace (*gratia gratum faciens*) brings this union about in three stages: rectifying and cleansing the soul through the theological virtues; freeing the soul and making it agile so it can move toward God through the gifts of the Holy Spirit; and perfecting the soul and uniting it to God through the Beatitudes. According to LaNave, Bonaventure locates holiness in the second stage: after the virtues, but before perfection. Holiness is the soul informed by the gifts of the Holy Spirit. Nevertheless, all three stages (virtues, gifts, and Beatitudes) function together. Each attains its own particular mode of theological knowing: virtues correspond to symbolic (creedal) theology; gifts correspond to theology proper (academic); and Beatitudes correspond to contemplative theology (both acquired and infused). Bonaventure assigns the three modes of theology to the three states of life in the Church: lay (virtues), clerical (gifts), and monastic or contemplative (Beatitudes). The intermediate stage especially pertains to the clerical state insofar as the priest is an intermediary between God and man. Bonaventure identifies a special obligation for those in sacred orders to cultivate academic theology.[8] I will return to this point in the conclusion. By placing contemplative theology as the highest form of knowing, the Seraphic Doctor is able to assert that, even without formal academic training, St. Francis was a theologian in the true sense and could surpass all other academic theologians.

   In order for us to arrive at what Bonaventure would consider a properly theological cognition, human reason—under the influence of sanctifying grace—will follow this threefold trajectory of transformation by the virtues, gifts, and Beatitudes. The process is a dynamic, lively interplay, a circumincession recapitulated at each level: first, faith, hope, and love (corresponding to man's intellect, memory, and will); followed by the gifts; and then the Beatitudes, wherein the soul itself becomes more perfectly conformed to the Trinity in Christ. Academic theology is included in this trajectory, yet it is not the terminal point. Beyond these three graced habits is the soul's union with God, which is characterized by two realities: the fruits of the Holy Spirit describe the graced soul's state of delight, while the spiritual senses are the graced soul's perception of spiritual realities, where knowing God becomes so immediate and real that it resembles the immediacy of knowing through the senses. The Sacraments, for their part, are a means of support and assistance to all of these operations.

Understanding the nature of theology and the doctrine of sanctifying grace in this way, we can now consider the trajectory itself in order to see faith's role in forging a reason suitable for theology. We do this while acknowledging that such a transformation is inseparable from that of the other two theological virtues of hope and love. The path concerning the virtue of faith seems most relevant to our exploration of why and how spirituality impresses a right method upon theology.

The Virtue of Faith

The virtue of faith establishes the human soul in a graced (and therefore unique) relationship with and orientation toward its object, thereby distinguishing the science of theology from the philosophical sciences in both object and mode. First, and perhaps most manifestly, faith brings to theology its specific material for reflection, those realities that are beyond the grasp of reason alone and are expressed in the articles of faith. However, faith's role is not merely limited to introducing the intellect to the God of Revelation through propositions. The grace operating in faith also has an effect on human reason itself.

When St. Bonaventure speaks of the faith operating in theology, he means an "informed faith" (*fides formata*), a living faith whose form is charity.[9] Informed faith is a graced virtue pertaining to the cognitive function of the soul whereby it thinks with assent. The habit of faith orients the soul to the first Truth and in this way, is similar to knowledge. Faith also involves free will because what is believed is unseen, thus distinguishing it from knowledge. Theology does not concern itself with what is seen, but with what is believed; this knowing is characterized more by reaching than possessing. In this view of the beatific vision, human knowledge of God always remains *in via*. Faith is, therefore, directed toward knowledge, but not in the usual sense. The truths of faith are not seen, but "salvific"; they are truths *secundum pietatem* (Ti 1:1), known through the authority of the highest truth, which draws the believer's heart. Through faith, God's self-knowledge begins to illuminate and direct the believer's intellect.

Every now and then in his treatment of faith in the *Sententiarum*, the Seraphic Doctor employs a suggestive phrase: through the habit of faith "the intellect is taken captive unto obedience to Christ and rests in the first Truth for its own sake" (2 Cor 10:5).[10] The words imply that this movement is not automatic, but a kind of struggle eventually resulting in a repose.[11] How does this transformation happen? To the extent that faith is a habit, it must be assigned in some way to the cognitive faculty. Bonaventure strongly qualifies the cognitive aspect of faith, giving a certain presiding role to the *affectus*.[12] Faith acts upon the intellect, inclining or extending it *by* the *affectus* (*ab affectu*). Moreover, faith extends the intellect *toward* the *affectus* (*ad affectum*), the final cause being the soul's union with God in love.[13] Thus, faith engages the speculative intellect, in that it believes what is true because it is true; the extended intellect, in that it believes voluntarily; and the affective faculty itself, in that it wills to assent to what unaided reason cannot attain. The speculative intellect cannot give this kind of assent itself, so faith inclines the intellect by and toward the *affectus* to make this assent possible.

Commenting on the description of faith given in the *Letter to the Hebrews*, Bonaventure also holds that faith is both substance (*substantia* or *hypostasis*) and evidence (*argumentum*).[14] As substance, faith is the foundation upon which the spiritual edifice of the soul is constructed; it establishes and sustains this edifice. As evidence, faith declares revealed truth to the intellect and illuminates it to come to a conclusion and firmly adhere to it in an even more convincing way, just as a true argument compels one to assent to a proven conclusion. In doing so, faith extends certainty to hope and charity through an experience greater than that of knowledge. St. Bonaventure makes a distinction between the certitude of speculation (*speculatio*) and the certitude of adhesion (*adhaesio*), the former belonging to the intellect and the latter, to the *affectus*.[15] This "more–certain–knowing" of faith could be called an "affective certitude," where the believer becomes more attached to the truth than to knowledge. The Seraphic Doctor, thus, argues that faith is the driver (*auriga*) of virtues because only through faith can one arrive at knowledge of the highest and truest Good.[16] Without this knowledge, there can be no desire for or love of the true Good. Through the grace operating in the virtue of faith, where the intellect is being extended by and toward the *affectus*, the soul becomes rectified in its cognitive function. By rectifying the soul in relation to the first Truth, faith disposes the soul to receive the Holy Spirit's gifts of knowledge and understanding, whereby the

cognitive faculty becomes more free and agile in its movement toward God.

We may gain a better understanding of informed faith
by comparing it to what Bonaventure calls "formless faith"
(*fides informata*), an inferior type of faith that lacks the form
of charity. Bonaventure examines formless faith as it appears
in human or demonic persons. In humans, formless faith
is understood as a virtue only in a broad sense because,
although it is somewhat guided by the uprightness of justice, it lacks charity and thus cannot attain its end or rectify,
invigorate, or direct the potency of the intellect because it
is not fully "captured" in subjection or submission to the
highest Truth.[17] The person may hear the apostolic preaching
and receive divine illumination, elevating the intellect in matters beyond it, but the intellect's assent is incomplete. There
is belief in the first Truth for its own sake, even though the
intellect is not directed toward Truth by loving it.[18] Infused
with sanctifying grace, formless faith can become informed,
taking away the deficiency and completing and perfecting the
original grace, like a seed that finally germinates.[19] Bonaventure's treatment of the qualified formless faith in demonic
persons is also illuminating.[20] The characteristics of this even
more deficient "faith" (produced, in part, by its original condition and, in part, by acquired knowledge) are: the complete
lack of clinging to the first Truth for its own sake and being
compelled to assent (*quasi extorta necessitate*) to the truths of
faith with a certain "grumbling" (*murmure*). Demonic persons
are not able to receive infused habits because their will is
more prone to attack the truths of faith than to give assent.
This corrupted and contemptible knowledge is the end result
of an intelligence deficient in love.

Informed faith moves the theologizing mind toward an affectively certain knowledge of its object. If theology is a true science, then there is a *ratio motiva*, a moving principle, a standard of knowledge impressed upon the human mind by God guiding the mind to this certain knowledge.[21] Here, Bonaventure focuses on man as an image of God. This means that man relates to God not only as effect is related to cause, but also as an object is related to cause. "Therefore," as LaNave observes, "the *ratio motiva* is also the *obiectum quo*—the object, not as that which is grasped (*obiectum quod*), but as the aspect under which that which is grasped is known."[22] Faith not only gives theology a unique content (*fides quae*) but also begins to transform the intellect itself, bringing about a unique way of thinking (*fides qua*). Faith is not only *data* but also a *principle* that directs thinking, giving it a new shape. LaNave draws a suggestive conclusion: "the infused virtue of faith moves the mind in its theologizing, and the content of faith is attainable by the mind insofar as the mind is transformed into the shape given by faith in its intelligibility. 'Putting on the mind of Christ' is a quite literal description of the scientific task of the theologian."[23]

The theological virtues initiate a life of holiness by rectifying the powers of the soul, bringing the fallen soul from *imago creationis* to *imago recreationis*. This rectifying work is essential. In the fallen state, God is still the object of the soul, but only implicitly. The soul can only know according to the degree that it is impressed by the eternal reasons as a moving principle. Sin produces obscurity in the soul, requiring grace to rectify the soul so that God can appear clearly, not only as its object but also as its end. Faith rectifies the rational power of the soul whose object is the Truth. Hope and love rectify

the affective power of the soul (in its irascible and concupis-
cible dimensions, respectively), whose object is the Good.[24]

According to Bonaventure, although the soul does not
attain theological wisdom in this first stage of the theological virtues, the believer can know the source or object of
theological wisdom which is beyond nature: God revealing
or God the revealer. The theologian, as one who studies
Divine Revelation, reveals what is hidden. Holy Scripture and
the threefold spiritual understanding of Scripture inherent
in the letter are essential to this endeavor. Without faith, the
theologian is unable to penetrate the allegorical meaning of
Holy Scripture. Hope and love are required for penetrating
the moral and anagogical meanings. The theologian must,
therefore, possess the theological virtues in order to receive
Divine Revelation in Holy Scripture with which to properly
engage the science. Faith opens the door for knowledge to
become wisdom.

The Gifts of Knowledge and Understanding

Bonaventure identifies two intellectual gifts of the Holy
Spirit that continue the transformation of reason: knowledge
(*scientia*) and understanding (*intellectus*). Faith orients the soul
toward its proper object, while knowledge and understanding provide the specific character of theological cognition.[25]
While these gifts do not bring new material to faith, they
bring a deeper recognition of what is believed. Bonaventure
connects the gift of knowledge to the practical intellect in its
relationship with created realities, and the gift of understanding to the speculative intellect in its relationship with uncreated realities.

The gift of knowledge is ordained to the practical not simply insofar as it knows the things of faith but, in particular, as the greatest of all created realities: the human nature of Christ. The deeper perspicacity attained from the gift of knowledge is knowing created reality through the eyes of faith—namely, how one should live beyond natural law according to the human nature of Christ. LaNave draws a striking conclusion from Bonaventure's idea: "The humanity of Christ does not function in theology as a mere datum of faith. To know the humanity of Christ by the gift of science is to possess it as a principle that directs action."[26] For its part, the gift of understanding offers the greatest specificity in the transformation of a reason fit for theology. With this gift, the soul apprehends the inner reasonableness and coherence of the things of faith, recognizing them as expressions of the eternal reasons. The cognition produced by the gift of understanding is the contemplation of truth (*cognitio veritatis*). Here, Bonaventure locates what we would call academic theology.

The genesis of theological knowing, therefore, begins with faith appropriating the content of faith, thereby providing a set of revealed principles for the foundation of a science. Faith also establishes a new relationship with God that functions as a *ratio motiva*. The gifts of knowledge and understanding deepen the relationship between man and God and generate principles for that understanding. A transformed reason knows created realities "according to a proper, ordered pattern of life" (the gift of knowledge) and "perceives creatures as manifestations of eternal Truth" (the gift of understanding).[27] These principles are evident only to a reason transformed by grace, now able to see the world in a graced way. This new knowledge is not incompatible with,

but rather perfects and elevates, what is known by natural
human reason. Thus, for theology to function properly, the
theologian must think with an informed faith, a faith that not
only accepts truths beyond the grasp of unaided reason, but
also reasons beyond natural reason through the gifts of the
Holy Spirit. Bonaventure argues that this trajectory from faith
into the gifts of knowledge and understanding is necessary
for proper theological cognition.

The trajectory of knowing traced thus far does not conclude with the *cognitio veritatis* of the God of Revelation, which
characterizes theology proper. Rather, the gifts of knowledge
and understanding dispose the intellect to receive the greatest
gift of the Holy Spirit, the gift of wisdom, whereby the intellect moves into an experiential cognition (*cognitio experimentalis*)
of God, which "consists in tasting the divine sweetness."[28]
Bonaventure insists that knowledge must pass into love. The
act of wisdom begins in cognition and is completed in the
affectus. Wisdom is both an intellectual and affective act that
begins in knowledge (with concomitant love) and ends in love
(with concomitant knowledge). The two acts proceed from
the same habit with the first ordered to the second. LaNave
highlights St. Bonaventure's remarkable appeal to Aristotle
in order to demonstrate that the act of wisdom is indeed
cognitive because there is no delight without the perception of suitability. Bonaventure also appeals to Dionysius
for the principle of knowing God through the *via negativa*,
which for Bonaventure does not indicate not knowing, but
rather a particular kind of knowing.[29] The act of wisdom
is ecstatic knowing, whereby the soul is drawn out and is
captured by its object, a pattern already seen with the virtue
of faith. This sapiential knowledge characterized by love

does not do away with speculative knowledge but amplifies it. According to Elizabeth Dreyer, Bonaventure uses the term "knowledge" "only with careful qualifications," preferring to call it "sensation."[30] What is noteworthy about Bonaventure's understanding of wisdom is that this ecstatic knowing need not be something exceptional; instead, it is "the normal fulfillment of the ordinary infusion of grace."[31] The gift of wisdom marks the transition from the gifts to the Beatitudes. Bonaventure holds that theology depends upon grace both formally (because the reason suitable for theology is a reason elevated by faith and the gifts of science and understanding) and finally (because the habit that perfects the intellect as extended *ad affectum* is wisdom).[32]

The Beatitude of Purity of Heart

Thus far, the trajectory followed has focused on how theological thinking requires "spirituality" ("holiness" for Bonaventure) in order to function properly with the virtue of faith and the gifts of knowledge and understanding that lead to the gift of wisdom. Sanctifying grace, however, has not yet completed its work of bringing the image of God in man into a real likeness of Jesus Christ. The gifts of knowledge and understanding work to make the soul agile and free in its movement toward God and dispose the soul to enter into the perfection of the Beatitudes. The Beatitude most clearly related to knowing is purity of heart, which for Bonaventure comprises moving into a direct intuitive knowledge of the Divine Persons. LaNave shows that the affective knowledge attained is not in any way anti-intellectual for Bonaventure. However, knowing at the level of Beatitude moves from the intellectual activity of analysis and synthesis into nondiscursive, restful knowledge. Affective knowledge is the deiform knowledge of "seeing" God.[33]

In the Beatitude of purity of heart, the soul is disposed to delight in the fruits of the Holy Spirit and the "use" of the spiritual senses. In this highest stage of knowing, God makes Himself present to the human soul in such an immediate and intense way that He is "sensed." Out of these theological virtues and gifts of the Holy Spirit there develops a spiritual *sensorium* corresponding to the corporeal senses. The knowing that occurs in the spiritual senses follows the same pattern whereby the soul's natural cognitive faculties (memory, intellect, and will) supernaturally apprehend God in a way that is unique to those who are made in His image.[34] Bonaventure conceives of man's response to God revealing himself not simply as "an apprehension of God by the graced faculties of intellect and will, but a fully human act of apprehension according to the logic of sensation."[35]

Jesus Christ is the object of the spiritual senses as the uncreated, inspired, and incarnate-crucified Word. The uncreated Word, splendor, and self-expression of the Father is the object of spiritual sight and hearing; the inspired Word is the object of spiritual smell; and the incarnate-crucified Word, as one would suspect, is the object of taste and touch. The virtue of faith believes. The gift of understanding understands what is believed. Subsequently, the Beatitude of purity of heart attains the vision of what is understood in an act of spiritual sight and hearing where the human soul gazes in radiant light upon the resplendent, most beautiful Spouse, hearing and aroused by His harmonious, resonant, sweet voice and His eloquent and instructive words of wisdom.[36] The soul delights in this seeing and hearing and is brought to a judgment about that perception in an experiential cognition. The whole trajectory leads to love and "being impressed with the touch of the crucified Word."[37]

Fathoming Jesus with the spiritual senses reveals that the human soul is participating in the divine light in a supernatural way, leading to experiencing a likeness to God, where "such knowledge is felt (*sentitur*) more than it is known (*cognoscitur*)."[38] The unity of the spiritual senses reveals the inseparable activity of the theological virtues at the beginning of the trajectory, as well as the spiritual–corporeal unity of man. As LaNave observes, the insight and originality of the Seraphic Doctor shines here. The soul's conformity to Christ involves an ultimate passing into (*transitus*) the love of Christ. However, given its corporality of St. Francis's stigmatization, this passing into is no longer construed in terms of Neoplatonic intellectual illumination, nor simply as a type of apophatic rapture. This progression is "wisdom," whereby the soul—because it has recovered the spiritual senses—can now "see" and "hear" God.[39] Moreover, Bonaventure's doctrine makes it evident that using the spiritual senses is not something gnostic or exclusive to just a few. It is, rather, the normal fruit of the Christian soul given over to the power of sanctifying grace.

It should be clarified that the ecstatic knowledge of transforming into Christ lies beyond the science of theology proper; yet, the Seraphic Doctor insists that academic theology is disposed toward it. Although theology proper has more to do with faith and the gifts, Bonaventure holds that the spiritual senses are nevertheless necessary for theology's proper functioning. LaNave finds support for this position in Bonaventure's theological argument, *ex pietate*, and his idea that theology is an affective knowledge.[40] The argument *ex pietate* comes into play when the theologian must adjudicate between several possible explanations for a truth of faith. The criterion for deciding which argument is strongest is the one that is most *ex pietate*, that is, the one that comes from "'thinking of God most piously'—thinking of him in a way that accords with one's highest knowledge of him."[41] Secondly, the science of theology is governed by an "affective cognition" resulting from a transformed reason. Theology is not merely rational knowledge of what is believed; it is essentially an affective knowledge flowing from an affective relationship with the object, which directs that knowledge beginning in faith, passing through the gifts, and arriving at Beatitude. We find in Bonaventure that theological reasoning requires a real and ongoing transformation of the theologian's reason, one that is continually rectified, illuminated, and united to God by sanctifying grace.

Five Implications

The first implication to be drawn from the preceding discussion is that St. Bonaventure would agree that spirituality (understood as holiness) impresses the right method upon theological studies. LaNave encapsulates Bonaventure's doctrine in the following way: "Theology is a true science; in order for it to be true to itself it must become a kind of wisdom; and the means by which it achieves its proper end is holiness."[42] Specifically, this impressing-upon involves the transformation of one's reason, beginning with extending the intellect by and toward the *affectus* in faith.

In his message in praise of Balthasar, Pope Benedict XVI added, "Theology, as [Balthasar] conceived it, had to be married to spirituality; only in this way, in fact, can it be profound and effective.[43] Here, I would suggest that the Seraphic Doctor goes further. The term "marriage" indicates two distinct realities that are subsequently conjoined. "Spirituality," understood as the trajectory from the theological virtues to the spiritual senses, is not a reality conjoined to theology; it comprises, and even encompasses, the very fabric of theological knowing. Without the theological virtues, the theologian cannot be properly oriented toward the object; without the gifts of the Holy Spirit, the theologian is unable to come to the specific knowing of theology; without understanding that theology must become a kind of wisdom that involves the transformation of one's reason, the theologian has altogether failed to understand the object of this science. Theology involves intense and rigorous intellectual activity, yet this activity happens within the ambit of grace, demanding that it transform one's reason. Not only would theology be unable to function properly without grace, it simply would not exist without it. Moreover, grace is not simply for the beginning of theology (that is, for the discovery of revealed realities unknowable to unaided human reason), but the way of proceeding in theology also falls under the influence of grace. Bonaventure's teaching, thus, unmasks the false dichotomy that considers intellectual rigor "real and objective," while spiritual affections are "soft and subjective."[44] Spirituality is shown to be interior to the rigorous, scientific thinking inherent in theology. Holiness is not extraneous to theology; it is inherent to its structure.

A corollary to this implication concerns the sapiential nature of theology. In *Fides et ratio*, Saint John Paul II wrote that philosophy needed to recover its sapiential character in order to overcome its current crisis of meaning, and that faith could help achieve such a recovery.[45] Perhaps Bonaventure would add, observing the present day, that theology must first rediscover its own sapiential identity before it can be in a position to assist philosophy. Only if our theological method leads to sapiential knowledge will it once again be in a position to help philosophy become a path to wisdom. Bonaventure's approach is very helpful in this regard.

A second implication of the Seraphic Doctor's teaching is that the theologian cannot properly engage the science of theology without his own reason undergoing a transformation by grace that begins with an informed faith. In other words, Bonaventure thinks it is impossible to be impartially engaged in theology. The subject matter of theology is not simply a collection of data for the intellect to consider, however rigorously. The subject matter is the living God of Revelation, the Blessed Trinity revealed in the Incarnate Son, Jesus Christ. Theology does not consider primarily an inert "what," but a living "Who." Bonaventure presupposes a theologian with a living faith, which by its very nature, rules out an uninvolved approach to the subject matter. The Seraphic Doctor views theology as demanding a form of life that attunes the theologian to the living and personal mystery under investigation. In a way, Bonaventure maintains that this mystery is so deep that the human soul cannot intellectually grasp it without actually entering into it. It is by personally entering into the mystery and being grasped by it that the intellect can truly discern its intelligibility. Although this position, strictly considered, bespeaks mystical theology, it can also be applied to theology proper in that it is ordered toward the mystical.

Bonaventure, therefore, would have us reject as inadequate any method involving curiosity or skepticism, any method that would permit a kind of "armchair theology." The intellectual stance of curiosity is anathema to Bonaventure. One's approach to theology must be consonant with the subject matter, and so the motive for theological investigation is crucial. Bonaventure contrasts the desire simply to know (*curiositas*) with the desire to know through an upright life (*studiositas*) that leads to conformity (*conformitas*) to Christ. The ultimate purpose of theology for Bonaventure is ultimately and always *ut boni fiamus*. Hence, Bonaventure's famous maxim, "If you wish to be true scholars, you must have piety."[46] The theologian, in imitation of Saint Francis, is seeking to be conformed to the reality he studies.[47] The God of Revelation is perceived and understood by way of conformity, not curiosity. The best way to think insightfully and well about the whole Christ is to become like Christ. The articles of faith, which as propositions can be captured by the human intellect, express the reality of Jesus Christ who actually captures the human intellect. The theologian, to be faithful to his science, must place himself in a constant state of personal abandonment to the mystery of Jesus Christ. Only this stance will create the possibility for adequate theological reflection. In other words, theology is about putting on the mind of Christ, inviting Him to think in me, that He may be expressed in me.[48] To use a more contemporary term, Bonaventure indicates the necessity for the theologian to be personally attuned to the presence of Jesus. One cannot encounter the living God and remain unchanged.

This raises several questions: Does the way theology is taught convey the theologian's personal engagement with

Christ and give evidence of that transformation through him? Are the theological virtues, the affective certitude of faith, the gifts of the Holy Spirit, and affection for Jesus Christ, the Father, and the Holy Spirit fostered in the classroom? Are they encouraged and intentionally cultivated as essential to theological method and proper intellectual formation? Are students invited to take what is taught in the lectures into their own meditative prayer and, likewise, bring the considerations of their meditative prayer back into the classroom? Does the way in which theology is taught create an environment that leads both theologians and students into the *cognitio experimentalis* of wisdom?

A third implication for Bonaventure is that vigor of mind must be preceded by, matched, and even surpassed by, conversion of heart. His doctrine highlights the fact that the human intellect and will are, in their present states, *fallen*, and that concupiscence not only affects our moral life, but our intellectual life as well. Mere curiosity is a kind of concupiscence of the mind; therefore, fallen human reason needs to be rectified and elevated by the theological virtues. Are theologians and seminary formators paying sufficient attention to this aspect? The virtue of faith rectifies the theologian's cognitive function in order to orient it toward its proper object, making it capable of penetrating the spiritual meaning of Holy Scripture. It must, then, be purified and illuminated by the gifts and united to the Blessed Trinity in the beatitudes in order to know God as He desires to be known by us. Because of the rigor necessary for theology, a talented but fallen reason very easily forgets its need to be captured, and perhaps even wrestled (Gn 32:24-26), into submission and obedience to Christ. Theologians and theological faculties can

be infected by presumption or, perhaps, by a subtle kind of
Pelagianism of the intellectual life, approaching the mystery
of the living God of Revelation without recognizing the
necessity for grace and without sufficient concern for personal and ongoing conversion.[49]

This implication may also provide the necessary link
between the lofty ideal that Bonaventure places before the
theologian and the theologian's own sense of sinfulness. An
honest theologian considering St. Bonaventure's doctrine
may look down upon his unstigmatized hands and into his
far-from-perfected heart and conclude, "I've never been
a theologian." To what degree does one have to pass into
Christ in order to be a theologian? I think the Seraphic Doctor—as a saint, as a priest, and as the Minister General of his
Order who well understood the vicissitudes of the sinner's
heart—would remind the person who would do theology that
one does theology not because one is holy, but so that one
may become holy, presuming that the requisite theological
virtues and *studiositas* are being cultivated. He would invite the
theologian to courageously and confidently set out upon the
path of holiness and engage theology with a living faith and
the habit of *studiositas* with the intention that he may become
conformed to Christ. With an abundance of grace and
human effort, theological wisdom will follow.

This leads to a fourth implication pertaining to the virtue
of faith. Bonaventure insists that theologians and students
of theology must possess an informed faith—that is, a living faith, a faith whose form is charity. Thinking with an
informed faith means allowing one's intellect to be extended
by and toward the *affectus*. Having an informed faith means
thinking with love, which results in the affective certitude of

the things of faith. Love is essential and intrinsic to what is taking place when faith encounters human reason. Only in this way does theological reflection adequately respond to the object of thought. Love is the genesis and culmination of Bonaventure's entire theological project. A formless faith is incapable of arriving at a properly theological cognition. A reason bereft of love is not simply deficient for theology; it is ultimately something demonic. Loveless reason lies at the origin of all evil, precipitating Lucifer's fall as well as man's, and as such, should be avoided at all costs, especially in theology. Bonaventure's teaching exposes and challenges our deep opposition to God, which would cling to an isolated, autonomous reason, erroneously concluding that conceding the necessity for grace would be "unscientific." Perhaps such resistance is due to an unconscious prejudice from believing Satan's lie that grace will harm or destroy our nature, or that God is "intruding" on what is ours. Bonaventure insists on the opposite: far from intruding upon, competing with, or destroying human reason, the Lord actually wishes to elevate it and make it like His. Grace renders human reason Godlike.

In addition to their having a living faith, Bonaventure also insists that candidates for the priesthood must already have a good command of the articles of faith (symbolic theology) in order to enter into theology proper.[50] Today, such competency cannot be presumed. It is, thus, necessary that formators resist the pressure to take shortcuts in catechetical formation, and instead insist upon an adequate catechetical preparation before allowing a seminarian to embark upon the study of theology. As we saw previously, the Seraphic Doctor links theology proper to the clerical state. This connection is important when considering the theological formation of priests. Theology proper is the kind of theological knowing most proportionate to our human powers of comprehension because it intellectually and critically considers the intelligibility of revealed and salvific realities in order that one may return to God and become like him. Thus, Bonaventure indicates that the clergy's mission on behalf of the Church is to show the intelligibility of the faith, thereby confirming believers in the faith. His position indicates the present-day need to overcome the anti-intellectual bias that has infected some seminary formation in recent decades, as well as the poor attitude and undisciplined approach toward studies among some seminarians. Perhaps in Bonaventure's time, the danger was *curiositas*. Today's danger may more likely be one where—with an environment where many candidates for priesthood suffer from a language barrier in the classroom—seminary faculties begin to succumb to the path of least resistance by dumbing-down the material or the rigor with which it should be treated. The priest must be able to speak intelligently about the faith and to demonstrate the intelligibility of the faith to others as part of the sacerdotal mission in the Church.

Finally, from the above implications, we can draw a fifth: the practice of theology is as much an issue of human and spiritual formation as it is an intellectual one. The Seraphic Doctor's system reveals and confirms the inseparability of intellectual formation from the other areas of formation.[51] In fact, the cultivation of an informed faith is *primarily* the work of human and spiritual formation. For example, when reflecting upon the gift of wisdom, Bonaventure himself writes that the first pillar of the "house" that wisdom builds is comprised of humility and chastity.[52] St. Bonaventure's doctrine reminds bishops, vocation directors, and seminary formators about the importance of evaluating whether a candidate has the requisite human and spiritual formation (the desire for God, the discipline necessary for receiving the theological virtues, and habit of prayer) to embark upon the study of theology.[53] It is worth noting the explicit reference that St. John Paul II makes to St. Bonaventure in *Pastores Dabo Vobis* when writing about the intellectual formation of priests: "Intellectual formation in theology and formation in the spiritual life, in particular the life of prayer, meet and strengthen each other, without detracting in any way from the soundness of research or from the spiritual tenor of prayer."[54] St. Bonaventure reminds us: "Let no one believe that it suffices for him to read if he lacks unction, speculate without devotion, investigate without admiration, look around without exaltation, be diligent without piety, know without charity, understand without humility, exert himself without divine grace, or see without divinely inspired wisdom."[55]

The inseparability of intellectual and human formation is, perhaps, most clearly exemplified by the trajectory of faith into the Beatitude of purity of heart. As shown above, academic theology is disposed toward that Beatitude. St. Bonaventure's doctrine highlights the essential connection between the cultivation of purity of heart through the virtue of chastity and the study of theology. How can theology be done adequately without also cultivating purity of heart among theologians and students of theology? This is an important question, although it extends beyond the limits of the present discussion. It does indicate that the seminary, perhaps more than the university, is the institutional setting where a renewal of theology can take place in the present time. One way human formation can assist intellectual formation is the strong role it plays in cultivating purity of heart. It seems clear that Bonaventure would be critical of any situation where the academic faculty oper-ates independently from the human, spiritual, and pastoral faculties because the latter three must fit around the first. He would instead insist upon close collaboration, even a mutual circumincession of the four areas of formation (human, spiritual, intellectual, and pastoral), following the pattern set by the theological virtues, the gifts of the Holy Spirit, and the Beatitudes.

NOTES

1.   "Spirituality does not attenuate the scientific charge, but impresses upon theological study the right method for achieving a coherent interpretation" (Pope Benedict XVI, "Message for the Centenary of the Birth of Fr. Hans Urs von Balthasar." *Libreria Editrice Vaticana*, October 6, 2005, http://www.vatican.va/holy_father/benedict_xvi/messages/pont-messages/2005/documents/hf_ben-xvi_mes_20051006_von-balthasar_en.html).

2.   All references to Bonaventure's writing are taken from the Quaracchi critical edition: Bonaventure, *Opera omnia*, 11 vols. Florence, Quaracchi 1882-1902.

3.   See Gregory LaNave, *Through Holiness to Wisdom: The Nature of Theology According to St. Bonaventure* (Rome: Istituto Storico dei Cappuccini, 2005), and Gregory LaNave, "Bonaventure," in *The Spiritual Senses: Perceiving God in Western Christianity*, eds. Paul L. Gavrilyak and Sarah Coakley (Cambridge: Cambridge University, 2011), 159–173. His emphasis on the importance of asking Thomistic questions of Bonaventure and Bonaventurean questions of Thomas seems a most promising and fruitful contribution for understanding both masters. I am grateful to Jared Goff for his helpful suggestions for interpreting Saint Bonaventure.

4.   LaNave elaborates on the distinctions between the *principium radicale*, the *totum integrale*, and the *totum universale* of the particular science of theology in Saint Bonaventure in his book, *Through Holiness to Wisdom*, 35–43.

5.   This is, in fact, the thesis that LaNave successfully demonstrates in his book, *Through Holiness to Wisdom*.

6.   See Ibid., 72.

7.   See, for example: Saint Bonaventure, *De triplici via.*

8.   See Saint Bonaventure, *De donis*, 4.17, and Saint Bonaventure, *Ad magistrumin nominatum.*

9.   What follows is a summary of III *Sent.* d. 23, a. 1, q. 1–2.

10.   III *Sent.*, d. 23, a. 1, q. 2: *"fides habitus est, per quem intellectus captivatur in obsequium Christi et innititur primae Veritatis propter se"*; see also d. 23, q. 1, a. 1; d. 23, a. 2, q. 1–2. The scriptural verse in the Vulgate reads: *"In captivitatem re digente somnem intellectum in obsequium Christi"*; in the Douay-Rheims: "bringing into captivity every understanding unto the obedience of Christ."

11.   In fact, Saint Bonaventure indicates such a struggle in *De donis*, 8.5. One cannot receive the gift of understanding unless one's intellect is first captured unto obedience to Christ. He writes that disordered concupiscent and irascible appetites impede the gift of understanding, but a

disordered rational appetite impedes this gift above all. The intellect must be "captured" if it is to take up this gift.

12.   See III *Sent.*, d. 23, a. 1, q. 2.
13.   See LaNave, *Through Holiness to Wisdom*, 51.
14.   See III *Sent.*, d. 23, a. 1, q. 5.
15.   See Ibid., d. 23, a. 1, q. 4.
16.   See Ibid., d. 23, a. 1, q. 1.
17.   See Ibid., d. 23, a. 2, q. 1.
18.   See Ibid., d. 23, a. 2, q. 3.
19.   See Ibid., d. 23, a. 2, q. 4–5.
20.   See Ibid., d. 23, a. 2, q. 3.
21.   See *De donis*, 8.15.
22.   LaNave, *Through Holiness to Wisdom*, 52.
23.   Ibid., 53. On page 194 of the same text, LaNave summarizes Bonaventure's idea that transformed reason is determined by two factors: "its illumination by the light of grace and its orientation to an object (the *totum integrale*) that expresses its supernatural principle (the *principium radicale*) in a way that can be perceived by the rational mind and thus become a first principle for its deductive reasoning."
24.   See Ibid., 162.
25.   See III *Sent.*, d. 35, a. un., q. 2–3; LaNave, *Through Holiness to Wisdom*, 53.
26.   LaNave, *Through Holiness to Wisdom*, 54.
27.   Ibid., 56.
28.   Ibid., 167. See also *De donis* 9.5–8, where Bonaventure describes the activity of the gift of wisdom as illuminating the cognitive power, gladdening the affective power, and invigorating the operative power, by which the human soul is built into a house of God with seven columns (see Mk 7:24, Prov 9:1).
29.   See Saint Bonaventure, *De scientia Christi*, q. 7; Saint Bonaventure, *Itinerarium*, c. 7.
30.   Elizabeth Dreyer, "'*Affectus*' in St. Bonaventure's Theology," *Franciscan Studies* 42 (1982), 14.
31.   LaNave, *Through Holiness to Wisdom*, 169.
32.   Ibid., 80.
33.   See Ibid., 82.
34.   What is significant here is the exemplarity present in Bonaventure's theology and, as we find in the *Itinerarium*, it does not mean knowing God as knowing a cause from its effect, but to "apprehend an object as an expressive likeness of God" (LaNave, "Bonaventure," 168).
35.   LaNave, *Through Holiness to Wisdom*, 108.
36.   See Fabio Tedoldi, *La dottrina dei cinque sensi spirituali in San Bonaventura* (Roma: Pontificium Athenaeum Antonianum, 1999), 182.
37.   LaNave, "Bonaventure," 169.

38. Ibid.

39. See LaNave, *Through Holiness to Wisdom*, 92.

40. LaNave, "Bonaventure," 172.

41. Ibid.

42. Ibid., 79.

43. Pope Benedict XVI, "Message for the Centenary of the Birth of Fr. Hans Urs von Balthasar."

44. See James Keating, "Teaching Seminary Theology," *Fellowship of Catholic Scholars Quarterly* (Spring 2011), 50.

45. See Saint John Paul II, *Fides et Ratio* (1998), sec. 81.

46. *De donis*, 3.17: "*Si vulti sesse veri scholares, opportet, voshabere, pietatem*" (see 1 Tim 6:3–4). Bonaventure's use of *pietas* should be understood in the Latin sense of "dutifulness" or "steadfast fidelity," which is evocative of the disciplined life required by *studiositas*, as well as in the Christian sense of a gift of the Holy Spirit, and not in the sometimes overly saccharine and emotive nuance of "piety" in English.

47. This theme also runs through the thought of Balthasar and Pope Benedict XVI. In his message praising Hans Urs von Balthasar, Pope Benedict XVI references "the profound existential interpretation" that characterizes Balthasar's theology. Tracey Rowland summarizes Joseph Ratzinger's position on this point: "The way of knowledge that leads to God and to Christ is a way of living. In order to know Christ it is necessary to follow him" (Tracey Rowland, *Ratzinger's Faith: The Theology of Pope Benedict XVI* (Oxford: Oxford University, 2008), 58).

48. Bonaventure's teaching also affirms the importance of externally expressing the unity of faith manifested, for example, in the theologian's public profession of faith and the reception of the *mandatum* from the competent ecclesiastical authority. Moreover, such consideration cannot overlook questions of institutional identity and governance. What is taught and how theology is taught are largely dependent upon the hiring and development of the faculty.

49. Here also, perhaps, is another connection between Saint Bonaventure and Pope Benedict XVI's praise of Balthasar: "One of the central topics on which he would voluntarily linger was that of showing the need for conversion. For him, the change of heart was a key point. Only in this way, in fact, is the mind freed of the limits that prevent its access to the mystery, and the eyes become capable of focusing on the face of Christ," (Pope Benedict XVI, "Message for the Centenary of the Birth of Fr. Hans Urs von Balthasar", October 6, 2005).

50. See United States Conference of Catholic Bishops, *Program of Priestly Formation*, 5th ed. (Washington DC: USCCB, 2006), secs. 137, 142, 203.

51. See Blessed John Paul II, *Pastores Dabo Vobis* (1992), sec. 51. I find the opening phrase particularly suggestive of Saint Bonaventure's view:

"Intellectual formation . . . is also deeply connected with, and indeed can be seen as a necessary expression of, both human and spiritual formation: It is a fundamental demand of the human intelligence by which one 'participates in the light of God's mind' and seeks to acquire a wisdom which in turn opens to and is directed toward knowing and adhering to God."

52. *De donis*, 9.10.

53. See *Pastores Dabo Vobis*, sec. 62.

54. Ibid., sec. 53.

55. *Itinerarium*, Prol., 4. The translation of the quote from Bonaventure is my own. Unfortunately, the official English translation available at *Libreria Editrice Vaticana* (www.vatican.va) for *Pastores Dabo Vobis*, sec. 53 seems to be missing part of Bonaventure's text. The *editio tipico* contains the entire phrase: "*Ne quis forte credat quod sibi sufficiat lectio sine unctione, speculatio sine devotione, investigatio sine admiratione, circumspectio sine exsultatione, industria sine pietate, scientia sine caritate, intellegentia sine humilitate, stadium absque divine gratia, speculum absque sapientia divinitus inspirata.*" The very same passage is quoted again in *Fides et Ratio*, sec. 105 this time with the entire phrase in English, but translated differently.

DOUBT AND THE TASK OF THEOLOGY IN THE NEW EVANGELIZATION

CHRISTOPHER COLLINS, SJ

At the beginning of *Introduction to Christianity*, Joseph Ratzinger makes a rather surprising proclamation of hope. Written in 1968 at the height of the "God is dead" movement, *Introduction to Christianity* asserts the great importance of the role of doubt in the context of a living faith in the modern world. Highlighting a scene from Paul Claudel's play *Le Soulier de Satin*, Ratzinger recalls a Jesuit missionary in South America, a shipwreck survivor now barely hanging on to life. "He himself has been lashed to a mast from the sunken ship, and he is now drifting on this piece of wood through the raging waters of the ocean."[1] Ratzinger uses this image as a foundational icon to establish the position of the believer in the contemporary world.

On the chaotic waves of the sea, Claudel's missionary proceeds with a prayer, "Lord I thank thee for bending me down like this. It sometimes happens that I found thy commands laborious and my will at a loss and jibbing at thy dispensation. But now I could not be bound to thee more closely than I am, and however violently my limbs move they

cannot get one inch away from thee. So I really am fastened
to the cross, but the cross on which I hang is not fastened
to anything else. It drifts on the sea."[2] And so, the place of
doubt becomes precisely the place from which faith must take
its starting point. As faith springs from this place of doubt,
so must theology, which remains today the practice of *fides
quaerens intellectum*. In doing theology, it is fruitful to let ourselves be found in that place of instability and uncertainty in
the world. Only then can the real dialogue between God and
humanity flourish and be true to itself.

In *Introduction to Christianity*, Ratzinger seeks to uncover
the ancient creedal structure of the faith. Destabilized by
doubt, this contemporary context is the locus of the one
who professes the words, "I believe. . . ." In Claudel's setting,
the profession of faith is made by the one who clings to that
piece of wood being tossed back and forth on the waters of
chaos; but this place of instability is precisely the place of
hope. This place of confrontation with reality seems to be
defeating the self; but it, in fact, opens up the possibility for
union of the self with God. In his second encyclical on hope,
Pope Benedict XVI notes: "It is not by sidestepping or fleeing
from suffering that we are healed, but rather by our capacity
for accepting it, maturing through it and finding meaning
through union with Christ, who suffered with infinite love."[3]
The place of suffering and insecurity that seems to undermine confidence gives way to the place of speaking in hope
and in love. It is in the speaking that the place of insecurity
becomes the place where one finds true security—in dialogue,
in relationship with the Lord who has already spoken to
humanity and who is also fastened to a piece of wood amid a
sea of chaos and instability.

Doubt as Common Ground

Doubt, Ratzinger explains, is the experience that "Wherever one looks, only the bottomless abyss of nothingness can be seen."[4] It is essential for Ratzinger—and for the task of theology—not to fear, but to embrace this reality in order to explore the depths of a believer's faith. Likewise, one should take seriously the concerns of nonbelievers so that intellectual and pastoral approaches to them are effective and fruitful. Thus, an essential aspect of the Church's mission in an age of doubt is to sow a seed of doubt, as it were, precisely in the field of doubt.

Ratzinger was apparently fond of recalling a story told by Martin Buber about an encounter between a rabbi and an atheist. After entertaining all of the atheist's arguments and doubts against the prospect of religious faith, the rabbi simply turned modestly to his interlocutor and asked, "But perhaps it is true after all."[5] In this sense, for Ratzinger, doubt "saves both sides from being shut up in their own worlds . . . becom[ing] the avenue of communication."[6] Communication, then, even from the setting of doubt, is necessary for the victory of life.

To put the *certainty* of the dogmatic atheist, for example, at an imbalance could well be enough for the task of evangelization. Indeed, the most chilling reality that causes doubt in the heart of the human person is death. In the Church's liturgy, it is telling that we speak of the "certainty" of death in contrast to the mystery and openness of the possibility of eternal life. For example, in the first preface offered in the *Roman Missal* for the Mass for the Dead, "The Hope of Resurrection in Christ," the celebrant prays on behalf of the

Church who is, in this moment, mourning, "In him the hope of resurrection has dawned, that those saddened by the certainty of dying might be consoled by the promise of immortality to come." The absolute reality of death and especially its *certainty* has the capacity to leave one without hope of a future beyond this life; therefore, speaking in the face of this apparent certainty is essential for the task of theology.

Silence and Communication in Death

The question posed by the certainty of death requires a word of response. Allowing this word of response is the basis for the spiritual foundation that becomes necessary for the work of theology. The question of spirituality also becomes necessary in the face of death. In a 2011 Angelus address, Pope Benedict XVI explored the mystery of death and the relationship that the person cries out for from within that reality. He explained, "Indeed, death represents a wall as it were, which prevents us from seeing beyond it; yet our hearts reach out beyond this wall and even though we cannot understand what it conceals, we nevertheless think about it and imagine it."[7] The desire of the human heart to "see beyond the wall"—indeed, the fear of not knowing if there is anything at all beyond that wall—is certainly central to the human condition. Pointing to this essential dilemma, Pope Benedict XVI does not shy away from reminding the audience that this wall cannot be scaled from our side. In the same address, he says it is Christ Himself who "destroys the wall of death" so that the communion of God and humanity can come to fruition. Only by the Word, spoken from God in Christ, specifically from the Cross, can we overcome our own isolation in the fear of death. Ratzinger notes in his earlier book about spiritual Christology, *Behold the Pierced One,* that "Death, which by its very nature is the end, the destruction of every communication, is changed by him into an act of self-communication . . . death, which puts an end to words and meaning, itself becomes a word, becomes the place where meaning communicates itself."[8]

The Cross: Word Spoken in Doubt

The Cross takes on the central place in the Christian imagination, becoming the central word from God to humanity and from humanity back to God. This is the place of dialogue. It is the place that stands between life and death; the place that stands in isolation from the support of human love and community; the place where every person must stand alone and rely only upon the power and love of God that is spoken from the Cross. False securities cannot take the place of this Word, which is ultimately love itself, in the face of darkness and alienation. Theology that does not proceed from this place of insecurity, within the dialogue between God and humanity, is fruitless.

A Way Forward for Theology

Ratzinger has frequently diagnosed the problem of the sterility of the theology that is too often produced in the modern era. His critique is not simply a function of the post-conciliar battles that many point out between so-called conservatives and liberals. He identified a problem dating back to his own seminary formation wherein much of the neo-scholastic theology he was being offered, while not erring in any essential way, still left the reader a bit cold with its "crystal-clear logic . . . too closed in on itself, too impersonal and ready-made."[9] He instead sought a recovery of theology that could be spoken in the language "not of scholars but of shepherds."[10] The prerequisite for a theology that is able to speak not only to the minds but also to the hearts, to the center of the human person in today's culture of disbelief, is precisely theology that has the dialogue between the human and divine as its foundation. This dialogue is not, of course, one between equals. It is an *asymmetrical* dialogue wherein God speaks first and humanity is primarily understood as "hearers of the word," as Rahner put it.[11] This dialogical structure is what sets the Christian vision apart for Pope Benedict XVI. He notes, "The novelty of biblical revelation consists in the fact that God becomes known through the dialogue which he desires to have with us."[12] This dialogue can only take place from a posture of spiritual openness and yet also must be embedded in history, taking seriously the concrete concerns of every human culture in each historical epoch.

History and Trinity

In his Apostolic Exhortation on the Word of God, *Verbum Domini*, Pope Benedict XVI notes that, in the intervening years since the Second Vatican Council (which, of course, placed new emphasis on this novelty of biblical revelation in history), we have witnessed a growing awareness of the "trinitarian and salvation-historical horizon of revelation"[13] against which Jesus Christ is to be acknowledged as "mediator and the sum total of revelation."[14] By way of encounter and dialogue with the person of Christ, humanity can be drawn up into the Trinitarian "conversation" at the heart of triune communion. For this reason, Saint John Paul II refers to authentic spirituality as "holy, familiar and attentive union with God the

Father through his Son Jesus Christ in the Holy Spirit."[15] The privileged point of entry into this communion is the place of contemplation of the Word of God, especially in the context of the liturgy. As *Dei Verbum* puts it, one way of thinking about the will of the Father is to consider the nature of His self-communication in Revelation, particularly in Scripture, for "in the sacred books, the Father who is in heaven comes lovingly to meet his children and talks with them."[16] A path toward the renewal of contemporary theology can be opened up by posing the question: "Is it possible for the practice of theology to enter into the same dynamic that is at the heart of Scripture?" The practice of theology would do well to let its starting point be the *fact* that the Father has already spoken in human words to those whom He wishes to adopt as His children. The deep critical analysis that follows, then, is the attempt to make sense of the Father's words and how they continue both to reveal and conceal in every new age and culture.

Performative Theology

Khaled Anatolios offers a model for this mode of doing theology in his book *Retrieving Nicaea: The Development and Meaning of Trinitarian Doctrine.*[17] He argues that the theological method used by many of the early Church Fathers reveals a process of theological inquiry, allowing doubts and challenges to be posed. From that context of uncertainty, reference is made to the whole of Scripture as normative, even if it is not clear just exactly what in Scripture is speaking to the place of doubt in the human subject. What emerges in the theologian, though, is a "performance" of the ecclesial and Trinitarian dynamics of the mysteries under consideration. Anatolios makes the case that, because the reality of God—precisely as triune communion—is the foundational framework for all of reality, we live within the triune reality now and at all times. This reality was only gradually uncovered and realized in the life of the Church well after the Death and Resurrection of Christ. This reality needs to be perpetually uncovered and realized. The way forward for theology today is to reinsert ourselves, ever anew, into this dynamic, this conversation, this dialogue that has been unfolding over the centuries. The challenge, as worded by Brian Daley in the Foreword to Anatolios's book, is to "come face to face with the origins of Trinitarian doctrine as a theological conversation on which our salvation, in one way or another, ultimately depends."[18] Entering into this conversation is not an exercise of abstraction in the realm of "the experts." Recalling the starting point for theological reflection in Gregory of Nazianzus's method, Daley reminds us, "The subject is nothing less than God."[19]

Doing theology well is not simply a matter of repeating the doctrines formulated throughout the course of the Church's history and handed down as authentic tradition. Further, it is not the deconstruction of those doctrines according to the analysis that comes with historical consciousness, standing at an "objective distance" from them. When this mistake is made, the reality spoken in the doctrines is vacated and the doctrines themselves are relegated to products of historically limited settings or imaginations, thereby becoming mere artifacts of the past. For theology to be done well, Anatolios argues, we must reject the split between historical and systematic theology. By this, he means to propose that the theologian "creatively re-perform the acts of understanding and interpretation that led to" the doctrinal statements that precede us.[20] These doctrines were originally formulated by allowing the experience of salvation in the present to come into contact with the understanding of God from the past in Scripture and tradition, and articulated in the context of worship. Doing theology within the "limits" of these boundaries, always springing from the context of contemporary doubts and uncertainties, guides a way for theology to continue to be a fount of renewal for the life of the faithful.

New Evangelization and Historical Consciousness

The human subject is engaged with the Divine Subject who spoke first. Yet, the process of theological reflection begins in earnest only when the question or doubt is spoken from the side of humanity. Perhaps this emphasis on the subjects—both human and divine—is confirmed in the teaching of Vatican II that was extended by St. John Paul II, Pope Benedict XVI, and certainly, manifested "more in deeds than in words," by Pope Francis. This post-conciliar direction for theology can be seen as the ever-deepening response to the crisis of modernity in its shift of attention from a cosmological worldview to one that places the experience of the human subject at the starting point. When we consider what ought to be the contours of the "new evangelization," this "turn to the subject" and the new philosophical personalism highlighted by Saint John Paul II (and what might be called the theological personalism of Pope Benedict XVI) surely present themselves as essential aspects of the Church's manner for proceeding in the missionary field. This perspective should also hold true in the classrooms of Catholic universities and seminaries.

By highlighting theological reflection's personalist aspect, we can embrace in a special way what had caused such angst early in the last century where Scripture study was concerned. Earlier generations of historical-critical exegetes' insistence upon "historical consciousness" often relativized, and ultimately dismissed, the scriptural witness in a destructive process of historicization. Thanks in part to the contributions of Pope Benedict XVI, a way has been opened up to theologically and spiritually integrate this historical consciousness. In his mind, the Council Fathers provided an impetus for theological reflection that was not limited to the definitional, propositional theology of neo-scholasticism, but rather drew mainly upon the "salvation-historical" framework for doing theology.[21]

For Pope Benedict XVI, letting the salvation-historical basis of Christian theology set the limits for theology includes, in today's context, entertaining the doubts of the day. In his theological expositions, Pope Benedict XVI repeatedly offers a robust articulation of the reasons *against faith* and appropriation of the truth contained in Scripture, as well as in dogma. By confronting the reader in this way, he immediately establishes a dramatic tension that makes the reader *vulnerable*, now looking for a way forward even though disbelief and doubt seem to be the only realistic options. A question is posed and a response is required. In Pope Benedict XVI's method, the ultimate response to these places of doubt is found in the Word of God itself. Deeper engagement with this Word offers the possibility of appropriation of divine revelation that meets the challenges of the day and transforms them. The dialogue, thus, begins. This dialogue is, in essence, the practice of "spirituality" and as such, it is the "proper method for theology."[22]

The Divine Subject

Asserting a spirituality that is dialogical in nature as the basis of theology indicates that, while theology ends up being "talk about God," the talk does not begin in the human person. Rowan Williams highlighted this point in his intervention at the recent synod on the new evangelization when he said that "all speaking about God presupposes God's own speaking."[23] Central to allowing a fruitful and generative theology to emerge would be to let God be the subject of theology.

Williams and Benedict agree on the point of needing to place God as the *subject* of theology. What they mean by this could be described in two ways. First, *God* must be the subject; that is, God must be the theologian's primary consideration, and not simply what people have thought about God over time. Second, in order for this to occur, God must be allowed to *speak*, to have the first Word. This is essential for understanding the grammatical framework of this endeavor of doing theology. God is the subject of the "sentence." We might say that the primary verb He uses pertains to speaking, and the object of God's speech is the Church, those who are made to hear. To be caught up in this Divine Speech is the basis for all evangelization and nourishment of the faith in the sacraments. Perhaps, in a special way, this dialogical model is especially fruitful for the *new* evangelization.

Doubt and Space for Dialogue

In a culture filled with noise, endless bits of information, and assertions of an often aggressive nature that advance preconceived notions of truth according to hardened ideologies, the Church can provide a place of refreshment, leading people saturated with information and trenchant ideological battles into a space of quiet and receptive listening to the Word of God. This is not a passive stance; it is a receptive one. Indeed, the person in the pew, the seminarian in the classroom, and the various audiences that make up the "market" of the new media are all confronted with significant challenges to faith, to the intelligibility of this life, to the possibility of love and meaning. Real doubts exist in every human heart. For many, these doubts have multiplied and been heaped upon one another at this moment in history like never before. These doubts and challenges must be brought into a place of quiet and listening. Those of us with these doubts must be encouraged to voice them within the Church and ultimately, to God. After voicing them, we would do well to be ready to listen to the Word of God, a Word that precedes even our concerns. We must speak our doubts; but once we begin to do so, we will soon realize that we are not the primary speakers—God precedes us in this dialogue. God is the subject, the One who speaks first.

This insight is essential to the renewal of theology. Another complementary way we might approach this question is to go back in the tradition and draw upon St. Anselm's formulation of the nature of theology as *fides quaerens intellectum.* As a theological virtue, faith is first and foremost a gift from God. Faith is not a human choice or the product of human effort. Faith begins with the Giver who is God. God takes the initiative. Once faith is given, then—and only then—is it possible to arrive at an *intellectum* of this *fides.*

Struggling to arrive at some understanding of the faith that precedes the very *possibility* of understanding is the theologian's task. In an even more fundamental way, it is the challenge for every Christian who is urged to always "be ready to give an explanation to anyone who asks you for a reason for your hope" (1 Pt 3:15). Ratzinger comments on this passage: "the Greek text is by far more expressive than any translation. Believers are enjoined to give an *apo-logia* regarding the *logos* of our hope. . . . The *logos* must be so intimately their own that it can become *apo-logia*; through the mediation of Christians, the Word [*Wort*] becomes response [*Antwort*] to man's questions."[24] Just as the ordinary Christian is charged with allowing the Word of God to penetrate his or her heart and then to give an account for the hope that comes from that encounter, Ratzinger argues that the true theologian must begin with the humility to allow God the first word. The theologian allows *God*—and not himself—to be the subject and to speak first.[25] It is for this reason that Scripture must be recovered as the soul of theology. Here, God speaks. The theologian should allow God the first Word and then, having spent time in contemplative silence, allow that Word to be received before a word of response can become *apologia*.

Communal Hearing

Perhaps what Pope Benedict XVI will be best remembered for is his constant insistence to the Church and to the world that Christianity is not about *ideas* to be believed or *rules* to be followed, but about a *person* to be encountered and spoken with . . . and loved. Christianity is about this relationship, specifically that the Catholic appropriation of this relationship is uniquely communal. It is not left to the individual to hear the word of God and act upon it, but rather, for the whole *qahal*, the whole *ekklysia*, to gather and hear the Word together.[26] Receiving the Word involves struggle, wrestling, as in the mode of Jacob, and then finally, allowing our response to be shaped by the "ecclesial I."[27] This community that is gathered to hear the Word is, of course, not just one comprised at any given moment, but one that stretches across history. The communal reception of the Word of God must also be a historical one, whose source is the living tradition of the Catholic faith, handed down to us from the Apostles and their successors.

In the Seminary

Allowing God to have the first word can—and must—be considered with some subtlety. There is no need (and the temptation in seminary formation must be resisted) to simply ignore critiques of the tradition that have been posed throughout the history of theology's development. The temptation to retreat into a posture that does not call into question currently accepted theological truths bears no fruit for the ongoing appropriation of the Word. It is evident that what we have received of God's self-revelation through Scripture and Tradition is the fruit of an ongoing dialogue that has been taking place throughout human history. In every time and in every culture, the Church must continue to hear the Word and realize that there is always more to the Word than what we are able to comprehend in the present moment. Facing the reality of "doubt," or at least a healthy "insecurity," about the nature of our relationship with the Lord actually proves fruitful. This is so not only due to the challenges of our current cultural context, but ultimately because this is the shape of Christian faith itself.[28] It is a gift from God who is, as Augustine puts it in *The Confessions*, both "interior *intimo meo et superior summo meo*"—more intimately present to me than my innermost being, and higher than the highest peak of my spirit.[29] As such, we are always rightly unsettled before the Lord. Yet, as we embark into dialogue with Him from the heart, that sense of being unsettled is transformed into a dynamic love that bears fruit in our lives and in our ministry to the people of God.

Retaining Spirituality as a Permanent Reality in Theology

In the effort to teach theology in such a way that keeps spirituality as its "correct method," it is first necessary to continually keep in mind the dictum that studying Scripture is "the soul of sacred theology."[30] We must also sustain recent developments to take seriously the liturgy itself as the primary source for theology. The liturgy is the *theologia prima* in which the people of God speak to God and, more importantly, allow God the first word.[31] Subjecting today's theological reflections to the framework of *lex orandi, lex credendi* is to let the dialogue with the living God become primary, and what we say about the dialogue afterwards, become secondary—important, but secondary. Focusing on the lives of the saints and their theological significance within the context of historical contingency gives flesh to present-day theology and allows the student to see this as a living and evolving tradition, one that has its constant basis in the Eternal Word, spoken in human words and living by the power of faith. Finally, consistent pastoral and ministerial encounters with the poor and vulnerable confront the student (and teacher) of theology with a constant need to cry out to Christ and listen to God's Word precisely in the setting among people who are weak, especially those whom we are not ultimately able to help or save by our own resources or good will. It is essential for the whole Church to choose to associate with the weak, the poor, and the vulnerable. Indeed, as Pope Francis is fond of saying, encounter with the poor and vulnerable is encounter, in a unique way, with the "flesh of Christ."[32]

The Church is *semper reformanda*. As such, there is ever the possibility of hope and new life, but this comes only when there is a preceding recognition that the life of the Christian and of the whole Church is always wanting, is always in a state of weakness and in need of redemption. Allowing confrontation with the reality of doubt and its accompanying vulnerability places the theologian on the same waves in the sea of chaos as the character in the Paul Claudel play, with only the Cross to cling to. It is precisely here that he begins to hear the Word.

NOTES

1. Joseph Ratzinger, *Introduction to Christianity* (San Francisco: Ignatius Press, 2004), 43.

2. Ibid., 43–44.

3. Pope Benedict XVI, *Spe Salvi* (2007), sec. 37.

4. Ratzinger, *Introduction to Christianity*, 43.

5. Ibid., 46.

6. Ibid., 47.

7. Pope Benedict XVI, "Angelus," *Libreria Editrice Vaticana*, April 10, 2011, http://www.vatican.va/holy_father/benedict_xvi/angelus/2011/documents/hf_ben-xvi_ang_20110410_en.html.

8. Joseph Ratzinger, *Behold the Pierced One: An Approach to a Spiritual Christology* (San Francisco: Ignatius Press, 1986), 24.

9. Joseph Ratzinger, *Milestones: Memoirs: 1927–1977* (San Francisco: Ignatius Press, 1998), 44.

10. Ibid., 121.

11. Karl Rahner, *Hearer of the Word: Laying the Foundation for a Philosophy of Religion*, trans. Joseph Danceel (New York: Continuum, 1994).

12. Pope Benedict XVI, *Verbum Domini* (2010), sec. 6.

13. Ibid.

14. Vatican Council II, "Dogmatic Constitution on Divine Revelation, *Dei Verbum* (1965)" in *Vatican Council II: The Basic Sixteen Documents: Constitutions, Decrees, Declarations*, ed. Austin Flannery (Northport, NY: Costello Publishing, 1996), sec. 2.

15. Vatican Council II, *Optatum Totius* (1965), sec. 8; see Blessed John Paul II, *Pastores Dabo Vobis* (1992), sec. 45.

16. Vatican Council II, *Dei Verbum* (1965), sec. 21.

17. Khaled Anatolios, *Retrieving Nicaea: The Development and Meaning of Trinitarian Doctrine* (Grand Rapids, MI: Baker Academic, 2011).

18. Brian E. Daly, "Foreword," in *Retrieving Nicaea: The Development and Meaning of Trinitarian Doctrine*, by Khaled Anatolios (Grand Rapids, MI: Baker Academic, 2011), xiv.

19. Ibid.

20. Anatolios, *Retrieving Nicaea*, 1.

21. Joseph Ratzinger, *Principles of Catholic Theology: Building Stones for a Fundamental Theology* (San Francisco: Ignatius Press, 1987), 176.

22. Pope Benedict XVI, "Message of His Holiness Benedict XVI for the Centenary of the Birth of Fr. Hans Urs Von Balthasar," *Libreria Editrice Vaticana*, October 6, 2005, http://www.vatican.va/holy_father/benedict_xvi/messages/pont-messages/2005/documents/hf_ben-xvi_mes_20051006_von-balthasar_en.html.

23. Archbishop Rowan Williams, "Address to the Synod of Bishops: To be Fully Human is to be Recreated in the Image of Christ's Humanity," *Zenit.org*, October 11, 2012, http://www.zenit.org/en/articles/archbishop-rowan-williams-address-to-the-synod-of-bishops.

24. Joseph Ratzinger, *The Nature and Mission of Theology* (San Francisco, Ignatius Press, 1995), 26.

25. Joseph Ratzinger, *Principles in Catholic Theology*, 321.

26. Joseph Ratzinger, *Called to Communion: Understanding the Church Today* (San Francisco: Ignatius Press, 1996), 30–31.

27. Ratzinger, *Principles of Catholic Theology*, 23.

28. Joseph Ratzinger, *God's Word: Scripture, Tradition, Office* (San Francisco: Ignatius Press, 2008), 123.

29. Saint Augustine, *The Confessions*, Edited by David Vincent Meconi, SJ (San Francisco: Ignatius Press, 2012), Book III, 6.11, p. 61.

30. Pope Paul VI, *Dei Verbum* (1965), sec. 24.

31. David W. Fagerberg, *Theologia Prima: What is Liturgical Theology?* (Chicago: Hillenbrand Books, 2004), 11-12.

32. Pope Francis, "Homily: Seventh Sunday of Easter," *Libreria Editrice Vaticana*, May 12, 2013, http://www.vatican.va/holy_father/francesco/homilies/2013/documents/papa-francesco_20130512_omelia-canonizzazioni_en.html.

Priestly Ministry:
Helping the Search for True Life

Peter Casarella

When we speak about the relationship between spirituality and theology, there is no need to begin a new interdisciplinary conversation between experts in spirituality and systematic theologians. Even more is at stake than rebuilding a bridge that collapsed at some point after the death of St. Bernard of Clairvaux.[1] There is also the question of how each of these disciplines offers a complementary contribution to the life of faith. Each one draws upon faith and promotes the faith Christians are called to put into practice. This essay attempts to show how the reintegration of spirituality and theology can shed some light on the true meaning of Christian life today by focusing on the ancient idea of *true life*.

The method that I employ is roughly that of the "theological phenomenology" that Hans Urs von Balthasar put forward when he studied the life of Thérèse of Lisieux. Von Balthasar said that "few things are likely to vitalize and rejuvenate theology, and therefore the whole of Christian life, as a blood transfusion from hagiography. Yet this must be done as a work of theology; the essence of sanctity has to be grasped

as truly evangelical, as belonging to the Church, as a mission
and not simply as an individual ascetical, mystical manifesta-
tion."[2] Like von Balthasar, I will consider the clerical styles
of concrete witnesses and attempt to shed light on the whole
question of true life through the collective luminosity of the
lived fragments.[3]

Rediscovering the Search for True Life

Pope Benedict XVI's 2005 message on the occasion
of the centenary of the birth of Hans Urs von Balthasar
included a personal witness to a beloved friend and, even
more emphatically, to von Balthasar's real legacy for theologians and for the Church today. Alongside Pope Benedict
XVI's embrace of von Balthasar's integration of theology
and sanctity lies this carefully crafted and heartfelt testimony:
"I can attest that his life was a genuine search for the truth,
which he understood as *a search for true life*. He searched for
traces of the presence of God and of his truth everywhere:
in philosophy, in literature, in religions, always managing to
break through the circuitousness that often imprisons the
mind to itself and opens it up to the spaces of the infinite."[4]
These words actually contain more than a eulogy or a shower
of praise. Pope Benedict XVI sees through and beyond the
theologian's works to the Christian stamping of his witness.
In the rather unique case of von Balthasar, says Pope Benedict XVI, the search for truth moved through *Germanistik*
(German cultural studies) to philosophy and theology and
then reached its apex through an opening to transcendence
that was not tied to any particular discipline.

The search for truth is directly linked to von Balthasar's
choice to embrace the state of life modeled by St. Ignatius of

Loyola, a choice initiated by God that took the young aesthete completely by surprise:

> Well, just as I was once constrained as a boy to plough my way through the entire undergrowth of Romantic music from Mendelssohn via Strauss to Mahler and Schönberg, before finally I was allowed to see rising behind these the eternal stars of Bach and Mozart—and for a long time now, these two have taken the place of all others a hundred times over—so, too, I had to clear my path through the jungle of modern literature, in Vienna, Berlin, Zürich and other places, until at last the kindly hand of God took hold of me . . . and chose me for a true life.[5]

By his own account, the mountains of interdisciplinary, pan-European wisdom that von Balthasar produced need to be seen as the fulfillment of a personal search for truth. That search took a decisive shape when the young student of *Germanistik* decided to enter the Society of Jesus. The Ignatian character of his entire life and theology has been noted by many scholars.[6] In short, von Balthasar's own theological breakthrough from Romantic aestheticism to the joy of Trinitarian communion was accomplished along just this path.

In 1971, von Balthasar published a small book, *In Gottes Einsatz Leben*, which lays out the foundations of the theology of election in the Old and New Testaments as the basis for Christian work and witness.[7] It introduces and even previews, as Margaret Turek notes, the expansive multi-volume *Theo-Drama*.[8] Von Balthasar explains how focusing on the encounter between the chooser and the chosen overcomes any dualism between prayer and works: "In the act of contemplation, we are at once drawn deeper into the springing source and at the same time thrust out from the source into our own channels of activity. If, however, we go about our active work in the *right* way, we shall paradoxically find ourselves penetrating yet deeper into the source. For the freedom we are looking for is in the last resort already given to us in the source."[9]

By recognizing that one's searching is a being searched, one discovers that the contemplative knows intimately what it means to go out to the so-called margins of the world in the imitation of Christ. Thus, von Balthasar himself sheds light on the dynamics of the search for true life. Readers of Joseph Ratzinger know that the idea of a "search for true life" also has a significant place in the writings of the Fathers of the Church.[10] The phrase appears in many places in the works of St. Augustine, including his *Confessions*. In the first book of the *Confessions*, Augustine refers to God as *"o vera vita, Deus Meus"* ("O true life, my God"), an acknowledgement of his own finitude and new dependence on the wisdom of Scripture. Here, he explains the false pride he took in a poetry recitation of the *Aeneid* using the notion of true life:

> What did all this matter to me, my God, my true Life? Why did my recitation win more praise than those of the many other boys in my class? Surely it was all so much smoke without fire? Was there no other subject on which I might have sharpened my wits and my tongue? I might have used them, O Lord, to praise you in the words of your Scriptures, which could have been a prop to support my heart, as if it were a young vine, so that it would not have produced this crop of worthless fruit, fit only for the birds to peck at.[11]

In Augustine's narration on the vanity of his rather substantial youthful achievements, God appears as the source of the true life Augustine failed to seek and is, thus, addressed *in the vocative* as true life itself. In *Confessions* Book IX, Augustine acknowledges that the source of all life is in God,[12] and God is personified as "My glory and my Life, God of my heart."[13] In Book X, Augustine also names God as "true Life," seeking to go beyond the seemingly limitless depth of memory in order to enter into union with the Lord.[14] God is Augustine's true life—beyond memory—precisely because the spiritual autobiography he wrote (the stamping of Augustine's Christian witness) is pervaded by a presence so powerful that memory's limitless caverns cannot contain it. As author of the early philosophical treatise *De Vita Beata*, Augustine had deep familiarity with what Seneca, St. Ambrose, and Plotinus thought about seeking God as life, true life, and the life of happiness, all of which he ultimately found too severe in their self-centered asceticism. The path to true life in the *Confessions* is deeply saturated with the declaration of John 14:6: "I am the way and the truth and the life." Augustine, therefore, addresses God as true life because he encountered a person who offered true life and a message that retained the character of a personal encounter.

The Augustinian search for true life left its mark on contemporary philosophers. Both Martin Heidegger and, more profoundly, Jean-Luc Marion draw out the phenomenological significance of this aspect of Augustine's personalism: "Life (precisely because I do not possess it but receive it from elsewhere) gives itself only on the condition that I receive it in each instant, therefore without stop or limit, in the situation in which I desire it also and necessarily as 'happy.' . . . When life is substituted for Being, it is already a matter of beatitude, intrinsic to desire and therefore unknown to Being that neither desires nor could desire."[15] Augustine shows us that the search for true life is the end of all our desires and every orientation to genuine happiness. Such a vibrant and existential search can never have a bloodless abstraction as its terminus. As Marion notes, the philosophy of life is an alternative to a bloodless metaphysics of being. In fact, Augustine turned to God as true life in the midst of life's crises, not as an excuse to turn away from them.

On this very point, Gregory of Nyssa's theology of true life is quite profound. Pope Benedict XVI also notes this connection in his catechesis on patristic theology.[16] According to Gregory of Nyssa, "true being is true life."[17] This statement is found in his book *Life of Moses*, in the section that deals with his doctrine of *epektesis* (perpetual progress)[18]; accordingly, the Christian life—even in its eternal reward—is marked by ever-greater movement toward God. Gregory offers a reading of the meaning of Exodus 33:21–23 according to the spiritual senses, drawing heavily upon the Platonic motif of *eros* as an intrinsically unattainable desire: "the ardent lover of beauty, although receiving what is always visible as an image of what he desires . . . longs to be filled with every stamp of the archetype."[19] Regarding the desire for this fulfillment, Gregory says that there is no promise of cessation or satiety.[20] In short, for Gregory, true life is surrender to God. The equation of true being and true life is a function of the path of negation. Moses entered into God's darkness. The biblical prohibition against being able to see God and live teaches us the unknowability of the divine nature. To highlight this apophaticism, Gregory calls the divine nature life-giving.[21]

Herein lies the paradox. The life-giving nature transcends all understanding, but we are also cautioned against taking the category of life as the introduction of a new "something" to be known: "It is not in the nature of what is not life to be the cause of life. Thus, what Moses yearned for is satisfied by the very things that leave his desire unsatisfied."[22] Moses teaches the Christian about a life of surrender before an "in-finite" God who empties his nature of all knowability and bounded-ness in order to be desired perpetually as true life.[23]

Johannine Reflections on the Search for True Life

"I am the way and the truth and the life" (Jn 14:6) is one of seven "I am" sayings in the Gospel of John. Two others ("Bread of Life" [Jn 6:35] and "Resurrection and the Life" [Jn 11:25]) are explicitly linked to Jesus' offer of life. Ratzinger summarizes the meaning of all the Johannine "I am" statements: "All these images are variations on the single theme, that Jesus has come so that human beings may have life, and have it in abundance (cf. Jn 10:10). . . . In the end, man both needs and longs for one thing: Life, the fullness of life—'happiness.'"[24] The offer of life is ultimately an offer of eternal life. This is stated sixteen times in the Gospel of John. Besides John 14:6, other statements speak more broadly about Jesus' offer of life. According to John 1:4: "Through him was life, and this life was the light of the human race." The Son of God gives life to whomever he wishes, according to John 5:21. Those who are unwilling to come to Jesus are not going to have life (Jn 5:40). The living bread gives life to the world (Jn 6:31, 35, 51). The Good Shepherd, for example, lays down his life for the sheep so that the Father may give life to him again (Jn 10:11, 15, 17). The abundance of life is joined to the Trinitarian communion in John 5:26: "For just as the Father has life in himself, so also he gave to his Son the possession of life in himself." Therefore, abundance is neither merely temporal nor a Platonic form. Abundance is the unfathomable generosity of the Father made visible and participable in and through the incarnate Son.

Life is, thus, the self-revelation and self-donation of the Word.[25] By a certain moralism, the search for a true life is narrowly viewed as a life in which only words are tested for their truth. The existentialist dissolution of the search, by contrast, considers the Word of life only in terms of self-fulfilling activism. According to philosopher Michel Henry, life is the true mode of the Word's revelation. He uses the term "self-generation" to differentiate between the mode of appearance of the Word of life and the mode of appearance of the life of the world. He presupposes an absolute distinction between the eternal Word and the finite world. Worldly words are exterior to the world. The world produces words in abundance without offering to receive anything that remains internal to the world's mode of self-expression. Absolute life is revealed in what is generated passively by the Word, and the Word reveals itself in the self-revelation of absolute life. I belong to the Word of life insomuch as I am called to participate in the self-generating activity that arises through participation at a distance in the Word. As the hymn in Colossians 3:1–3 states, we are called to new life in Christ and, on that basis, to living ex-centrically in the Word.[26] My belonging to the "world" is of a wholly different sort. If I recognize that the Word through whom God creates the world is, in fact, consubstantial with the Father, then I am still encompassed by the self-generation of the Word. In that case, I am in the world but not of it (Jn 17:14–15).[27]

What should one do if one encounters true life in the person of Jesus Christ? Conversion and Baptism are offered to the woman at the well and many others in the Gospel of John.[28] Does the Gospel of John provide other clues that could be offered to the faithful regarding the daily practice of, or discernible guideposts to, true life? Or do the antinomies between darkness and light, between the Word and the world, preclude the formation of a real form of life? As a matter of fact, the truth in the Gospel of John is not just seen; one acts upon it. One practices the truth: "But whoever lives the truth [ὁ δὲ ποιῶν τὴν ἀλήθειαν] comes to the light, so that his works may be clearly seen as done in God" (Jn 3:21).[29] Other statements in John confirm that judgments will be made based upon whether our deeds [τὰ ἔργα] are good or evil (Jn 3:19).[30] Likewise, according to 1 John 1:6, "If we say, 'We have fellowship with him,' while we continue to walk in darkness, we lie and do not act in truth [ψευδόμεθα καὶ οὐ ποιοῦμεν τὴν ἀλήθειαν]."[31]

Seen through the lens of theological phenomenology, life itself is the self-generating, self-revealing Word. What makes life true is not one or even a series of true utterances or blameless acts. The unforeseen abundance of life in the Word belies such calculations. The confession of faith must be ready unto death. On the other hand, the one beckoned by the attractiveness of the Word, by the invitation to be reborn, is not left empty-handed. The practice of the truth is a hands-on project; it is what we learn from the saints. By linking the practice of the truth or the way of holiness to the search for true life, we are on the way to discovering the proper sense in which spirituality is the correct method for theology.

Priestly Ministry Aiding in the Search for Truth:
The Witness of Romano Guardini

In 1997, the remains of Romano Guardini were transferred to St. Ludwig's, the University Church in Munich, where he preached from 1942 to 1961. There one finds the following saying on his memorial plaque: "*So meine ich es mit meiner seelsorglichen Arbeit—helfen durch die Wahrheit.*"[32] This citation has served as the subtitle and common thread of this essay. Guardini wrote this epithet as holder of the chair of the "Catholic *Weltanschauung* (Worldview)" in Munich. As von Balthasar writes, "Any appointee to a professorship for 'Catholic *Weltanschauung*,' especially at a non-Catholic university, must ask himself which area of truth thus falls under his responsibility."[33] Guardini gave a fairly precise answer to this question, but the question itself illustrates the challenge of interpreting his legacy. I will confine my remarks to explicating the meaning of the epithet on the memorial plaque and in the process, draw upon Guardini's legacy as seen by Joseph Ratzinger and Hans Urs von Balthasar.

A first clue can be found in Guardini's interpretation of John 1:4: "Through him was life, and this life was the light of the human race." The two words "life" and "light" belong together, writes Guardini. "They explain, interpret, and fulfill one another."[34] The life that God breathes into the world is intelligible and radiates with consciousness, freedom, and responsibility. We see here the priority of *logos* over *ethos* that was so dear to Guardini. He resisted the desire to see truth solely through the modern lens of a *verum factum*, that is to say, a man-made reality.

Der Gegensatz (opposite) is the guiding leitmotif of Guardini's entire worldview. The German term is less of a static antinomy. It refers to the polar nature of reality and the countervailing rhythms that make existence dynamic, free, and riddled with paradox. Relativism is, thus, countered in an original way—not by imposing a pre-existing unity but by searching in the past and the present for a whole that is greater than its individual parts. There is a very distinctive idea of worldly difference here. First, the differences in the world need to be considered in terms of polarities that exist on both the categorical and the transcendental level.[35] What unfolds on both levels as "polar" is a tribute to the power of unity that holds the polarities in tension. The world's meaning, which is essential to passing the truth on to others, lies precisely in this conviction.

Guardini is most famous for his work *The Spirit of the Liturgy*.[36] Ratzinger reminds us that his theory of worship is equally important. Guardini, Ratzinger says, saw worship as a form of obedience to being (*Anbetung als Gehorsam des Seins*). On this point, Ratzinger draws an interesting contrast between Guardini and Odo Casel. Ratzinger says that the antimodern predilections in the style of worship of Guardini and Maria Laach obscure a more fundamental difference. Ratzinger writes: "Guardini's glance to the Middle Ages is of a wholly different sort. He is not in search of a lost past. He desires rather a breakthrough to being itself, a search for what is essential, for what lies in the truth and not in a dissipated form."[37] Guardini revered the medieval past but was not its prisoner. He was in search of a new idiom for articulating a sense of reality that still remained loyal to the past.

All of Guardini's efforts at reform—what von Balthasar calls "Reform from the source"[38]—needs to be seen in this light. Guardini was so convinced of the priority of the Logos that he maintained that freedom is truth.[39] He feared that the dying of the modern world heralded an "unpagan paganism" and a view of created reality that divorced all things from their source in God. Von Balthasar writes that Guardini "reconciles for a final time the inevitable fracture line between the ascending worldly anticipations and the descending, divine, final decisions."[40] Guardini's diagnosis, according to von Balthasar, centers on the modern untruth that God is wholly other than the world. Following Nicholas of Cusa, Guardini seeks to counter the drift toward secularism by finding new forms of expression for God's non-otherness (*li non aliud*).[41] Herein lies the metaphysical and theological thrust of Guardini's entire reorientation to the truth. It is the rediscovery that God is "not 'an other' but is that Being in whom my existence is established, my truth preformulated, and the significance of my existence contained."[42]

Robert A. Krieg marks Guardini as a forerunner of *Gaudium et Spes*.[43] Krieg also documents the breadth of his reception in North America. Virgil Michel embarked on a life of liturgical reform after reading Guardini. Thomas Merton said: "Guardini is speaking of the true situation of the Christian in the world today: called by what does not yet exist, called to help it come into existence through and by a present dislocation of Christian life."[44] The writer Flannery O'Connor chided Guardini for relying too heavily on his own "spiritual intuition" in the interpretation of Scripture but still said of his book *The Lord*: "In my opinion there is nothing like it anywhere, certainly not in this country."[45] Guardini had lasting influence on a generation of Catholics in Europe and North America because of his dual dedication to articulating basic Christian truths with clarity and simplicity, and thoughtfully—and artfully—communicating the utter seriousness of faith as a truly attractive proposal.

What, then, does it mean to identify priestly ministry with "helping by dint of the truth?" Does such an outlook simply provide cover for a priest who happens to be a University Professor? Even if one concedes that a priest in some fashion holds the title of magister, has Guardini adequately formulated the difference between the self-determining art of Socratic midwifery and the *gratia gratis data* (grace freely given) for the sake of leading others to the truth? Here Guardini is not confusing the Crucifixion with the death of Socrates. On the contrary, he knows the lesson of the Good Shepherd from the Gospel of John and took it to heart. Guardini wrote about the Catholic *Weltanschauung* for the sake of ecclesial reform.

At the same time, his concept of reform out of the origin is not firstly an institutional program. In seminary education, for example, the maturity of affect is just as necessary as spiritual and intellectual formation.[46] Accordingly, reform out of the origin is also based upon the model that Guardini finds in divine revelation alone, of seeking a softer heart and begging Christ for divine mercy. As he says in *The Lord*: "Men actually did not know that God must be as he is in order to be able to forgive, for what they formerly meant by forgiveness was no true forgiveness, but a covering up, a looking away, a gracious ignoring, cessation of anger and punishment. Genuine forgiveness is as far superior to creation, as love to justice, and if the mystery of creation out of nothing is already impenetrable, all human concepts are completely lost when faced with the mystery of God's power to render a sinner sinless."[47] Thus, the model for priestly ministry in Guardini is both intellectual and affective. *"Durch die Wahrheit helfen"* means that the minister must free himself to pass through the Paschal Mystery of Christ and face the Lord as the merciful guarantor of justice in order to emerge as a collaborator in the vineyard where true life is nourished and bears fruit.[48]

True Life in Society

True life extends to social life. In seeking the common good of society and promoting structures and sound policies that incorporate a more just order into the social fabric of people's lives, we also seek to discover some image of eternal life. The image is expressed through the medium of a city built with the cybernetic artifices that we could call "human hands." Since St. Augustine, Christian thinkers have labored to articulate the proper ends of true life in this way. Here I will consider two thinkers who dedicated their priestly ministry to the betterment of the true life of the earthly city: Luigi Sturzo and Félix Varela.[49]

Luigi Sturzo was a founder of Christian democracy in Italy. He was born in Catania to an aristocratic farming family. Educated at the Gregorian University in Rome, he was able as a young priest to deploy the Thomistic social teaching of Pope Leo XIII and provide detailed information on the negative effects of the expansion of industrial capitalism on the farmers, craftsmen, and middle class in Southern Italy. At the beginning of the twentieth century, he lectured on Catholic

principles of political economy and founded the powerful
Partito Popolare in 1919 with little opposition from the Vatican.[50] By 1924, however, the Vatican had begun to collaborate
with the Fascists, a move that put pressure on Sturzo to end
his leadership role in the party and flee to exile in London
and later the United States. He did not return to Italy until
after the war. Only at the end of his life did he accept a
Vatican request that he not be directly involved in politics. In
spite of that ban, he received the honorific title of lifetime
Senator of the Italian Republic in 1953. Sturzo deserves
credit for opposing fascism in the name of Catholic social
principles more consistently than the Vatican. His political
theology still has shortcomings, and his involvement in Italian
politics can never be considered outside of the context of
the loss of the Papal States in 1870 and the signing of the
Lateran Treaty of 1929 between the Vatican and Mussolini.

Sturzo still has his admirers today. For example, John Milbank praises Sturzo in the first edition of his book, *Theology
and Social Theory*.[51] Both Sturzo and Milbank use Giambattista
Vico, and both severely criticize the radical empiricism of the
social sciences as an adequate basis for discerning the mission
of the Church in the world today. More importantly, Paul
Hanly Furfey (1896–1992), chair of sociology at The Catholic
University of America and collaborator with Dorothy Day
from the 1930s, modeled his own "Society in the concrete"
on that of Sturzo.[52] Through Furfey, Sturzo's ideas had a
brief—but potent—reception among some Catholic sociologists in this country.

Sturzo's book *The True Life: Sociology of the Supernatural*
begins with an epigram from Augustine's Tractate 120 on
John: "*ad vitam quae vera vita est* [to life, which is true life]."

Sturzo writes: "True sociology is the science of society in its concrete existence and in its historical development. If the supernatural is an historical and social fact, it must fall within the field of sociological investigation."[53] Sturzo saw society as a sum total of its individuals. He thought that Marxist determinism and scientistic positivism were not capable of grasping the real traits that marked social configurations. Drawing upon the humanistic method of eighteenth century philosopher Giambattista Vico as well as the thought of Maurice Blondel, Sturzo developed an anti-Hegelian historicist method that left the outcome of social analyses open to the entrance of the divine into history.[54] As an Augustinian, Sturzo did not accept the popular sociological dogma that secular progress is the driving force in modern society. Sturzo tried to give an account of the processual character of social laws that was neither deterministic nor secular:

> The sociology of Luigi Sturzo, based on history, and with a dynamic orientation, and a concern for the poor, can help in our movement towards greater rationality. If society is to be transformed, it will be only through the exercise of individual freedom. Free and individual initiative must work to change the social environment. Social structures or scaffolding are necessary for the social action of individual men. Integral sociology looks for the presence of the supernatural initiatives of human beings whereby the divine action enters into the life of society. This initiative involves not only the work, animated by actual grace, but also the shaping of goals under the influence of faith.[55]

Few in the West have even considered a grand vision
of social theory driven by Catholic social teaching and its
premodern sources. Sturzo's ideas rival the theories of Russian writers Vladimir Solovyov and Mikhail Bulgakov in their
scope and aim. Giovanni Battista Montini (later Paul VI)
came to admire and defend Sturzo on account of his own
father, who was an active politician and official in the ranks
of Sturzo's *Partito Popolare*.[56] It is not always clear that Sturzo
carefully attended to the asymmetry between Trinitarian
communion and social solidarity, but his insights into the
Augustinian basis of democratic principles were timely and
necessary for Italy in the first half of the twentieth century.[57]

Father Félix Varela (1788–1853) is unknown to most
North Americans even though his priestly activity directly
influenced the life of Catholics throughout the United States
in a period of virulent anti-Catholicism. On the other hand,
he is venerated by Cubans within and outside of the island.
This high esteem by Cubans, and also by recent popes,
derives from his passion to impart philosophical learning, his
quixotic and perilous attempt to defend Cuban independence
from Spain and the end of slavery in the Spanish Cortes, and
his innovative pastoral activity in the Archdiocese of New
York. His pastoral activity was done on behalf of poor Irish
immigrants, many of whom found themselves in New York
City to help build the Erie Canal.

Varela assiduously sought true life and, as a consequence,
was a remarkable pastor. He began as a learned professor of
philosophy in Havana and was a highly regarded professor
in the seminary. As a result of his passion for Cuba and vast
learning in multiple domains, he was elected in 1821—at the
age of thirty-three—to the Spanish Cortes in Madrid. At the

time Puerto Rico and Cuba were the only Spanish colonies still loyal to the king. In Spain, Varela proposed the *Project for Colonial Autonomy* modeled on a British system of self-government. His second initiative was even bolder because it involved arguing for the end of slavery. He considered slavery to be on the same level as an inequality of rights. Varela's progressive thinking might have gained a hearing had King Ferdinand VII of Spain not formed an alliance with Russian, Prussian, Austrian, and French troops. Ferdinand disbanded the Cortes and sought to take vengeance on all who posed a threat to his despotism.

As a result, Varela found himself as an exile in New York City in 1823. His career there was astoundingly successful, and some think that the Archbishopric of New York was kept from him only because the Spanish crown intervened. One year after his arrival, he embarked on a journalistic career with the publication of *El Habanero, Papel Político, Científico, y Literario*. He produced other national publications, including *Children's Catholic Magazine*. His translations included rendering Thomas Jefferson's *Manual of Parliamentary Procedure* into Spanish. He edited and published the works of notable poets, organized musical concerts in parishes, took over fiscal administration of the Church of the Transfiguration, and served at the First, Third, and Sixth Provincial Council of Baltimore.[58]

Varela's life and thought extends beyond the boundaries that separate Cuba and the United States. As a small child, Varela spent time in St. Augustine, Florida. In his last years, he faced difficulties with his health and died during a restorative visit to his childhood home. The most penetrating study of Varela's pastoral life and thought was written

by a fellow Cuban. As a child, Rev. Felipe Estévez emigrated
under the infamous "Operation Peter Pan" to the Diocese
of Fort Wayne-South Bend and is now the current Bishop of
St. Augustine.[59] Estévez rightly notes that Varela's *Letters to
Elpidio* contain valuable insights into his ideas about priestly
ministry. Two volumes of letters were composed, and a third
was also envisioned but never published.[60] The recipient,
Elpidio, might have been a student or other close friend.
Varela invokes the name repeatedly, but leaves the actual identity a mystery. This has lead most scholars to conclude that
he was writing to Cuba's young people, in particular, and all
people of good will who were looking for *elpis* (hope) in the
midst of social despair.

Two social factors need to be considered before engaging
the vision of true life in the letters. Varela arrived in North
America as a champion of social progress and modern
freedom. He was already inclined to favor Anglo-Saxon
parliamentary procedures over colonialism and held an irenic
attitude towards Protestantism; yet, he found himself the
pastor of poor Irish immigrants whose "Popish" faith was
being ridiculed by revivalists. As a pastor, Varela produced
apologetic material for all ages that rebuked the anti-Catholic
tirades and attempted to make the literary, historical, and
scientific riches of the Catholic tradition of learning better
known in the United States. The second factor has to do with
his increasingly strained relationship with Cuban leaders. In
general, the Cuban Church, much like Rome itself, was allied
with the state and took little interest in national autonomy
or other forms of liberal thinking. Lay intellectuals turned
to the European Enlightenment, particularly in France, for
an alternative. Varela himself sided with the latter and held a

special interest in the Catholic liberalism of Hugues Felicité Robert de Lamennais, a controversial priest and philosopher in France. However, when he criticized the bigotry that he encountered in the United States, the anticlerical intellectuals on the island seemed to have lost interest in Varela's calls for reform. Their vision of freedom was more secular, and they apparently could not appreciate the dialectical position of enlightened Catholic freedom that Varela was attempting to articulate.

Accordingly, the *Letters to Elpidio* take on two "monsters:" irreligiosity and superstition.[61] The former targeted the secular, anticlerical, and antireligious excesses of modern freedom. The latter was not limited to an isolated belief in unfounded miracles, but held in view a surprisingly diverse collection of idolaters:

1. Catholic clergy who did not practice what they preached (notably including bishops who appointed such deceitful pastors);

2. Anyone in any Christian regime who used religious rhetoric for the sake of usurping temporal power; and

3. Protestants who professed Christianity as a new form of freedom from tyrannical oppression and then irrationally turned their modern principles against the Catholic faithful.

The timeliness of Varela's *Letters* emerges, in my opinion, once one reflects upon the underlying motivation that led him to join in battle against both irreligiosity and superstition. Both departed (with equally disastrous consequences) from the true life oriented to genuine happiness. At heart, Varela was a Thomist who dressed up his social and political writings with a great deal of humor, wit, and early-nineteenth century French liberal Catholicism. However, he maintained that he never swerved from St. Thomas on theological matters. Among his favorite texts was Thomas's defense of the pagan religions, which Varela then contrasted with Protestant invectives against Catholicism.

Priests today must heed the call to speak out on behalf of religious liberty. Without it, there is no true life. If religious liberty is restricted to the cultic realm, as seems to be one dominant strand proposed by the United States federal government today, then there can be no true life for Catholics whose lives and testimonies—by necessity—extend beyond the parish. Both Sturzo and Varela knew the pain of exile, and both sought against all odds for reconciliation with their compatriots at home. Both resisted the temptation of the sacred power of the crown and defended the fragile idea of a constitutional democracy to fight for allowing the Catholic witness to become a more vital witness in society. Sturzo's "supernatural sociology" may have unwittingly inclined too far in the direction of what Charles Taylor calls "the immanent frame."[62] Varela speaks more clearly of the relevance of a separation of Church and state both as a Thomist and also on the basis of a physical threat to his life. *Gaudium et Spes* picked up this theme under the heading of *the iusta autonomia* (rightful autonomy) of earthly affairs.[63]

Eternal Life:
Spirituality as the Correct Method for the Study of Theology

Pope Benedict XVI's words of praise for von Balthasar's theology in his address of October 6, 2005 also include the statement that spirituality is the correct method for the study of theology. "Method" here is a precise term, but it is not as rigid or formal as it might appear at first glance. Pope Benedict XVI is not asking that a systematic method be replaced by an affective one; nor is he advocating a *via media*. The method of integration is articulated, as he notes, in von Balthasar's groundbreaking essay on theology and holiness.[64]

The corrective to contemporary theology that spirituality provides cannot avoid eschatology either in its form or its content. Integration here is cut of the same cloth as what von Balthasar calls the "eschatological reduction."[65] It is, therefore, fitting, before we conclude this meditation on true life, to add a word specifically about the concept of eternal life. The first clue can be found in Adrienne von Speyr's little classic, *The Gates of Eternal Life*: "Because the Son translated his life from eternity into time, we can conceive what it will be like when God translates our life from time into eternity."[66] The incarnate Word translates into our own language and way of understanding how the eternal life of God is present to us in the here and now. "All creaturely being and becoming is oriented to the eternal, incarnate Son."[67] There is no entry point into this mystery that can circumvent the encounter with the flesh of the Word. In his enthusiasm to translate the Gospel into a social project, Sturzo sometimes misses this point. Any adequate letter to Elpidio written today would also have to take this methodological principle into account more explicitly than Varela did.

Two other distinctive features of von Balthasar's theology of eternal life are noteworthy in this context. The first concerns the ideas of process, development, self-enrichment, and even "surprise" in God.[68] In some sense, this follows from the path of negative theology charted by Gregory of

Nyssa and later refined by Maximus the Confessor, Thomas
Aquinas, and St. Bonaventure. When von Balthasar claims
that there is a becoming rooted in the absolute being of God,
he is not succumbing to the panentheistic schemes of modern process theology. On the contrary, he is positing that the
identity of procession and mission carries with it an eternal
superabundance of love flowing forth from the triune God.
Von Balthasar's search for true life ended in this growing
awareness of Trinitarian self-enrichment.

Second, for von Balthasar, seeking eternal life begets a
consideration of the Trinitarian inversion whereby "all the
apparently negative things in the *oikonomia* can be traced back
to, and explained by the positive things in the *theologia*."[69]
Although often misunderstood, this principle is actually the
backbone of von Balthasar's argument against divine mutabil-
ity. It follows from his reflections on cross and Trinity: "What
we see in Christ's forsakenness on the cross, in ultimate
creaturely negativity, is the revelation of the highest positivity
of Trinitarian love."[70] Although von Balthasar's formulation
has been critiqued for being too speculative, any priest who
seeks to minister by dint of the truth needs to find a way to
communicate the truth about eternal life that sees our path to
God's love as centered on the Cross.[71]

Sacred Silence: Intellect and Affect in the True Life of a Seminarian

One could object that this array of witnesses sets a daunting bar for the average seminarian. Does a young seminarian
have to ascend to the heights of an Augustine, Hans Urs von
Balthasar, Romano Guardini, Luigi Sturzo, or Félix Varela
simply to live a true life and to be able to communicate that
gift to others? What concrete steps might a seminarian take

today in order to follow in these seemingly extraordinary footsteps? In more practical terms, how might one teach a seminarian about true life?

One point to keep in mind is that the search for true life is not as formidable as a search for *a* true life. By touting exemplary witnesses, we fall prey to the perfectionist illusion that the only way forward is to be a perfect copy of another saintly person. Life in Christ is the true life, and in each of our lives we can strive to partake *in some fashion* of Christ's truth and Christ's life. Moreover, to communicate Christ's message about true life today is, by its very nature, to recognize that many people feel exiled from it.[72] The dynamism of searching is never exhausted along the way for seekers of true life. The path itself is one of learned ignorance even for the most seasoned seekers. In a seminary one might still find oneself encircled by an indifference to true life, if not to life itself. Indifference pervades the lives of young people in our culture, and it affects family life. If indifference has been wrested away from the hearts of the seminarians themselves, then it is still a familiar reality in the lives of their families and of the families to whom they will minister. Indifference to true life is not an attitude for which we blame others if we allow ourselves to confront our own indifference to it. Exile and retreat are necessary circumventions in the search for true life. On the earthly path to true life there is no exit ramp, only a regular need for spiritual GPS updates.

A second point to consider with respect to today's seminarian concerns their devotional life. "Seminarians, perhaps especially seminarians today, take an intense interest in the Liturgy," notes Msgr. Gerard McCarren.[73] For Christians, there is no true life without Liturgy and prayer. Liturgical formation is obviously a major element of seminary life. Different themes arise in liturgical formation that immediately point to a need for linking personal and academic development in multiple theological areas (not just liturgical studies), such as the direct encounter with the Word of God, the need to seek repentance, the expression of joy and gratitude in word and song, and the mutual participation of the presider with the assembly in the body of Christ.

One theme highlighted by McCarrren stands out as especially challenging and necessary for today's seminarians—the cultivation of anamnetic silence.[74] McCarren records several practical points, such as teaching the seminarian how to free himself for the Lord in the moments of silence that precede and accompany the celebration of the Mass. I know from abundant personal experience that a genuinely prayerful presider leads the community into deeper communion with the Lord. However, there is also the salient fact of cultural saturation with what Augustine calls the *regio dissimilitudinis* (a place of unlikeness). When we walk into the desert to pray, it is not enough to switch off our cell phones and temporarily refrain from engaging social media. We must actively struggle to set aside the barrage of instant verbal and mental images that plague us willy-nilly. Never before have we faced a challenge as daunting as finding a truly empty space to ponder all the good that the Lord has done for us. The medieval dictum *nudus nudem Christum sequi* takes on new relevance in our age.

The proper devotional and liturgical mediations demonstrate that the path to true life rests upon a hard won equilibrium between intellect and affect, solitude and communal prayer, retreating within and missionary apostolic action. By focusing on the encounter with the person of Christ, what often appears as insoluble antinomy can be resolved into a life of genuine communion. The priest today is engaged in the fascinating adventure of reconstructing a people.[75] He needs practical guidelines in order to embark on this adventure. The Christic mind, as James Keating reminds us, is one of pure receptivity to God that recognizes that paying attention is the root of true communion.[76] This does not mean that the introvert has to become an extrovert or vice versa.[77] It does mean that both types of personalities are called to enter into a process of discernment in which they "listen for truth from the mouth of truth;"[78] for example, Christ speaking through the Spirit of God. Safeguarding against either a privatization or a socialization of the faith is the conscious effort to root one's own choice of life "in a *conscience publicly formed* and in *a community that reverences individual conscience* as subjectively ultimate in authority."[79] Figures like Romano Guardini and Félix Varela recognized this spiritual exchange between conscience, community, and culture in myriad ways. In teaching a seminarian to search for true life, it is important to keep those lessons in mind. Each seminarian will have to reflect carefully on the spiritual foundations of a well-formed conscience and the need to reach out to local families, student organizations, ecclesial movements, Catholic Worker homes, prayer groups, ethnic or national compatriots, or other forms of support to find his own path to true life.

Conclusion

The final word must be that God is love. The truth of life is ministered and administered through love.[80] The love shared in the Holy Spirit is, at the end of the day, the true parish administrator. The radical availability of a priestly existence is the sign and fruit of God's love for humanity. The priest is called to thank God for the gift of a true life and even more so for the free gift that can be shared with others. The Catholic priesthood today faces pressures like never before, both internally and externally. Psychological, spiritual, and physical fatigue can take their toll, but they cannot obscure what remains perpetually valid about the priesthood. The gift of sharing true life with others is a unique gift. The priestly share of this gift is not just exercised in a counseling session, from the pulpit, or from the comfort of a university professorship. A contemplative like St. Thérèse prays for such souls and renders an invaluable missionary service to the ecclesial communion in that fashion. Lay missionaries and women religious have given remarkable life to the Church through their witness of faith. A priest, as Pope Francis has recently taught us, goes out to the existential margins and becomes an evangelizing shepherd marked by the unpleasant odor of the sheep.[81] This priestly encounter with the people of God is equally personal and sacramental. It is hard for me to imagine any other form of existence in the world today that can effectively or truly live out this particular mission. Without this witness of priests, the body of Christ would suffer an irreparable wound.

NOTES

1. Much has been written about the history of the divorce between spirituality and theology and how to face its consequences. Some key sources include: Louis Dupré, Don E. Saliers, and Jon Meyendorff, eds., *Christian Spirituality III: Post-Reformation and Modern* (New York: Herder & Herder, 1991); Julia A. Lamm, ed. *The Wiley-Blackwell Companion to Christian Mysticism* (Oxford: Wiley-Blackwell, 2012); Den s Turner, *The Darkness of God: Negativity in Christian Mysticism* (New York: Cambridge University Press, 1995); Hans Urs von Balthasar, "Theology and Sanctity," in *The Word Made Flesh*, vol. 1 of *Explorations in Theology* (San Francisco: Ignatius, 1989), 181–209; and Peter J. Casarella, "'Modern Forms Filled with Traditional Spiritual Content:' On Louis Dupré's Contribution to Christian Theology," in *Christian Spirituality and the Culture of Modernity*, ed. Peter Casarella and George Schner (Grand Rapids, MI: Eerdmans Press, 1998), 275–310.

2. Hans Urs von Balthasar, *Two Sisters in the Spirit: Thérèse of Lisieux and Elizabeth of the Trinity* (San Francisco: Ignatius, 1992), 39.

3. Hans Urs von Balthasar, *Studies in Theological Style: Clerical Styles*, vol. II of *The Glory of the Lord: A Theological Aesthetics* (San Francisco: Ignatius, 1984), especially 22–30. In his introduction to this volume, von Balthasar refrains from saying anything whatsoever about the theology of the priesthood or the question of priestly ministry. See, however, Hans Urs von Balthasar, *Priestly Spirituality* (San Francisco: Ignatius, 2013).

4. Pope Benedict XVI, *"Messagio di Sua Santità Benedetto XVI ai Partecipanti al Covegno Internazionale in Occasione della Celebrazione del Centenario della Nascità del Teologo Hans Urs von Balthasar"* Oct. 6, 2005. Translation mine; emphasis mine.

5. Hans Urs von Balthasar, *My Work in Retrospect* (San Francisco: Ignatius, 1993), 10.

6. Werner Löser, an eminent professor at the Jesuit faculty in Frankfurt, has studied this aspect of von Balthasar's biography more thoroughly than anyone and explains von Balthasar's role as an Ignatian retreat master: "The Ignatian Exercises in the Work of Hans Urs von Balthasar," *Sankt Georgen*, January 28, 1999/accessed March 22, 2014, http://www.sankt-georgen.de/leseraum/loeser3.html.

7. Hans Urs von Balthasar, *In Gottes Einsatz Leben* (Einsiedeln: Johannes, 1972).

8. See Margaret Turek's Foreword to: Hans Urs von Balthasar, *Engagement with God: The Drama of Christian Discipleship*, trans. R. John Halliburton (San Francisco: Ignatius, 1975), x.

9. Ibid., 48.

10. Space does not allow for anything but a few examples here. Besides recognizing the paradigmatic instances of Augustine and Gregory of Nyssa, one should also note that Cyril of Alexandria sees the appropriation of divine life as a process that encompasses the whole of the Christian life. See Daniel A. Keating, *The Appropriation of Divine Life in Cyril of Alexandria* (Oxford: Oxford University Press, 2004).

11. Saint Augustine, *Confessions*, trans. R. S. Pine Coffin (New York: Penguin, 1961), Book I, 17, p. 38. Other references to "God as life" in Book I can be found in I, 4, p. 23; I, 6, p. 26 (*summa vita*); and I, 13, p. 33.

12. Ibid., Book IX, 10, p. 197, citing *Psalm* 35:10 (36:10).

13. Ibid., Book IX, 13, p. 203.

14. Ibid., Book X, 17, p. 224.

15. Jean-Luc Marion, *In the Self's Place: The Approach of Saint Augustine* (Stanford: Stanford University Press, 2012), 86.

16. Pope Benedict XVI, *The Fathers of the Church: From Clement of Rome to Augustine of Hippo* (Grand Rapids, MI: Eerdmans, 2009), 71.

17. Gregory of Nyssa, *Life of Moses* (New York: Paulist Press, 1978), sec. 235, p. 115.

18. See Hans Urs von Balthasar, *Presence and Thought: An Essay on the Religious Philosophy of Gregory of Nyssa* (San Francisco: Ignatius, 1995), 89–95.

19. Gregory of Nyssa, *The Life of Moses* (New York: Paulist, 1978), sec. 231, p. 114.

20. Ibid., sec. 232, p. 115.

21. Ibid., sec. 234, p. 115.

22. Ibid., sec. 235, p. 115.

23. There is a cruciform dimension to Gregory's mysticism in *Life of Moses*, sec. 274 and elsewhere.

24. Pope Benedict XVI, *Jesus of Nazareth: From the Baptism in the Jordan to the Transfiguration* (New York: Doubleday, 2007), 353. Here he draws upon both Rudolf Schnackenburg and C. K. Barrett.

25. What follows here draws freely from Michel Henry, *C'est Moi la Verité: Pour une Philosophie du Christianisme* (Paris: Éditions du Seuil, 1996), 269–291.

26. For commentary, see Joseph Ratzinger, *Eschatology: Death and Eternal Life* (Washington, DC: The Catholic University of America Press, 2000), 170–171.

27. "I gave them your word, and the world hated them, because they do not belong to the world any more than I belong to the world. I do not ask that you take them out of the world but that you keep them from the evil one." (Quotation added from USCCB: http://www.usccb.org/bible/john/17) This passage introduces the notion of being consecrated by the Word to the truth.

28. See Peter J. Casarella, "Conversion and Witnessing: Intercultural Renewal in a World Church," *Proceedings of the Catholic Theological Society of America* 68 (2013): 1–17.

29. See also Hans Urs von Balthasar, *Wahrheit Gottes*, vol. II of *Theologik* (Einseideln: Johannes, 1985), 31.

30. See also John 18:37, which links testifying to the truth with responding to the Lord's voice: "So Pilate said to him, 'Then you are a king?' Jesus answered, "You say I am a king. For this I was born and for this I came into the world, to testify to the truth. Everyone who belongs to the truth listens to my voice." For a discussion on the Cross as the supreme testimony of the Word's truth, see Mansueto Bianchi, "La testimonianza nella tradizione Giovannea. Vangelo e Lettere," in *Testimonianza e verità: Un approccio interdisciplinare*, ed. Piero Ciardella and Maurizio Gronchi (Rome: Città Nuova, 2000), 136–137.

31. See also 1 John 2:21–25 and 2 John 1:4.

32. "This is what I set out to do in my pastoral work: 'Helping by dint of the truth.'" See the pamphlet distributed on the fiftieth anniversary of St. Laurentius Church by the Archdiocese of Munich: "Romano Guardini: Ein Wurzel der Gemeinde," *Erzbistum München und Freising*, accessed March 24, 2014, http://www.erzbistum-muenchen.de/media/pfarreien/media3877720.PDF. For the influence of Guardini's model of ministry on Joseph Ratzinger, see Emery de Gaál, *The Theology of Pope Benedict XVI: The Christocentric Shift* (New York: Palgrave/Macmillan, 2010), 20.

33. Hans Urs von Balthasar, *Romano Guardini: Reform from the Source* (San Francisco: Ignatius, 1995), 21.

34. Romano Guardini, *Drei Schriftauslegungen* (Würzburg: Werkbund Verlag, 1958), 15.

35. Hanna Barbara Gerl, "Durchblick auf Ganzes," in *Wege zur Wahrheit: Die bleibende Bedeutung von Romano Guardini*, ed. Joseph Cardinal Ratzinger (Düsseldorf: Patmos, 1985), 61.

36. Romano Guardini, *The Spirit of the Liturgy* (New York: Crossroad, 1998).

37. Joseph Ratzinger, "Von der Liturgie zur Christologie," in *Wege zur Wahrheit*, 136–137.

38. Hans Urs von Balthasar, *Romano Guardini: Reform from the Source* (San Francisco: Ignatius, 2010).

39. Ibid., 135, citing *Auf dem Wege*, 20.

40. Balthasar, *Reform from the Source*, 50.

41. Romano Guardini, *Welt und Person: Versuche zur christlichen Lehre vom Menschen* (Würzburg: Werkbund-Verlag, 1950), 23–29. Massimo Borghesi suggests that Guardini's search for a new idea of creation is a search for a concrete Platonism, one inspired by his early studies of St. Bonaventure. See Massimo Borghesi, *Romano Guardini: Dialettica e antropologia* (Rome: Edizioni Studium, 1990), 142–152.

42. Romano Guardini, *Freedom, Grace, and Destiny* (New York: Pantheon, 1961), 81.

43. Robert A. Kreig, *Romano Guardini: A Precursor of Vatican II* (Notre Dame, IN: Notre Dame Press, 1997).

44. Thomas Merton, *Conjectures of a Guilty Bystander* (Garden City, NY: Doubleday, 1966), 284–285, as cited in Robert A. Krieg, *Romano Guardini*, 195, note 45.

45. Flannery O'Connor, *The Habit of Being: The Letters of Flannery O'Connor* (New York: Farrar, Strauss, and Giroux, 1979), 99.

46. Daniel Trapp, "Benchmarks for Affective Maturity in Graduate Seminary Formation," in *Seminary Theology II: Theology and Spiritual Direction in Dialogue*, ed. James Keating (Omaha, NE: The Institute for Priestly Formation, 2011), 102.

47. Romano Guardini, *The Lord* (Washington, DC: Regnery Publishing, 1954). See also the short summary on Christ's Lordship in Romano Guardini, "Das Herrentum Christi," in idem, *Glaubenserkenntnis* (Würzburg: Werkbund Verlag, 1949).

48. On Christ as judge, see Romano Guardini, *Die letzten Dinge* (Würzburg: Werkbund Verlag, 1952).

49. See also Joseph Ratzinger, *Die Einheit der Nationen: Eine Vision der Kirchenväter* (Salzburg: Pustet, 1971), which contains the young Joseph Ratzinger's essays on the Fathers' relevance for political theology today.

50. For this and what follows see Francesca Piombo, "Don Luigi Sturzo: A Christian Democrat in Exile," in *Exile and Patronage: Cross-cultural Negotiations Beyond the Third Reich*, ed. Andrew Chandler, Katarzyna Stokłosa, and Jutta Vinzentat (Berlin: LIT Verlag, 2006), 153–166.

51. John Milbank, *Theology and Social Theory: Beyond Secular Reason* (Oxford: Blackwell, 1993), 223–225.

52. Paul Hanly Furfey, *Three Theories of Society* (New York: Macmillan, 1937). On Furfey's indebtedness to Sturzo and on his relevance today, see Nicholas Sergeyevitch Timasheff, *The Sociology of Luigi Sturzo* (Baltimore: Helicon, 1962), and Michael John Baxter, "Blowing the Dynamite of the Church: Catholic Radicalism from a Catholic Radicalist Perspective," in *The Church as Counterculture*, ed. Michael L. Budde and Robert W. Brimlow (New York: State University of New York Press, 2000), 195–212.

53. Luigi Sturzo, *The True Life: Sociology of the Supernatural* (London: Geoffrey Bles, 1947), 9.

54. Ibid., 182–240.

55. George P. Graham, "Luigi Sturzo: A Prophet for Today," *Catholic Culture*, March 24, 2014, https://www.catholicculture.org/culture/library/view.cfm?recnum=8725.

56. See their correspondence now published in: G. Montini and G. B. Montini, *Affetii familiari spiritualità e politica: Carteggio 1900–1942* (Brescia:

Istituto Paolo VI, 2009). I would like to thank Father Michael Paul Gallagher for pointing out this connection to me.

57. My own reflections on the present-day relevance of the Trinitarian social analogy can be found in Peter J. Casarella, "Thinking Out Loud about the Triune God: Problems and Prospects for a Trinitarian Social Ethic in a Procedural Republic," in *A World for All? Global Civil Society in Political Theory and Trinitarian Theology*, eds. William Storrar, Peter J. Casarella, and Paul Metzger (Grand Rapids, MI: Eerdmans Press, 2011), 122–134.

58. For this and what follows, one may consult Joseph and Helen M. McCadden, *Félix Varela: Torch Bearer from Cuba*, 3rd ed. (San Juan, P.R.: Ramallo Bros., 1998).

59. A summary of his thoughts can be found in his booklet: Felipe J. Estévez, *El perfil pastoral de Félix Varela* (Miami: Ediciones Universal, 1989), which is based upon a doctoral dissertation completed at the Gregorian University in Rome in 1980.

60. For the Spanish, see Félix Varela, *Cartas a Elpidio sobre la Impiedad, La Spuerstición, y el Fanaticismo en sus Relaciones con la Sociedad* (Miami: Editorial Cubana, 1996).

61. The third "monster" was fanaticism, the subject of the third unwritten volume. On this point, Bishop Estévez has some interesting reflections. See his "Introduction" to *Félix Varela: Letters to Elpido*, ed. Felipe J. Estévez (New York: Paulist, 1989), 18–19.

62. Charles Taylor, *A Secular Age* (Cambridge, MA: Harvard University Press, 2007), *passim*, especially 542-57.

63. Pope Paul VI, *Gaudium et Spes* (1965), sec. 33.

64. Balthasar, "Theology and Sanctity," 181–209.

65. Hans Urs von Balthasar, *Seeing the Form*, vol. I of *The Glory of the Lord: A Theological Aesthetics* (San Francisco: Ignatius, 1982), 679–683.

66. Adrienne von Speyr, *The Gates of Eternal Life* (San Francisco: Ignatius, 1983), 133.

67. Hans Urs von Balthasar, *The Last Act*, vol. V of *Theo-Drama: Theological Dramatic Theory* (San Francisco: Ignatius, 1998), 80.

68. Ibid., 77–98.

69. Ibid., 511–521, at 516.

70. Ibid., 517.

71. To this end, Cyril O'Regan adds considerable nuance to the lively discussion of this issue by considering von Balthasar's refutation of the immanentism inherent in Hegelian Trinitarian thought as a paschal apocalyptic. See Cyril O'Regan, *Hegel*, vol. 1 of *The Anatomy of Misremembering: Von Balthasar's Response to Philosophical Modernity* (New York: Crossroad, 2014).

72. I would like to thank Father Christopher Collins for pointing this out.

73. Gerard McCarren, "Encountering Christ in Teaching and Prayer," in *Seminary Theology II*, ed. James Keating, 51–74, at 52.

74. Ibid., 58. See also Pope Benedict XVI, "Silence and the Word: Path of Evangelization" (Message for the 46th World Communications Day), *Libreria Editrice Vaticana*, May 20, 2012, http://www.vatican.va/holy_father/benedict_xvi/messages/communications/documents/hf_ben-xvi_mes_20120124_46th-world-communications-day_en.html.

75. Camisasca, *Together on the Road*, 113–115.

76. See James Keating, "Theology as Thinking in Prayer" (*Chicago Studies*, 53:1 2014).

77. James Keating, *Listening for Truth: Praying our Way to Virtue* (Ligouri, MO: Ligouri, 2002), 65.

78. Ibid., 61-63.

79. Ibid., 65, emphasis in the original.

80. See Hans Urs von Balthasar, *Truth of the World*, vol. I of *Theo-Logic: Theological Dramatic Theory* (San Francisco: Ignatius, 2000), 120–130.

81. Pope Francis, "Chrism Mass," *Libreria Editrice Vaticana*, March 28, 2013, http://www.vatican.va/holy_father/francesco/homilies/2013/documents/papa-francesco_20130328_messa-crismale_en.html.

The Union of Sanctity and Theology in the Thought of Hans Urs von Balthasar: Implications for Seminary Formation

Larry S. Chapp

What follows is outlined in three steps. First, I will lay out the basic problem of the rupture between theology and sanctity. Second, I will ground Balthasar's theology regarding the union of theology and sanctity within his broader ecclesiology. Finally, I will make some observations concerning the implications of this theological analysis for seminary formation.

The Rupture between Theology and Sanctity

We hear a lot these days about the "new evangelization." This seems to be a rather protean phrase because it has been interpreted in many different, if not contradictory, ways. Various groups have adopted (some might say co-opted) the idea for the sake of their respective ecclesiological agendas. However, if one looks at the teaching of the last three pontificates, a clear pattern emerges as to what the Magisterium thinks of the "new evangelization" (a not unimportant point, as it was precisely the Magisterium, in the person of St. John Paul II, that first proposed the idea). In order for the Church to be credible in the modern world, it must be discernibly centered on Christ in a radical way (evangelical); stripped of all that is inessential or obscures Christ (clericalism, juridicism); and focused on that "pearl of great price" (the joy of knowing God). This focus is, in its own way, nothing other than a challenge to live out the universal call to holiness articulated by Vatican II. In other words, the last three popes have called on the Church to strive for the sanctity of cruciform love in an increasingly cold and loveless world. Thus, the new evangelization is not concerned with the political categories of "right" and "left," or "liberal" and "conservative." Theologically, this translates into a need for a renewed ecclesiology where the deep union of the institutional/sacramental and the spiritual/Marian elements of the Church are brought into sharper focus.

Hans Urs von Balthasar once famously wrote that all true Christian theology should be a theology of prayer, a theology "on its knees."[1] Some have criticized him for this assertion on the grounds that it robs theology of its "scientific" and "academic" objectivity, reducing it to an act of pious poetry in the service of a subjective faith. This criticism is woefully misguided in its understanding of theology as primarily an exercise of secular reason applied to the doctrines of the faith, where the latter are judged in the light of the former.

In light of this serious defect of understanding, it is troubling that this view of theology continues to persevere in our Catholic universities and seminaries. This approach presumes a rupture or dualism between the orders of faith and reason insofar as the doctrines of the faith seem to have no intrinsic or constitutive role in how we conceive of "reason" in the first place. For Balthasar, no such dualism is allowed to the Christian, who must view all things as created within and for the Trinitarian *perichoresis* of love. Thus, the single "objective" criterion of truth for the Christian theologian is Revelation, which is to say, the Trinity, as made manifest in the life, death, and resurrection of Christ.[2] This criterion changes everything. A distinction can certainly be made between nature and grace, as well as faith and reason. However, they are not grounded in a reality conceived of in a bifurcated way, where secular reason is presumed to be the default position of human nature with the posture of faith ("religion") added on top like sprinkles on ice cream. Rather, the proper distinction between faith and reason is grounded in a theological truth: because the sole criterion for all truth is the Trinity, then the legitimate autonomy of nature as that which is "not God" is itself a Trinitarian reality. In other words, it is the Trinity that makes nature "natural."

Here, Balthasar immediately adds a cautionary warning. If we speak of the Revelation of God's triune nature as the criterion for truth, we need to be clear that we are not talking about something that is merely didactic, as if the Trinity were some kind of divine "factoid" that we can now add to the aggregated and fragmented storehouse of the rest of our knowledge of "things." Rather, the Trinity is made manifest in the lived action of the life of Christ. What this tells us, theologically speaking, is that no truth can be discerned apart from its action in the world. There is no "pure theory" but theory as understood through praxis. As he puts it: "From the standpoint of revelation, there is simply no real truth which does not have to be incarnated in an act or in some action, so that the incarnation of Christ is the criterion of all real truth (1 Jn 2:22; 4:2), and 'walking in the truth' is the way the believer possesses the truth."[3]

In the early Church, therefore, it was not uncommon— indeed it was the norm—that the Church's greatest theologians were also some of her greatest saints. The idea would have been utterly foreign to the Church fathers that one could discern the truth of Revelation without living them. This too accounts for the fact that most of these early theologians were also pastors and bishops who sought to orient theology toward its lived application among the faithful. As Balthasar further notes (with all due nods in the direction of *ex opere operato* and the condemnation of the Donatists), the early Church expected her theologians, pastors, and bishops to be men of sanctity and prayer. Even the great Augustine, the archnemesis of the Donatist error, would not have thought that the opposite position would also be true: that the personal sanctity of the shepherd is unimportant because there is no constitutive link between the ability to perceive theological truth and lived holiness.[4]

This view of the inner link between theology and lived holiness begins to weaken in the early Middle Ages with the growth of new universities and the rise of the scholastic form of theology that was taught in those universities. There is, thus, a momentous shift in location: theology that was once chiefly practiced in the monastery and the pastor's study was subsequently practiced in the university. As Balthasar puts it: "Theology was, when pursued by men of sanctity, a theology at prayer; which is why its fruitfulness for prayer, its power to foster prayer, is so undeniable. As time went on, theology at prayer was superseded by theology at the desk. . . . 'Scientific theology' became more and more divorced from prayer."[5]

Aristotle also played a role in the shifting focus of theology during this period. Balthasar is very clear that his introduction was both necessary and good, for Aristotle brought a new methodological precision wherein the relative autonomy of the profane disciplines from theology came to the fore. As Balthasar notes, this was a necessary set of distinctions and brought in its wake great advances in theology, philosophy, and the sciences. As practiced in the hands of its masters (such as Albertus Magnus, Aquinas, Anselm, and Bonaventure) the scholastic method was at once academic and deeply spiritual, holding in view the proper distinctions between faith and reason (or nature) and grace, all the while grounding those distinctions in a theological criterion. Following in their wake was an era of epigones who could not hold the synthesis together, and so theology began to degenerate into an arid, rationalistic, formalism that viewed the task of theology as an exercise in the deductive application of the first principles of Revelation to a host of topical theological "issues." After the Reformation, the scientific revolution, and the Enlightenment, this hypertrophy of the deductive moment within theology was contaminated with the bacillus of a kind of Cartesianism that sought logical certitude above all things. It thus degenerated into a theology in full defensive, reactionary mode, intent on "proving" the truth of faith to the nonbelievers through a putatively "certain" philosophical propaedeutic, with an equally rationalistic rigor applied to the theological debates with the Protestants.

The upshot of all of this was the complete rupture between dogmatic theology and "spiritual theology," the latter being increasingly associated with an analysis of the internal psychological states that accompany the path to the mystical Carmel. Balthasar, somewhat surprisingly given his emphasis upon contemplation, is rather critical of the Carmelite spirituality of people like John of the Cross and Theresa of Avila. He accepts, of course, that they are doctors of the Church, but it does not stop him from pointing out that their theological contribution to the Church would have been even greater had their writings been more profoundly integrated with the central truths of Revelation dealt with in dogmatic theology. This is what the Fathers did. This is what great medieval thinkers did. This is what late medieval saints like Catherine of Sienna and Catherine of Genoa did. This is even what the Rhineland mystics, like Hildegard, did. However, by the time we arrive at the era of the great Carmelites, anyone who wanted to take the spiritual life seriously had to speak in the language of interiority. The emphasis on various mystical states in their writings is certainly true as far as it goes, but is itself a deep symptom, according to Balthasar, of the bifurcation between spirituality and theology.[6]

One could quibble with Balthasar here and view his critique of Carmelite theology as a bit harsh, but there can be little doubt of the truth of his central point. The increasing association of sanctity with a flight into interior mystical states has more in common with a generic kind of spirituality of the flight of the soul to God than it has with the historical particularities of Christian Revelation and its explication in dogmatic theology. This has implications for the type of spiritual formation men studying for the diocesan priesthood should receive, as I will later note.

I will make one last point before I move on to the next

section. Notice how what we think of as a "saint" shifted on a popular level to a more extrinsic focus on the saint as a kind of supernatural hero, or at least a moral hero who represents an "ideal" or "exemplar," but who, at the end of the day, remains strangely foreign to the day-to-day lives of average people who cannot attain such lofty heights. I am not saying this is how the saints view their own witness, but that their witness is blunted by a spiritual obtuseness in the Church caused by the rupture that Balthasar details. Contrast this with the proper notion of the saints as expositors of Revelation, as living witnesses to the truth of Christ lived out, in full flesh, in the here and now. It is, therefore, no accident, as Balthasar points out, that this bifurcation led to the fact that few modern theologians are saints and few modern saints are theologians (in the didactic sense, because, according to Balthasar, the saints are the true theologians in that the witness of their lives are an exposition of Revelation).[7]

A Renewed Ecclesiology

Balthasar does not leave us without hope as he scopes out a theological solution to this unfortunate rupture between theology and sanctity. The solution involves retrieving an understanding of the Church that is at once the body of Christ and the bride of Christ. As the body of Christ, the Church has, as one constituent feature of this fact, the juridical Church of Office and Magisterium. Balthasar associates this aspect of the Church with the "Petrine" dimension and likens it to the skeleton on a living body that makes it possible to flesh out the rest. As the Bride of Christ, the Church is Marian. Balthasar associates this aspect of the Church with her internal holiness, which he views as superior to the

Petrine Church, though not in opposition to it.[8] The institutional Petrine Church is absolutely necessary, but is merely a means to an end, which is the subjective holiness of the Church, grounded in Mary's *fiat*.

This brings into focus Balthasar's development of the necessity for a perfect subjective holiness in the Church that acts as the recipient of the objective holiness of the institutional Office. Without the role of Mary, the empirical nature of the subjective holiness of the Church could be called into question. Such "holiness" would remain an abstraction to be sought after, always seeming to be unreal in the face of the overwhelming sinfulness of the members of the Church. Balthasar's approach to the role of Mary addresses this problem by emphasizing that Mary represents much more than a figurative theological abstraction, but is, in fact, a concrete, historical reality. The holiness of the Church does not, according to Balthasar, exist simply as a Platonic ideal in the heavenly realm, nor is the Church's holiness completely explained by the objective efficacy of grace in the sacraments. The holiness of the Church finds its ground and personal center in Mary's Immaculate Conception and perfect act of faith.[9]

Does the Church, therefore, have two "subjects," one represented by Mary and the other by Christ? This is a difficult issue to judge in Balthasar's theology because his use of masculine and feminine archetypes as an explanation for the relationship between the objective and subjective holiness of the Church could easily lead one to posit two subjectivities in the Church. However, according to Balthasar, a single consciousness grounds the Church's holiness, and that consciousness is Christ's. There can be no question here of establishing Mary's fecundity for the Church on the basis of some "power" which she herself possesses. Mary's faith is prototypical for the Church and, therefore, she is the "mother" of all believers; however, she should not be seen as an autonomous "goddess of fertility."[10] In a sense, one can say that insofar as the Church is the body of Christ, then He is the subjectivity of the Church. However, insofar as the Church is a response to Christ, as a bride to her bridegroom, then Mary is the Church's subjectivity. Because one cannot "carve up" the movement of grace in this manner, one must say that grace "opens up" the believer to Christ through Mary. The relationship between Christ and Mary becomes paradigmatic for the Church as a whole: the grace of Christ, predicated upon the model of the Incarnation with its union of "unmixed" natures, creates a union between the believer and Christ that does no violence to the inner integrity of the response of the believer. In other words, Mary's faith, though totally dependent upon the grace of Christ, is, nevertheless, a genuine response of her own. Thus, Mary's perfect act of faith can be seen as the center of the Church's subjectivity, insofar as the Church's response to Christ is genuinely its own. This dual emphasis on Mary and Christ represents, therefore, the concrete personification of an abstract theological principle: the Church is both totally dependent on Christ and identified with Christ as His very body, yet is concurrently distinct from Christ.[11] What is involved is not a philosophical contradiction, but a theological paradox involving the complex and mysterious relationship between nature and grace.

What this means with regard to the personalizing mission of each individual believer is that Mary "stands behind" each person as the ground, taking up the imperfect act of faith into her own and making it available to Christ. The ultimate goal of each and every mission in the Church is the glorification of God. This glorification takes place as each individual's mission is "molded" into a Christological form. In other words, the believer must "give birth" to Christ by opening himself or herself to an ever-greater vessel of Christ's grace.[12] This opening up is accomplished with Mary's help, as her universal *fiat* is "used" by Christ to give birth to himself again and again in the various missions of each individual: "[Mary] took part, as an intermediary, in the creation [of the Church] by the universality and unrestrictedness of her *Fiat*, which the Son is able to use as an infinitely plastic medium to bring forth from it new believers, those born again. Her presence with him at the Cross, her eternal role as the woman in labor (Rev 12), show how fully her self-surrender is universalized to become the common source, the productive womb, of all Christian grace."[13]

Therefore, wherever there is faith, love, and hope, there the Church functions by drawing all humanity into a unified, Christological glorification of God. Furthermore, it is essential that the Church's spiritual core be seen as the primary reality around which it is constituted. The external or objective side of the Church is only a means to this spiritual end. The institutional aspects of the Church flow out of the Church's spiritual core and have no other function than to create the conditions necessary for the Spirit to flourish.[14] There is also an objective holiness to the institutional Church because only the Office of the Church makes possible the guarantee of Christ's total presence to us in the sacraments. Balthasar brings this point home by reiterating: "The abiding structure of offices in the Church (the 'institution') means that we are guaranteed the possibility of participating in the original event at any and every time."[15]

According to Balthasar, this points to the impossibility of driving an artificial wedge between the "life" of the Church and the "form" of the Church. Balthasar draws upon analogies from the natural world and states that things as simple as protozoa "have their inner law of form, and the higher the level of conscious life, the higher is the complexity of the structure that supports it."[16] The institutional and spiritual dimensions of the Church may be formally (and even sometimes materially) distinct from one another, but they may never be seen as "contrary" to one another (as if comprised of opposing principles). Even though a simplistic phenomenology of the Church might be tempted to see the Church's spiritual side as coming directly from Christ while the institutional side is seen as something artificial, a more profound theology recognizes that it is only the Church's office—in the sacraments—that guarantees the presence of Christ, "the bridegroom," for His Church, "the bride." The institutional side of the Church renders it historically visible and concrete, guaranteeing the contemporaneousness of Christ for the believer. Office and sacrament "feed" the spiritual side of the Church by making Christ truly present in a physical, tangible, and visibly historical manner: "Far from being the antithesis of the nuptial "event," the institution actually makes it possible for this event to be a here-and-now reality at every point through history. The institution guarantees the perpetual presence of Christ the Bridegroom for the Church his Bride. So it is entrusted to men who, though they belong to the overall feminine modality of the Church, are selected from her and remain in her to exercise their office;

their function is to embody Christ, who comes to the Church to make her fruitful."[17]

Obviously, many themes in ecclesiology need attention and renewal. However, in this brief essay I wanted to highlight the aspect of ecclesiology most in need of renewal with an eye toward integrating the spiritual and intellectual formation of seminarians. Indeed, it takes no genius to see how baneful the effects are of any approach to seminary formation that does not seek to bring together the sacramental-public and spiritual-subjective elements in the life of the priest. I will now turn to some concrete applications of the brief theology outlined in the previous sections.

Seminary Formation

I should begin by pointing out that, in my youth, I spent seven years in the seminary: three in minor seminary and four in a theologate (Mount St. Mary's in Emmitsburg, Maryland), so my interest in seminary formation is more than academic. I also like to think that my years in seminary formation (1978–1986) are not so distant as to render my experiences obsolete to the contemporary situation. Knowing, as I do, many current seminarians studying for the diocesan priesthood, I do not believe that they are. Basing the following analysis on my own experiences, I would like to begin by stating the principle that will guide all that follows: seminarians need, above all else, to be formed into holiness before they are formed into priests. There are two corollaries of this first principle. First, in order to be formed into holiness, seminarians need to be formed into human beings who are well integrated morally, socially, emotionally, intellectually, and psychologically. Second, in order to be formed into holiness, seminarians need truly to learn (existentially) a theology that unites holiness and doctrine so that they can teach it to others in their lives and in their words. I could say a lot about the main principle and about the first corollary, but that is not my charge in this essay. I will instead focus on the second corollary, which I will now elaborate upon in the following two points.

As Balthasar noted above, the disastrous bifurcation between spirituality and dogmatic theology in modern Catholicism must be overcome. In the seminary, one all too often finds this bifurcation take on a living form in the divide that emerges between seminarians who are academically gifted and who excel in their theological studies, and those who are not so gifted, but who thrive on prayer and devotional practices. A certain amount of this kind of thing will happen in any setting because people are different; but what is striking in seminary formation is how sharp this divide can be, and that neither side really sees how academic theology relates to prayer and spirituality. After all, how does reading—devotionally—the writings of the Little Flower help one understand the nuances of the use for the *communicatio idiomatum* at Ephesus? Conversely, how does arguing over de Lubac's interpretation of Aquinas on nature and grace help one live a deeper prayer life as one tries to ascend the slopes of Mt. Carmel with Theresa of Avila?

C. S. Lewis once said that theology is the most "practical" discipline of all because its statements are geared toward an explication of the concrete facts of historical Revelation and how those facts are lived in the lives of the saints and, indeed, in all of us. As Balthasar says, dogmatic theology must take its message from Revelation itself, such that what is central to Revelation should be central in theology and what is peripheral in Revelation should be peripheral in theology. However, the reality of modern theological education is that it has fragmented into a cacophony of various disciplines, creating an atmosphere where integration of one's learning with one's life is thoroughly discouraged. What is central to Revelation is the confluence of goodness and truth in Christ, and the call for all of us to join with him in that union. This call is radical: "Be perfect, just as your heavenly Father is perfect" (Mt 5:48). This radical call is really a call to the holiness of knowing Christ. Theology, in other words, is about Christ and should bring us to Christ, so that we can know Christ. How can we expect seminarians to "learn theology" if they do not first equate learning theology with learning about Christ?

The reform of theological education in the seminaries, therefore, is a reform in the direction of teaching seminarians a type of theology that is Christocentric, and radically so. Joseph Ratzinger pointed out that what made Vatican II truly unique and different was just how Christocentric it was. In fact, he said that such a Christological concentration had never before been seen in the Church's history. This should influence the form of our theology. What this means concretely will have to be worked out in practice. At the very least, it most certainly means that no theological discipline can be thought to be more "removed" from Christology than other disciplines.

Nowhere is this last point more sharply focused than in the disaster that is modern Scripture studies. The theological writings of the Church Fathers were saturated in the Scriptures. Furthermore, contrary to popular opinion, so were the great scholastics. A single principle guided both the Fathers and the scholastics as they interpreted Scripture: the entirety of the Word of God is about Christ. Accordingly, a true biblical theology permeated their writings such that this Christological focus was allowed to act as the hermeneutical key for understanding the whole. In short, the Bible was treated as a true canon of writings, despite all of the differences in language, authorship, manuscript integrity and variants, historical context, literary genre, and ideological deformation. It was understood that, absent Christ, the entire thing would fall apart, like the single loose thread on a wool sweater that, once pulled, unravels all the rest.

Even in many seminaries today, modern Scripture studies work against this unification in Christ and give the impression that only a trained philologist can understand God's Word. Do not get me wrong—I am not arguing against the use of the historical-critical method or of the need for seminarians to learn languages, and so forth. I am not arguing anti-intellectually here at all, but quite the reverse. The need to bring seminarians to holiness of life so they can do proper theology requires that the Bible be allowed, once again—even in our Scripture classes—to be viewed as "Holy Scripture." This can only happen where the whole hangs together as a gestalt or form. Therefore, when it comes to the interpretation of Scripture, as Balthasar says, it is the "*Endgestalt*" that is normative. In other words, the Scriptures must be read backwards, with the resurrected Christ acting as the interpretive key for the whole. However, seminarians need guidance here, and I would argue that there are no better guides than the Church Fathers. Seminarians should begin by reading de Lubac's works on the medieval "senses of Scripture" and then move on to a study of the Fathers themselves in their biblical theology. Only then will they have the grounding needed to study the more modern critical methods.

There can be no growth in the kind of holiness required for knowing Christ, and thus for doing good theology, without a total immersion in the Scriptures. In order to heal the rift between theology and sanctity noted by Balthasar, we need to heal the rift between the critical study of Scripture and biblical theology as such. In seminaries, biblical theology should be viewed as the heuristic discipline within which historical-critical studies find themselves as subdisciplines. Furthermore, the recovery of an invigorating and Christologically-focused biblical theology will only increase understanding of the Church within the framework of covenant theology as mentioned above.

Conclusion

Three things hang together to form a fitting conclusion to this essay. First, theology must engender holiness and holiness must exegete theology in a mutually enriching unity. When one is teaching theology to seminarians, one must make every effort to show how the theological points in question relate to the most critical issues of what it means to be human. Theology, therefore, must have a humanistic dimension at all times. Second, in order to do this theology, the theology must be Christologically centered in all of its disciplines. There can be no question of treating some theological disciplines as more centered on Christ than others. Third, this Christological centering requires reforming modern Scripture studies in the seminary, placing critical exegesis at the service of a higher biblical theology. Theological education that does not make the reading, studying, and praying of Scripture a central focus is not in any way a Catholic theological education.

NOTES

1. Hans Urs von Balthasar, "Theology and Sanctity," in *The Word Made Flesh*, vol. I of *Explorations in Theology* (San Francisco: Ignatius Press, 1989), 206.

2. Ibid., 194.

3. Ibid., 181–82.

4. Ibid., 182–83.

5. Ibid., 208.

6. Ibid., 189–192.

7. Balthasar states: "In the whole history of Catholic theology there is hardly anything that is less noticed, yet more deserving of notice, than the fact that, since the great period of Scholasticism, there have been few theologians who were saints. We mean here by 'theologian' one whose office and vocation is to expound revelation in its fullness, and therefore whose work centers on dogmatic theology," (Ibid., 181).

8. See Larry S. Chapp, "Who is the Church? The Personalistic Categories of Balthasar's Ecclesiology," *Communio: International Catholic Review* (Summer, 1996), 322–338.

9. Hans Urs von Balthasar, "Who is the Church?" in *Spouse of the Word*, vol. II of *Explorations in Theology* (San Francisco: Ignatius Press, 1991), 177.

10. "Mary is the prototype of the Church, not only because of her virginal faith but also equally because of her fruitfulness. This is, indeed, not autonomous (as that of the goddess of fertility), but wholly ancillary, since it is Christ, not Mary, who brought the Church into being by his Passion," (Ibid., 165).

11. This process of "personalizing" and "making concrete" of what, at first glance, is a theological abstraction is a direct result of Balthasar's fusion of personalistic and aesthetic categories. This is a constant theme in Balthasar's protological and eschatological theologies, drawing heavily upon the philosophical theology of Romano Guardini. Like Balthasar, Guardini, sees a danger to Christian theology whenever the dialogical and personalistic nature of the ground of being is forgotten.

God is not an abstraction, but a "Thou" who encounters the human "I" in the very depths the latter's being. If the universe does, in fact, tend toward some of theological or cosmological "omega point" (to use a Teilhard rase), then it must not be forgotten that awaiting us is not a "what," but a "who;" not an impersonal light, but a "face." This protological and eschatological personalism is also reflected in Balthasar's ecclesiology and Mariology: the rejection of the Protestant "either-or" for the Catholic "both-and." The philosophical "tension" created by the more inclusive Catholic model is overcome by positing the ground of possibility for all of these tensions within the "difference within unity" of the Incarnation and the Trinity. However, these are also personalistic in some sense: the hypostatic union is only possible because of the integrating power of the "person" of the "Logos." The Trinitarian plurality is made possible within the unitary consciousness of God. In ecclesiology, therefore, all apparent dichotomies find their "resolution" in engraced personalistic categories. For instance, both collegial authority in the Church and its concretization in the Petrine office are universal aspects of God's grace and its particular presence in the Christologically grounded sacraments. In all of these cases, what is most theologically abstract and universal finds its ultimate resolution in that which is concrete, particular, and personalistic. See Hans Urs von Balthasar, *The Theology of Karl Barth* (San Francisco: Ignatius, 1992), 326–363; Romano Guardini, *The World and the Person* (Chicago: Henry Regnery Company, 1965).

    12.   Hans Urs von Balthasar, *Dramatis Personae: The Person in Christ*, vol. III of *Theo-Drama: Theological Dramatic Theory* (San Francisco: Ignatius Press, 1992), 353: "Together with Mary, the Church brings Christ into the world in the shape of its members; and the individual Christian, insofar as he is *anima ecclesiastica*, enters into the mystery of Christmas and repeats it in his heart."

    13.   Balthasar, "Who is the Church?" 165–166.

    14.   Ibid., 158.

    15.   Balthasar, *Dramatis Personae: The Person in Christ*, 355.

    16.   Ibid.

    17.   Ibid., 354.

THE UNITY OF SPIRITUALITY AND THEOLOGY IN PRIESTLY EXISTENCE: JOSEPH RATZINGER'S HOMILIES AT A NEWLY ORDAINED PRIEST'S FIRST MASS

FR. EMERY DE GAÁL

The indissoluble unity of the personal faith decision (the *fides qua*) and its creedal content (the *fides quae*) become apparent in the homilies that Joseph Ratzinger delivered at the first Masses of newly ordained priests. A daily, lived relationship with Christ is the font for celebrating the sacraments and preaching. A seminarian's spiritual formation and theological training receive their unifying culmination in ordination to the priesthood and first Mass.

The Genre of a Homily at a Priest's First Mass

Over the course of history, it became customary for someone other than the newly ordained priest to deliver the homily at the neomyst's (or newly ordained priest's) first Mass. A newly ordained priest's first Holy Mass[3]—referred to in Latin alternately as *Missa solemnis, Missa cantata, Prima Missa* or *Primitiae* (first fruits), and in German as *Primizmesse*—is

even to this day one of the highlights in the history of a
continental European Catholic parish and of the local body
politic. It illustrates and celebrates "the considerable dignity
and sublimity of the presbyteral office" and the indissoluble
link between the priest and the Mass as sacrifice on the one
hand, and the inseparable unity of the priests and the people
of God on the other hand.[4] This is the case *a fortiori* in southern Germany, the German speaking parts of Switzerland,
and the former crownlands of Austria—the area home to
Pope Benedict XVI. It is one of the prerogatives of the yet-
to-be ordained priest to select the homilist. The *ordinandus*
takes great trouble to secure a good homilist for his first
Holy Mass, preferably someone he knows well and who has
guided him on his way to the priesthood. To express the high
significance such an event plays in the lives of the Catholic
population, Germans appropriately say in the vernacular "one
walks off a pair of shoes in order to participate [interiorly
and fully] in a first Holy Mass."[5] The Church and the town
square, along with the young priest's home—and frequently
also the pulpit where the homilist will deliver his sermon—
are all richly decorated with wreaths made of foliage, flowers,
and pine branches.

Part of the *Ordo of St. Amand*, the *Ordo Romanus* 39 (probably compiled by a Frank monk) is the oldest source to record
in detail a newly ordained priest's first Eucharist. It relates this
practice for the city of Rome in the eighth and ninth centuries without explicitly mentioning a homily.[6] In his homiletic
sketches, the thirteenth century Dominican master general
Humbertus de Romanis (+1277) offers the first glimpses
into the nature of homilies delivered on the occasion of a
first Holy Mass. Under the heading *In noua Missa*, Romanis

discusses, in general terms, the nature of the priesthood (for example, the power to consecrate is given neither to angels nor to any other human being) as one of the outstanding characteristics of a priest that needs to be mentioned in a homily. A homily should also call the faithful's attention to the priest's power to bind and loose in the Sacrament of Reconciliation, as well as his ability to perform the other sacraments. In addition, reference is made to the fact that people kiss the hands of a newly consecrated priest as "the Lord showers greater graces during such a Mass."[7] Thus, the specific genre of a homily for a first Holy Mass must be dated back to at least the thirteenth century. At that time, it seemed meaningful and, in fact, taken as a matter of course.[8]

Indicative of Joseph Ratzinger's own understanding of a homily delivered on the occasion of a priest's first Mass are observations from his former prefect of studies in the Freising seminary and later professor for pastoral theology, Father Alfred Läpple (1915–2013). Läpple warns homilists not to delight in "baroque and emotional pathos."[9] Living in a theologically churned-up age characterized by technical sobriety, the homily held at a priest's first Holy Mass is oftentimes "a relict of a blissful faith of seemingly uncontested days." Such a homily must confidently and joyfully enunciate the sacerdotal role and spirituality of the neopresbyter while not denying the prospect of a future decline in vocations and the need for a radical restructuring of ministry.[10] At the same time, it must use this opportunity to reorient the Church spiritually. It ought to present an orienting model for the role of a priest ("*ein priesterliches Leitbild*"), as well as localize the position and mission of the priest within the people of God.[11]

Joseph Ratzinger's Homilies at Priests' First Holy Masses

Joseph Ratzinger's prayer card for the occasion of his ordination to the priesthood and first Holy Mass quotes Paul, saying of the priest that he does not lord over people's faith but is "servant of your joy" (2 Cor 1:24).[12] These words are significant as they shed some light on Ratzinger's understanding of the priesthood and the prevailing mood of both his own life as priest and the ideals he wanted his homilies to share with newly ordained priests and the faithful.[13] Using this programmatic quotation, Ratzinger deliberately parts ways with the instruction–theoretical or propositional understanding of faith that was still so characteristic of the nineteenth century and Neo-Scholasticism, in general. The priest's Christ-centered existence is decisive. The people of God— much stressed later by Vatican II[14]—are now acknowledged as a subject of faith.

Research has turned up a total of five homilies preserved in written form that Joseph Ratzinger delivered as a young priest, professor of theology, or cardinal for a priest's first Holy Mass. These are reprinted in volume 12 of Ratzinger's *Gesammelte Schriften* (Collected Works) or in *Ministers of Your Joy*.[15] At least two other homilies that Ratzinger delivered at the first Masses of newly ordained priests exist only as audio recordings.[16]

Excursus: A Seminarian's Trial Homily

By way of introducing Ratzinger's thoughts on the nature of priesthood it is worth mentioning a trial homily he delivered while still a seminarian at lovely *Heilig Geist* Church in Freising, Germany on January 21, 1951. This homily is based on the parable of the laborers in the vineyard (Mt 20:1–16).

He opens this sermon by acknowledging that the selected pericope is very familiar. God finds people on the strangest of paths, including those for whom God's mercy might reach very late in their lives. "This would truly suffice to make it [the parable] good news. However, originally," Ratzinger informs us, "its intention had been larger and more comprehensive. Over the gospel hovers the shadow of the ultimate decision. Jesus is for the last time on the way to the holy city . . . at the end of which his death stands."[17] Christ's disciples are aware that he must mean the salvation of the Jewish people and of the whole world. Only the Jews had remained loyal to God amid the numerous pagan cults proliferating in the ancient world. In the eyes of practicing Jews, the heathen must be those who aimlessly loaf around.

Ratzinger points out to his audience that, at this moment, something "strange and intolerable" occurs: pagan people also receive "the same one Dinar of the Kingdom of God" as the pious Jews.[18] The heathen shall come to God just in time to receive the same reward as the Jews. Even more unsettling, they will receive salvation before the Jews. Are there not both just men and sinners among the Jews? This is a provocation because the heathen are sinners. Rhetorically, Ratzinger asks his audience: "Is it not terrifying that the same salvation is proclaimed to both?"[19] He continues by admitting, "Yes, this is the actual mystery of Christ. The mystery, that God descends and makes just the sinner."[20] Justification occurs groundless. "The mystery of Christ is the unfounded goodness of God, the charity with which God loves, simply because he is full of charity, even and exactly then when we do not love him, when we are sinners."[21] Ratzinger impresses upon his listeners, "This is something we may never lose sight of: Not because we were good, did we become or remain Christians, but because first God was good. We all are people brought home from sin, into which we were born and into which we entered so often."[22]

Ratzinger the seminarian then points out something that might disturb us deeply. If there is parity between the gentile and the believing Jew in Our Lord's parable, is it not better to remain a sinner? In fact, Ratzinger probes, are we not worse off as believers because we might be envious and begrudge the redeemed pagan? Baptism did not simply justify us; it made us Christians and, he elaborates, "a part of Christ Himself, the continuation of Christ into our time. In us Christ walks through the streets of this world, in us he continues to live through the centuries."[23] If this is, indeed, the case, then we Christians are not part of the laborers in the parable, but are "meant [to reference] the Lord Jesus Himself, who narrates this parable."[24] We are part of the one Jesus Christ who proclaims God's charity to the sinners and are "ourselves this charity."[25] In the time of Jesus Christ, this charity was imparted to people and became visible and tangible in them. When departing again, Our Lord left this charity with us "so that those seeking and wandering aimlessly may continue to see and sense in us, what they once had seen and sensed in Him: this closeness of God, whose mysterious nature becomes apparent in us. And this mysterious nature is just this strange, unfounded charity."[26]

Ratzinger continues, stating that such charity is unmerited and lives from its inner divine plenitude: "A holiness that is content with itself is not Christian—it would position us on the side of the Jews."[27] Yet Ratzinger elaborates, we humans could not fulfill such expectations were we not bearers of such grace. This compels us to seek His proximity ever anew. It obligates us to struggle again and again to become as He is. For the point is not only myself, but whether many other people will see Christ. He concludes this sermon with the words: "We should always be mindful that others await us. And pray that God may grant us to serve them well."[28]

This little known trial homily describes Ratzinger's understanding of Christian discipleship and priesthood, and sets the tenor for the subsequent homilies he will give at first Holy Masses. Christians are precious, but concurrently humble, vessels because they are acutely aware that they have been given a gift they are not worthy of. *A fortiori*, a priest should existentially bear this insight out.

Fishers of Men

The first recorded homily for a newly ordained priest that Ratzinger delivered was on July 4, 1954 during the first Mass of Father Franz Niegel in the Bavarian mountain town of Berchtesgaden. Throughout Fr. Niegel's life, Ratzinger maintained close contact with him. In Niegel's last assignment as pastor in Unterwössen, Ratzinger visited him at least thirty times, delivering homilies there for Monsignor Niegel's sixtieth birthday on Easter Monday 1986, on his fortieth ordination anniversary in 1994, and again on Niegel's seventieth birthday in 1996. Both enjoyed music. As Archbishop of Munich, Ratzinger once delivered a talk for Advental singing (*Adventsingen*) in Unterwössen.[29]

The Gospel for Fr. Niegel's first Mass was that of the Fisher of Men (Lk 5:1–11). By way of introduction, Ratzinger poetically establishes a parallel between the natural beauty of Galilee and his Bavarian home country. However, he continues, this is but the context for a "far greater and more significant" parallel uniting 2000 years. In the morning hours of a human being's life, "he receives a call and commission." Peter again casts out a net—this time hauling in "a heavy, miraculous freight" which is "not his own achievement," beginning something altogether novel. "The Lord tells him 'henceforward you will catch human beings.'"[30] Directly addressing the priest, then-seminary professor Ratzinger says that no matter how little success he may have, he should carry on undaunted, "drawing people home to the coasts of eternity, who resist and block in the false pretense of [holding fast to] their supposed happiness."[31] These morning hours of a human life still occur today, 2000 years later.

When an ordaining bishop speaks to deacons about their tasks as priests in terse and sober words reminiscent of former Roman rulers, this is but "an echo of the Lake Gennesaret. . . . [The priest] chooses just a few rays of light hidden in fullness of light: To sacrifice, bless, preside, preach [and] baptize."[32] Ratzinger then describes the ministry of preaching God's Word. He enjoins the priest to preach well and emphasizes his point by quoting the ecclesiastical writer and doctor Hippolytus (ca. 170–236): "The birth of Christ is not yet finished. Constantly Christ the Lord is born in this world. The Church gives birth to this Christ, by teaching all peoples and preaching to them. . . . By the Church announcing, without wavering, God's Word to a world where lie, deception and sensation trump, she creates God's place in the midst of the world." Without God's Word, the world would be infinitely impoverished. "God is still [like the Holy Family] on the search for accommodations and is provided a home: Christ is born anew."[33] He reminds everyone to awaken "the humility of the listener in us." Next to the pulpit for the homily lies the pulpit of everyday life, where everyone is called to give birth to Christ anew. Such homiletic endeavors succeed only if a new sense of "humility of listening is awakened." Such humility leads to "the courage of speaking, which Christians need more than ever." By living the preached Word, all of the faithful provide for "the homeless God space in this world."[34]

Bringing God's blessing to the homes of people after his first Holy Mass, the neomyst becomes aware that he is now, by his very nature, a man who blesses. "The priest blesses children in school, he blesses the faithful during Holy Mass, he blesses the hikers on the mountains or (those) travelling far away, he blesses the sick and dying in the hour of their affliction and those of extreme forsakenness, which only God's merciful hand can enter. He still imparts the last blessing at the grave across into eternity."[35]

The priest reminds us that all human hope and success "ultimately depend on the charity of the eternal God."[36] Quoting the Italian poet and philosopher Dante Alighieri (1265–1321), Ratzinger observes that, eclipsing economic calculations, all is indebted to that eternal charity "which also moves the sun and stars."[37] It is provocatively "strange"[38] he continues, that this blessing begins with the Sign of the Cross. It reminds one of both Jesus Christ's afflictions and of the afflictions lying hidden in all things. It reminds us "that all blessings arise from sacrifice … the third and highest task of a priest."[39] Using the first person plural, he continues: one needs "to enter wholeheartedly this first holy sacrifice."[40] Ratzinger wishes Fr. Niegel to ask God to grant him the ability "to live from the strength of this sacrifice"[41] so that Fr.

Niegel may receive from it the fullness of blessing for himself, as well as the strength to bless others. "All blessings originate in the cross. . . . On the luminous morning hour of a vocation follows three years later the definitive hour of sending forth . . . [culminating in] denial, cross and resurrection."[42]

When a priest's hands are firmly bound by a bishop during the ordination ceremony and "these bound hands will raise the chalice, then this is an echo of Christ telling Simon Peter someone else will gird him" (cf. Jn 21:18).[43] The days of "dreamy hope," when a multitude of options are open to a human being, are gone "forever; he placed his bound hands into God's hand. Henceforth God, God alone determines the path and the possibility."[44]

Ratzinger concludes this homily by referring to the day's processional hymn, which sings, "The Lord is my light and my salvation" (Ps 27:1). Ratzinger finishes with Our Lord's words "Be of good cheer for I have overcome the world."[45]

The Priest—A Man Who Blesses

Ratzinger delivered his second homily, "The Priest—A Human Being Who Blesses," on the occasion of a first Holy Mass for his friend, Fr. Franz Niedermayer, in Kirchanschöring on July 10, 1955. Niedermayer and Ratzinger had attended the high school seminary in Traunstein together, where Niedermayer had been a conscripted, but civilian air force helper. Due to severe injuries he sustained as a prisoner of war during World War II, Niedermayer was ordained four years after Ratzinger. The Niedermayer family continues to remain in contact with Ratzinger even after Fr. Niedermayer's death.[46]

The bishop sends priests "on to God's farm field, which awaits its reaper."[47] he bishop first asks the archdeacon "*Scis illos dignos esse*—do you know whether they are worthy?"[48] He then silently places his hands on the *ordinandi*. This is, Ratzinger emphasizes, "according to the teaching of the holy Church,"[49] the actual moment of consecration. The homilist continues: "It was for me an unforgettable and touching moment, also I was permitted to lay my hands on our reverend *Herr Primiziant*, my dear friend."[50] Ratzinger then relates that Fr. Niedermayer had spent two and a half years in a Russian prison camp and, upon his return, found his father seriously sick. Almost blind, his father knelt at the altar (*Primizaltar*) of his son's first Mass. After ordination, the concelebrating priests held their hands over the *ordinandi*. Ratzinger considers this gesture as the "deepest symbol" for the priest's mission: to be a man who blesses.[51] "Whose hand is not there to curse and to hit, and likewise not for [the sake of] technology or activity, but to bless."[52] Here one detects the influence of Romano Guardini (1885–1968) and his critique that modern man's way of perceiving all reality is exclusively technical, ignoring God as the actual architect.[53] As a seminarian, Ratzinger had both read Guardini's books and attended some of his much-celebrated homilies in St. Ludwig, the university church in Munich.[54]

Ratzinger develops man's dependence on God's grace in three steps. The miraculous multiplication of loaves illustrates man's inner helplessness. This is woefully apparent in this era when man solipsistically becomes his own yardstick and standard. In contradistinction, the priest is called to be "witness and servant,"[55] the shepherd leading people to the true, Good Shepherd's pastures. "One does not become priest for one's own sake, but rather for others . . . to be a servant to the servants of God."[56] As memorably put by Ratzinger's lodestar, Augustine (354–430), "In the confessional he must listen almost daily to the sins and filth of humankind. . . . Even in his highest commission, in the celebration of the Holy Eucharist the priest is actually not privileged, but celebrates Holy Mass as your table servant. . . . The priest does not enter heaven easier than others."[57] Rather, it is more difficult for him because he comes alone. Ratzinger quotes from a late-Medieval priest's prayer from the Salzburg region in Austria: "A priest needs to be completely big and completely small . . . completely different from me; pray for me!"[58] To illustrate this, Ratzinger points to the figure of St. Francis of Assisi (ca. 1181–1226) who introduced himself to thieves that were about to rob him as "a herald of a great king."[59] It is precisely for this reason that he remained a deacon.[60] The priest participates in Jesus Christ's pastoral office, as well as in the Lord's teaching office. He performs his tasks, mindful that "in front of the great realities of God, in fact, every human being is but a stammering child."[61] When praying the *Orate Fratres*— "Pray brethren that your and my sacrifice may be pleasing to God"[62] the celebrating priest is, in a consoling way, aware that people also pray on his behalf to God Almighty. Ratzinger closes this homily with the words: "Pray brothers, that this priest's and all priests' life-sacrifice may be pleasing to God the Lord. Amen."[63]

There Are Always Seeds That Bear Fruit for Harvest

On the eve of the epochal Second Vatican Council, Ratzinger was asked to give a homily in the Rhineland on Sexagesima Sunday, 1962.[64] Echoing Luke 8:4–15, it is titled:

"There are always seeds that bear fruit for the harvest."[65] Amid this optimistic statement, a sense of *Kulturpessimismus* shines through: most of Christ's followers "were only fellow-travelers without roots and without depth who would abandon him at the first approach of danger" the then-professor at the University of Bonn informs his congregation.[66] A vocation is defined by the two nouns "contestation" and "discouragement."[67] Ratzinger thinks of "the almost hopeless situation of the peasant in Israel who gathers his harvest from a soil that at every moment threatens to revert to desert."[68] Our Lord wants to say that everything truly fruitful is, at first, "small and hidden"[69] indeed, the world could not survive without it being thus. Christ's words originate in an inconspicuous corner of Galilee, yet for exactly this reason, they do not pass away. God also speaks in the divine incognito today. The efforts of Christians are not in vain. "Secretly the world lives from the fact that in it people are still continually believing, hoping and loving."[70] The "image of the sower of the gospel is . . . an image of the priest, to whom it tells of the misery and the splendour of his ministry."[71] Yet, it would be an oversimplification if we were to assume that we are "those who are on God's side" and not the "others."[72]

> We shall have to ask ourselves quite honestly whether to a considerable extent we ourselves do not also belong among them. . . . Jesus calls weathervanes, who cannot stand firm but simply let themselves be driven by the current of the age, who are at the mercy of "them," of the great mass of people; who are continually asking only what "they" are doing, what "they" are saying and thinking, and who have never known the sublimity of

the truth for whose sake it is worthwhile to stand out against "them"?[73]

Despite such fickleness "Jesus says to the disciples: 'To you it has been given to know the secrets of the kingdom of God.'"[74] On the part of the believer and—in a most deliberate way—on the part of a priest, it is required that he die like "a grain of wheat falls to the ground and dies" (Jn 12:24). Such a Eucharistic disposition, Ratzinger argues, permits the Christian to become a genuine disciple and priest. "Thus the bread of the Eucharist is for us at once the sign of the Cross and the sign of God's great and joyful harvest. . . . It is the priest's finest and sublimest ministry that he can be the servant of this Holy meal, that he may transform and distribute this bread of unity. . . . He must add a piece of his heart's blood—himself. His fate is tied to God. . . . In the midst of weakness the triumph of grace is fulfilled."[75] In this confidence, the priest may pray with the psalmist: "'And I will come to the altar of God, the God of my joy' (Ps 43 [42]:4)."[76]

Meditation on the Day of a First Mass

This precious text begins with the observation of the French author and aviator Antoine de Saint-Exupéry (1900–1944), "there is only one real problem in this world: how to give men once again a spiritual meaning and a spiritual restlessness; how to make something like a Gregorian chant drop its gentle dew upon them. Do you not see: people can no longer live on refrigerators, politics, balance-sheets, and crossword puzzles. They simply cannot do it . . . —the light, the clouds, the heavens with their stars—these we no longer understand."[77]

A witness from the totalitarian Soviet Union, Alexander Solzhenitsyn (1918–2008), seconds this sentiment: "We need cathedrals . . . spaces for the soul."[78] Ratzinger draws the conclusion "we need men who . . . are solicitous for the human soul and seek to help men not to lose their souls in the turmoil of everyday life."[79] He alerts his readers to the fact that kings in the Fertile Crescent were described as "shepherds." "Jesus, the Son of God, is the true Shepherd ... backing the currency of his Word with his own precious blood."[80] The priest brings the Word to "a world that lacks such words" and has become "infinitely boring and empty . . . cheerless . . . a trackless waste."[81] Ratzinger recalls Johann Wolfgang von Goethe's (1749–1832) remark that the Church's sacraments "take possession of and transform all the important moments of life."[82] The priest primarily effects this through the sacraments of Penance and the altar (Eucharist) and through his existential configuration to the person of Christ. The priest is the visible sign of the world's transformation by "sacrificing together with Christ."[83] This is foretold in Samuel (1 Sam 3:1–10) who receives his calling as "a burden that he must carry through the toil and hardships of a long life . . . in the midst of people's indifference."[84] This sobering Old Testament example is actually the cause for him to ask the community to thank God with him for sending a newly ordained priest into their midst.

So That God's Word Remains—On the Burden and Joy of a Prophet

Already a professor at the newly founded University of Regensburg, Ratzinger delivers his next homily in his hometown of Traunstein for Father Karl Besler in 1973. It carries the title "So that God's Word remains—on the burden and joy of a prophet." [85] Ratzinger reminisces back to 1951 when he celebrated his first Mass in the same church. The three neopresbyters at the time, who had celebrated their first Holy Masses on the same Sunday in the same parish church, had not become "masters of that day, but keepers, who are measured by their loyalty."[86] Ratzinger then quotes the motto for his own ordination, "servant of your joy" (2 Cor 1:24). The readings chosen by Fr. Besler were Ezekiel 2:2–5; 2 Corinthians 12:7–10, and Mark 6:1–6a. All three figures—Ezekiel, Paul, and Jesus—describe aspects of priesthood. Ratzinger observes that, during Ezekiel's deportation from Israel to Babylon, he discovers that God is not limited to Jerusalem and the temple, but is the Lord of "heaven and earth,"[87] also living in the midst of the Israeli deportees. Speaking after the profound cultural upheavals of 1968, Ratzinger points to the parallels between the situation of the Israeli deportees of the sixth century BC and the profound cultural upheavals of the 1970s: both are uprooted after "a spiritual destruction of the Temple."[88] The catchphrase, "God is dead," is attractive, and precepts handed down for generations are no longer relevant. As Ezekiel did then, people nowadays acknowledge how very necessary God is. "We begin to recognize increasingly that the merely useful [utilitarian] does not save people, that cities in which people only plan and think become unbearable, that they need the breath of eternity, so that they are habitable by human beings; that people must again learn how to recognize God's reflection(s) in one another and in creation, so that they support one another, enjoy life, and so that they again recognize what love truly means."[89]

He circumscribes the task of a priest "to be above all the servant of the humane."[90]

Ratzinger then turns the faithful's attention to Paul and asks rhetorically whether "sinners and the Church as a whole can be bearers of justice, truth, loyalty, purity, love, selflessness . . . and bearers of a divine message?"[91] Laypeople are challenged to "see in priests messengers of something greater."[92] It is their "duty and right to force the priest, so to speak, against his own despondency to be that to which he is called, to will him as priest, and to assist him, so that the Word of God remains vivacious and life-giving in this world. Only together can they bear the call, can they struggle and look after each other. His authority remains present."[93]

The glaring asymmetry between message and messenger, Ratzinger implies, is exactly *the challenge*, but also *the chance* to live out faith. For this reason, Ratzinger quotes the Doctor of the Church, St. Ambrose (ca. 339–397), "God did not call philosophers but fishermen."[94] "Precisely the messengers' weakness attests to the truth of the message."[95] The priest may not adulterate God's Word, but should transmit it in a disinterested manner, "stepping back behind the greater" reality he may point to.[96]

Ratzinger turns to the logical questions that now surface: Is disinterested priesthood a reasonable and intelligent task for a human being? How is someone to find his identity if he is to be disinterested? He provides an answer by way of a story narrated by the Swedish novelist and Nobel laureate Selma Lagerlöf (1858–1940). In the Middle Ages, there was a brutal, violent, and egoistic knight who suddenly had the inexplicable *idée fixe* of bringing a burning flame from the Holy Land home to upper Italy. In Ratzinger's own inimitable diction: "And through the self-lost [in the sense of self-denying] service to this flame, which now becomes the only law of his way, he becomes someone different. For he may not look back any longer on what becomes of himself, exclusively the flame is the content of his way and of his life. In this service to the other he becomes free of himself, does he become healed, does he become mature, does he become kind, does he become warm, develops in him that what he truly could be."[97]

Ratzinger concludes: "It appears to me this is a very deep image of what a true priestly vocation can be."[98] This flame is a parable for God's Word, entrusted to the care of priests. Without it, the world would become infinitely impoverished and boring. People would become soul-less, "mere images of their machines [and not] remain God's images. And only in this connection can the Eucharist as *Kreuzesopfer Jesu Christi* [Jesus Christ's sacrifice on the cross] be celebrated."[99] In celebrating the Eucharist, priests become "carers of souls" (the literal meaning of the German word *Seelsorger*), lest churches degenerate into meaningless museums and the beautiful Mozart Mass in C Minor evolves into *l'art pour l'art*, a self-referential art event. Ratzinger addresses all present, calling on them to keep churches alive by "living the Church." Then, "the yesterday owns its today and the future is present in them."[100]

Concluding Observations

These homilies are thoroughly biblical, patristic, pastoral, contemporary, and spiritual in orientation. At no point are they dogmatic or moralizing. No theological tractate nor Denzinger theology is presented. A facile functionalistic *ex opere operato* schema is long *passé* to Ratzinger's thinking. Priesthood is never simply office but is eminently sacrament to Ratzinger's mind. Never does he stress the sublimity of the Eucharist without underlining the celebrant's unworthiness. He calls on all to become more Christ-centered. While critical of the ruling *Zeitgeist*, the tenor is never *larmoyant*. It is worthy to note how unsparingly realistic and prescient Ratzinger already was regarding the future perspectives of Christianity in his first homily—delivered in 1954—when attendance at Mass among Catholics in West Germany still averaged around 80 percent.

Amid a prevailing emphasis on self-determination and the attendant, pervasive crisis of the priest's identity, Ratzinger unfolds the priest's grandeur and beauty from the mission given to Jesus Christ from His eternal Father within the Blessed Trinity, in whose house He must abide (Lk 2:49). The priest places his complete being and life at the service of Christ. The priest realizes his dignity by being a servant of the Word and sacraments. The prevailing tenor is joyful, spiritual, and edifying. This is achieved not by exalting Catholic faith or the priesthood, but by being clairvoyant about the *conditio humana* and the future of the Occident, and interpreting it spiritually so as to enter deeper into the mystery of Christ.

Indeed, only if a priest's spirituality is Christ-centered, can he speak the Christian truths about God. Ratzinger preached to newly ordained priests that a spirituality rooted existentially in Christ enables and compels the priest to preach sound theology. Here, one detects hints of a critical nuance made by John Henry Newman (1801–1890): existential realization is required, not only notional assent.[101] The priest lives from a real nexus between spirituality and theology. Propositional certitude is hollow if it is not grounded in a personal, spiritual experience. The priest should thereby be able to show that "truth possesses us, not we truth."[102]

Far from celebrating clericalist triumphalism, Ratzinger draws a picture of a priest who is very human and as equally threatened as other Christians. Without ever raising his voice, he calls upon priests to be existentially veracious. So that God's eternal Word might become ever anew incarnate, he repeatedly develops how a priest must respond to "the signs of the time,"[103] but never accommodate the negative aspects of the prevailing *Zeitgeist*.

Using the Continental European distinction between the terms "culture" and "civilization," Ratzinger argues by implication that people are often completely enraptured by civilization's achievements, at risk of becoming uncultured and, hence, inhumane. It is the priest's high task to protect the *humanum*. Resonating in the background, one hears the great Jesuit theologian and inspiration for Ratzinger's own understanding of Catholic faith, Henri de Lubac (1896–1991), whom Ratzinger read extensively in his formative years as seminarian and student.[104] Catholicism is not a lifestyle nor a denomination, but the highest and fullest realization of being human.[105]

Modernity and postmodernity can be defined as studied attempts to deny life's tragic content—the signal discovery of Greek antiquity. On the festive day of a priest's first Mass, Ratzinger does not temper, but sobers, all festivity to a joy in the Cross. The inherently tragic nature of human existence is not denied by Christianity, but receives its deepest meaning, and even unsurpassable beauty, in the Cross of Jesus Christ, who through the Eucharist continues to impart on us the strength to persevere amid life's vicissitudes and give everything its most sublime meaning in Christ.

From Ratzinger's very first homily onward, the universal erudition of a Renaissance humanist shines forth. Throughout, one appreciates his poetic vein (*poetische Ader*). However, something significant and characteristic about Ratzinger must not go unmentioned. His thoughts are profound and his eloquent language is, at times, hauntingly beautiful; yet, the beauty of his words occurs to the reader or listener only afterwards. His style is not elegant; it does not intend to demonstrate the greatness of the speaker, but to point to the *magnalia Dei*, the marvels of God. Very similar to John the Baptist and his patron saint, Joseph, the author Ratzinger becomes noble as he enters Christ's *kenosis*, God's self-emptying humility.

NOTES

1.   Bartolomé de Las Casas, "Historia de las Indias," in: Juan Pérez de Tudela y Bueso and Emilio Lopez Oto, eds., *Biblioteca de Autores Españoles* 96 (Madrid: Atlas, 1957), 137f. It is also noteworthy because de Las Casas had already been ordained in Rome in 1506 or 1507. No reason is given for the delay of the first Holy Mass; however, delays were not uncommon at that time. In addition, because no ships had recently arrived from Spain, there was no wine to consecrate. See also, Gustavo Gutiérrez, *Gott oder das Gold: Der befreiende Weg des Bartolomé de Las Casas* (Freiburg: Herder, 190), 167, note 4.

St. Ignatius of Loyola celebrated his first Holy Mass at Saint Mary Major in 1538 after he found it impossible to celebrate it in Bethlehem. He had been ordained on June 24, 1537 in Venice. Winfried Haunerfeld, *Die Primiz: Studien zu ihrer Feier in der lateinischen Kirche Europas* (Regensburg: Pustet, 1997), 25.

2.   Jean Chrysostome, *Sur le sacerdoce (Dialogue et Homélie)*, introduction, texte critique, traduction et notes par Anne-Marie Malingrey, *Sources Chrétiennes*, vol. 272 (Paris: Cerf, 1980), 365–419.

3.   See D. Dietlein, "First fruits (in the Bible)," in *The New Catholic Encyclopedia*, vol. V (Washington, DC: McGraw-Hill, 1967), rubric 936f.

4.   Alois Hierzer, "Das Priesterbild in spätmittelalterlichen Primizpredigten steirischer Handschriften: Eine vorreformationsgeschichtliche Studie" (Ph.D. diss., Notre Dame, IN: University of Notre Dame, 1964), 38 and 26 respectively. For France, see "Discours pour la première messe d'un jeune prêtre sur les grandeurs du sacerdoce catholique (l'abbé Breton)," in *Encyclopédie de la Prédication contemporaine*, Tome XVIII (Marseille: Mingardon, 1885), 591–597; "Discours sur le sacerdoce. Par M. l'abbé J. Jousset (held Sept. 3, 1876)," in *Encyclopédie de a Prédication contemporaine*, Tome XIX (Marseille: Mingardon, 1881), 167–185; "Le sacerdoce (held on Sept. 14, 1882 by Celestin de Werviq)," in *Les Orateurs sacrés contemporains*, Tome LX (Marseille: St. Thomas d'Aquin, 1886), 365ff.

5.   "Man muß ein Paar Schuhe durchlaufen, um an einer Primiz teilnehmen zu können." Franz Niderberger, *Sagen und Gebräuche aus Unterwalden*, 3rd ed. (Zürich: Olms, 1989), 557. (Translated by author).

6.   Michel Andrieu, *Les Ordines Romani du haut moyen-âge*, (1951; reprint, Louvain: Spicilegium Sacrum Lovaniense, 1961), 271–280.

7.   "In tali Missa maiorem gratiam effundat Dominus." Humbertus de Romanis, *De eruditione praedicatorum* 2, 45 *In noua Missa* (*Maxima Bibliotheca Veterum Patrum* 25, ed. by Marguerin de La Bigne) (Lugduni: Anissonius, 1677), 424–567, at 536.

8.   For a surprisingly modern understanding of a *Primizpredigt* rejecting extraneous elements and pompous descriptions of the priesthood, see the

homilies of Johann Michael Sailer, *Vermischte Schriften*, in: ‚Johann Michael Sailer, *Sämmtliche Werke*, ed. by Joseph Widmer, vol. 40, 2nd rev. ed., (Sulzbach: J.E. v. Seidel, 1841).

For a neopresbyter's reaction to Sailer's homily at his first Holy Mass, see also Christoph von Schmid, "Sailer, der liebevolle, treue Lehrer," in *Die Apostel Deutschlands* (1846; reprint, Augsburg: Wolff, 1953), 163–167 and Joseph Cardinal Ratzinger, "'Gott spricht zu uns.' Predigt beim Pontifikalgottesdienst zum 150. Todestag von Bischof Johann Michael Sailer am 16.5.1982," in *Beiträge zur Geschichte des Bistums Regensburg* 35 (Regensburg: Pustet, 2001), 475–479.

9. "Wer das Wort ‚Primizpredigt' gebraucht, weckt bei nicht wenigen die Erinnerung an barockes und gefühlsbetontes Pathos, vielleicht auch Erinnerungen an überdimensionale Ansprachen, die das zusammengeströmte und festlich gestimmte Gottesvolk geduldig über sich ergehen ließ. Wie viele Primizpredigten sind im Laufe der letzten hundert Jahre gehalten worden! Welches Echo aber haben sie gehabt? Fast möchte es scheinen, als sei die Primizpredigt inmitten einer theologisch aufgewühlten und gleichzeitig auch von der technischen Sachlichkeit mitgeprägten Zeit ein letztes Relikt aus glaubensseligen und scheinbar unangefochtenen Tagen. . . . Jede künftige Primizpredigt auch vor jedem Hauch eines billigen und wahrhaft unzeitgemäßen Triumphalismus (zu) bewahren. Mit den Durakkorden der Freude vermischen sich die herben Mollakkorde der Zukunftssorgen der Kirche. Das Kirchenvolk soll gerade anläßlich der feierlichen Erstlingsmesse eines Neupriesters von der schmerzlichen Tatsache des bedrohlichen Priestermangels erfahren, denn es wird—vielleicht eher, als wir ohnehin schon befürchten—mit dem dadurch heraufbeschworenen Seelsorgsnot und den eventuellen Umstrukturierungen der Seelsorge überhaupt fertig werden müssen." Alfred Läpple, "Die Primizpredigt: Bestandsaufnahme—Anregungen" in *Mitten in der Gemeinde* (München: Don Bosco, 1968), 185–193, at 185f.

The seminarian Ratzinger had been master of ceremonies at Läpple's first Mass, celebrated in Partenkirchen in 1947. Alfred Läpple, *Benedikt XVI und seine Wurzeln: Was sein Leben und seinen Glauben prägte* (Augsburg: St. Ulrich, 2006), 71. [Quotations translated by the author.]

10. Ibid.

11. Läpple, "Die Primizpredigt," 185–187.

12. "Nicht Herren eures Glaubens sind wir, sondern Diener eurer Freude." Joseph Ratzinger, *Künder des Wortes und Diener euer Freude: Theologie und Spiritualität des Weihesakraments*, vol. 12 of *Gesammelte Schriften* (Freiburg: Herder, 2010), front inside cover page. [Translated by author].

13. Joseph Ratzinger, *Diener eurer Freude: Meditationen über die priesterliche Spiritualität* (Freiburg: Herder, 1988); in English: Joseph Ratzinger, *Ministers of Your Joy: Scriptural Meditations on Priestly Spirituality*, trans. Robert Nowell (Ann Arbor, MI: Servant Publications, 1989).

14. See, for example: Pope Paul VI, *Dei Verbum* (1965), sec. 8; Paul VI, *Ad Gentes* (1965), sec. 15; Pope Paul VI, *Lumen Gentium* (1964), sec. 30; and Pope Paul VI, *Gaudium et Spes* (1965), sec. 88.

15. Ratzinger, *Gesammelte Schriften*, vol. 12, 664–692; Ratzinger, *Ministers of Your Joy*, 11–23. It would be interesting to compare Ratzinger's homilies on the occasion of a priest's first Holy Masses with those of Karl Rahner. Karl Rahner, *Die Gnade wird es Vollenden*, (Munich: Ars Sacra, 1957).

16. Vinzenz Pfnür (ed.), *Papst Benedikt XVI. Joseph Ratzinger—Das Werk: Die Gesamtbibliographie,* (Augsburg: Sankt Ulrich, 2009), 232 and 344. Ratzinger delivered one such homily at St. Oswald Church in Traunstein, Germany on July 8, 1983 Date cannot be verified and likely one more at the same location on May 27, 2001.

17. Pope Benedict XVI, *Mitteilungen, Institut Papst Benedikt XVI*, Jahrgang 2, ed. Rudolf Voderholzer, Christian Schaller, and Franz-Xaver Heibl (Regensburg: Schnell & Steiner, 2009), 17–18, at 17.

18. Ibid., 17.

19. Ibid.

20. Ibid.

21. Ibid.

22. Ibid., 17f.

23. Ibid., 18.

24. Ibid.

25. Ibid.

26. Ibid.

27. Ibid.

28. Ibid.

29. Ratzinger, *Gesammelte Schriften*, vol. 12, 664-669. See also *Mitteilungen. Institut Papst Benedikt XVI.*, Rudolf Voderholzer, Christian Schaller and Franz-Xaver Heibl eds., Jahrgang 2, 21-25. Alfred Läpple, *Benedikt XVI. und seine Wurzeln* (Augsburg: St. Ulrich, 2006), 111-114.

30. Ratzinger, *Gesammelte Schriften*, 664.

31. Ibid.

32. Ibid., 665.

33. Ibid.

34. Ibid.

35. Ibid., 667.

36. Ibid.

37. Ibid., 667f.

38. Ibid.

39. Ibid., 668.

40. Ibid.

41. Ibid.

42. Ibid.

43. Ibid., 669.

44. Ibid.
45. Ibid.
46. Ibid., 670–677, at 670.
47. Ibid., 670.
48. Ibid.
49. Ibid.
50. Ibid.
51. Ibid., 671.
52. Ibid.
53. Romano Guardini, *Letters From Lake Como: Explorations on Technology and the Human Race*, trans. Geoffrey William Bromiley (Grand Rapids, MI: Eerdmans, 1994), 121. Originally published in German 1927.
54. Emery de Gaál, *The Theology of Pope Benedict XVI: The Christocentric Shift* (New York: Palgrave MacMillan, 2010), 39.
55. *Gesammelte Schriften*, vol. 12, 674.
56. Ibid., 674.
57. Ibid.
58. Ibid., 675.
59. Ibid., 677.
60. Ibid.
61. Ibid.
62. Ibid.
63. Ibid.
64. Ratzinger, *Das Werk*, 127. [Author Note: No additional information can be gleaned from this entry in Ratzinger's bibliography.]
65. Ratzinger, *Ministers of Your Joy*, 11–23.
66. Ibid., 12.
67. Ibid., 16.
68. Ibid.
69. Ibid.
70. Ibid.
71. Ibid., 17.
72. Ibid.
73. Ibid., 18.
74. Ibid., 19.
75. Ibid., 20f.
76. Ibid., 23.
77. Joseph Ratzinger, *Dogma and Preaching: Applying Christian Doctrine to Daily Life* (San Francisco: Ignatius, 2011), 369–375, at 369f. This particular text's context and origin cannot be reconstructed.
78. Ibid., 370.
79. Ibid.
80. Ibid.
81. Ibid., 373.

82. Ibid.
83. Ibid., 374.
84. Ibid.
85. Ratzinger, *Gesammelte Schriften*, vol. 2, 685–692.
86. Ibid.
87. Ibid., 687.
88. Ibid.
89. Ibid.
90. Ibid., 688.
91. Ibid., 688f.
92. Ibid.
93. Ibid., 689.
94. Ibid., 690.
95. Ibid.
96. Ibid.
97. Ibid.
98. Ibid.
99. Ibid.
100. Ibid.
101. John Henry Newman, *An Essay in Aid of a Grammar of Assent* (Notre Dame, IN: Notre Dame, 2001). Ratzinger was exposed to Newman's thinking via Alfred Läpple (1915-2013) and especially his *Doktorvater*, Gottlieb Söhngen (1892–1971). See also Emery de Gaál, *The Theology of Pope Benedict XVI: The Christocentric Shift*, 33–36.
102. *Gesammelte Schriften*, vol. 12, 690.
103. See Vatican II: *Gaudium et Spes*, secs. 4 and 11; *Presbyterorum Ordinis*, sec. 9; and *Unitatis Redintegratio*, sec. 4.
104. de Gaál, *The Theology of Pope Benedict XVI*, especially 36–38.
105. Henri de Lubac, *Catholicism: Christ and the Common Destiny of Man*, trans. By Lancelot C. Sheppard and Sister Elizabeth Englund, OCD, (San Francisco: Ignatius, 1988); first printed in French in 1947.

CPSIA information can be obtained
at www.ICGtesting.com
Printed in the USA
FFOW03n1844190115
10317FF

9 780988 76132